# HOW TO
# cheat
## IN
# After Effects

## Chad Perkins

AMSTERDAM • BOSTON • HE
PARIS • SAN DIEGO • SAN F..

Focal Press is an imprint of Elsevier

ELSEVIER

 Press

Focal Press is an imprint of Elsevier
The Boulevard, Langford Lane, Kidlington, Oxford, OX5 1GB, UK
30 Corporate Drive, Suite 400, Burlington, MA 01803, USA

First published 2011

Notices

Knowledge and best practice in this field are constantly changing. As new research and experience broaden our understanding, changes in research methods, professional practices, or medical treatment may become necessary.

Practitioners and researchers must always rely on their own experience and knowledge in evaluating and using any information, methods, compounds, or experiments described herein. In using such information or methods they should be mindful of their own safety and the safety of others, including parties for whom they have a professional responsibility.

To the fullest extent of the law, neither the Publisher nor the authors, contributors, or editors, assume any liability for any injury and/or damage to persons or property as a matter of products liability, negligence or otherwise, or from any use or operation of any methods, products, instructions, or ideas contained in the material herein.

British Library Cataloguing in Publication Data
A catalogue record for this book is available from the British Library

Library of Congress Control Number: 2010932688

ISBN: 978-0-240-52202-9

For information on all Focal Press publications visit our website at www.focalpress.com

Book cover art and concept by Chad Perkins. Photography by Zombie Crush Photography. Models: Pink Tattillac, Hot Rod Heidi, Holly Rose, and Jordan Daryn Knightley.

Printed and bound in the United States

10 11 12  10 9 8 7 6 5 4 3 2 1

## Working together to grow libraries in developing countries

www.elsevier.com | www.bookaid.org | www.sabre.org

ELSEVIER    BOOK AID International    Sabre Foundation

# Contents

The cheat format.................... vi
Acknowledgments.................. viii
How to use this book ................1

## 1  Cool Tricks Appetizer!  2

Fireball . . . . . . . . . . . . . . . . . . . . . 4
Growing Vines . . . . . . . . . . . . . . . . . 6
Tracked Text. . . . . . . . . . . . . . . . . . 8
Blooming Flower . . . . . . . . . . . . . . 10
Tilt Shift. . . . . . . . . . . . . . . . . . . . 12
Ink Spatter. . . . . . . . . . . . . . . . . . 14
Damaged Film . . . . . . . . . . . . . . . . 16
The Master Solid . . . . . . . . . . . . . . 18

*Interlude: Using the Help* . . . . . . . . . . .20

## 2  Lights and Cameras  22

Creating Basic Shadows. . . . . . . . . . .24
Stained Glass Shadows. . . . . . . . . . . .26
Controlling Shadows. . . . . . . . . . . . .28
Negative Light. . . . . . . . . . . . . . . . .30
Film Noir Lighting . . . . . . . . . . . . . .32
Creating Depth of Field . . . . . . . . . .34
Rack Focus. . . . . . . . . . . . . . . . . . .36
Lens Distortion. . . . . . . . . . . . . . . .38
Multiple Camera Angles. . . . . . . . . . .40
3D Camera Path. . . . . . . . . . . . . . . .42
Orient to Camera. . . . . . . . . . . . . . .44

*Interlude: Lighting is the Secret*. . . . . . .46

## 3  3D Objects  48

The Parallax Effect . . . . . . . . . . . . . .50
3D in Repoussé . . . . . . . . . . . . . . . .52
Photoshop 3D in After Effects. . . . . . .56
3D Shatter Scenes. . . . . . . . . . . . . . .58
3D Text. . . . . . . . . . . . . . . . . . . . .62
3D Postcards . . . . . . . . . . . . . . . . . .64
3D Objects from Solids. . . . . . . . . . . .66
3D Distortion . . . . . . . . . . . . . . . . .68
3D Planetscape . . . . . . . . . . . . . . . .72
Echospace . . . . . . . . . . . . . . . . . . .76

3D in Nested Compositions . . . . . . . . . .78

*Interlude: Picking a 3D App* . . . . . . . . . 80

## 4  Compositing  82

Making a Garbage Matte . . . . . . . . . . .84
Removing a Green Screen . . . . . . . . . .86
Pulling a Luma Key . . . . . . . . . . . . . .88
Refining a Matte. . . . . . . . . . . . . . . .90
Using Multiple Mattes . . . . . . . . . . . .92
Intro to Compositing. . . . . . . . . . . . .94
Blending Away Dark . . . . . . . . . . . . .96
Blending Away Light. . . . . . . . . . . . .98
Compositing Textures . . . . . . . . . . . .100
Temporal Alignment . . . . . . . . . . . . .102
Compositing with Color . . . . . . . . . . .104
Compositing with Animation. . . . . . . .106
Compositing with Focus. . . . . . . . . . .108
Motion Blur . . . . . . . . . . . . . . . . . . 110
Matching Color . . . . . . . . . . . . . . . . 112
Premultiplied Alpha Channels . . . . . . . 114
Tracking with Mocha . . . . . . . . . . . . . 116
Mocha Shapes. . . . . . . . . . . . . . . . .120
Using Roto Brush. . . . . . . . . . . . . . .122
Restoring Opacity . . . . . . . . . . . . . .124
Manual Shadow. . . . . . . . . . . . . . . .126
Guide Layers . . . . . . . . . . . . . . . . .128

*Interlude: Shooting Better Green Screen*
*Footage* . . . . . . . . . . . . . . . . . . . . . 130

## 5  Animation  132

The Puppet Pin Tool . . . . . . . . . . . . .134
Puppet Overlap . . . . . . . . . . . . . . . .136
Puppet Animation. . . . . . . . . . . . . . .138
Bouncing Ball . . . . . . . . . . . . . . . . .140
Parenting . . . . . . . . . . . . . . . . . . . .142
Waving Sail . . . . . . . . . . . . . . . . . .144
Animating the Blob. . . . . . . . . . . . . .146
Animating a Photo: Part 1 . . . . . . . . .148
Animating a Photo: Part 2 . . . . . . . . .150
Displacement Mapping. . . . . . . . . . . .152

# Contents

Resizing Animation . . . . . . . . . . . . . . . . .154
Text Messaged Animation . . . . . . . . . . .156

*Interlude: Walt's Principles.* . . . . . . . . . 158

## 6 Light Effects 160

HDR . . . . . . . . . . . . . . . . . . . . . . . . . . .162
Volumetric Light . . . . . . . . . . . . . . . . . .164
Silhouettes. . . . . . . . . . . . . . . . . . . . . . .166
Light Whips . . . . . . . . . . . . . . . . . . . . . .168
Stage Lights. . . . . . . . . . . . . . . . . . . . . .170
Energy Cube. . . . . . . . . . . . . . . . . . . . . .172
Searchlights. . . . . . . . . . . . . . . . . . . . . .174
Sheen . . . . . . . . . . . . . . . . . . . . . . . . . .176
The Glow Effect. . . . . . . . . . . . . . . . . . .178
Laser Beams. . . . . . . . . . . . . . . . . . . . . .180
Trapcode Shine . . . . . . . . . . . . . . . . . . .182

*Interlude: High Dynamic Range* . . . . . . 184

## 7 Masks and Shapes 186

Mask Options. . . . . . . . . . . . . . . . . . . . .188
Instant Vignette. . . . . . . . . . . . . . . . . . .190
From Video to Shape Layer. . . . . . . . . . .192
The Vegas Effect . . . . . . . . . . . . . . . . . .194
Luma Matte . . . . . . . . . . . . . . . . . . . . . .196
Track Matte . . . . . . . . . . . . . . . . . . . . . .198
Animating Masks. . . . . . . . . . . . . . . . . .200
Motion Paths from Illustrator . . . . . . . .202
Trapcode 3D Stroke. . . . . . . . . . . . . . . .204

## 8 Particles 206

Particle Bootcamp. . . . . . . . . . . . . . . . .208
Sparkles . . . . . . . . . . . . . . . . . . . . . . . .210
Smoke Trail . . . . . . . . . . . . . . . . . . . . . .212
Foam Basics. . . . . . . . . . . . . . . . . . . . . .214
Custom Particles . . . . . . . . . . . . . . . . . .216
Simple Rain . . . . . . . . . . . . . . . . . . . . . .218
Basic Snow. . . . . . . . . . . . . . . . . . . . . . .220
Windblown Snow . . . . . . . . . . . . . . . . .222
Molten Gold. . . . . . . . . . . . . . . . . . . . . .224

Light Ribbons. . . . . . . . . . . . . . . . . . . . .226
Steam. . . . . . . . . . . . . . . . . . . . . . . . . . .230
3D Fireworks . . . . . . . . . . . . . . . . . . . . .232
Psychic Waves . . . . . . . . . . . . . . . . . . . .234
Particle Deflection. . . . . . . . . . . . . . . . .236
Star Field . . . . . . . . . . . . . . . . . . . . . . . .238
Confetti . . . . . . . . . . . . . . . . . . . . . . . . .240
Water Surface Disruption. . . . . . . . . . . .242
Flowing Chocolate. . . . . . . . . . . . . . . . .244
Trapcode Form: 4D Fractal . . . . . . . . . .246
Particular: 3D Light Streaks . . . . . . . . . .248

*Interlude: Particle Alternatives.* . . . . . . 250

## 9 Color Correction 252

Reading a Histogram . . . . . . . . . . . . . . .254
Cinematic Color: Warmth. . . . . . . . . . . .256
Cinematic Color: Horror . . . . . . . . . . . . .258
Cinematic Color: Flashback . . . . . . . . . .260
Day for Night. . . . . . . . . . . . . . . . . . . . .262
Reference Monitor . . . . . . . . . . . . . . . . .264
Before and After . . . . . . . . . . . . . . . . . .266
Colorizing. . . . . . . . . . . . . . . . . . . . . . . .268
Hue Shift . . . . . . . . . . . . . . . . . . . . . . . .270
Stylizing . . . . . . . . . . . . . . . . . . . . . . . . .272
Faking Dimension . . . . . . . . . . . . . . . . .274
Secondary Color Correction . . . . . . . . . .276
Spot Color Correction . . . . . . . . . . . . . .278
Color Finesse Basics . . . . . . . . . . . . . . . .280
Color Finesse "Looks" . . . . . . . . . . . . . .282
Using Color Lookup Tables . . . . . . . . . . .284
Improving 3D Renders. . . . . . . . . . . . . .286
Checking Dark Areas. . . . . . . . . . . . . . .288
Magic Bullet Looks . . . . . . . . . . . . . . . .290

*Interlude: Shooting Filmlike Video* . . . . 292

## 10 Backgrounds and Textures 294

Fire Texture . . . . . . . . . . . . . . . . . . . . . .296
Candle Flame. . . . . . . . . . . . . . . . . . . . .300
Creative Playing. . . . . . . . . . . . . . . . . . .302
Hot Grill . . . . . . . . . . . . . . . . . . . . . . . . .306

It's Curtains for You!. . . . . . . . . . . . . . . .308

Background Bars . . . . . . . . . . . . . . . . . . .310

Basic Water . . . . . . . . . . . . . . . . . . . . . .312

Better Water . . . . . . . . . . . . . . . . . . . . .314

TV Noise . . . . . . . . . . . . . . . . . . . . . . . .316

Ornate Vintage Patterns. . . . . . . . . . . . .318

Cells Through a Microscope . . . . . . . . . .320

Retro Video Game Maze. . . . . . . . . . . . .322

Quick Variations . . . . . . . . . . . . . . . . . .324

Animation Presets. . . . . . . . . . . . . . . . .328

Presets and Adobe Bridge. . . . . . . . . . . .330

Library of Custom Textures. . . . . . . . . . .332

*Interlude: Generic Background Texture*

*Recipe* . . . . . . . . . . . . . . . . . . . . . . . . 334

Index. . . . . . . . . . . . . . . . . . . . . . . . . . .336

# The cheat format

This whole "cheat" thing was created by Steve Caplin for the epic book, How to Cheat in Photoshop, which I think is in its zillionth edition (give or take). So, I'm proudly and unashamedly ripping off of Steve's brilliance in creating what I consider to be the ultimate software training book format.

Instead of going through and describing stuff as most computer software books do (including my previous book, The After Effects Illusionist), this book tackles one trick (aka "cheat") at a time in a very visual way. There are a few steps to follow, and pictures guiding you the whole way. It's a very visual process, and in my opinion, it's a fun way to make a computer book.

Because this book is more focused on little mini recipes of sorts (usually 2 pages, and rarely up to 4 pages), we're going to be focusing more on what to do than how to do it. Against every tendency in my body, I'm just going to be barking out orders (such as "set this property to this value", etc.) without much explanation. Although, I admit that I do fight convention and try to explain things as much as possible. But that's not really the point of this book.

I mentioned the recipe metaphor, and that's precisely what this book is like. On a cooking show, the veggies are all pre-cut, the spices are already measured out and in their own separate bowls, and the chef/host doesn't always explain why they are baking at a certain temperature or what the heck cardamom is doing in the dish. They just make the dish in a very visual way, so that it is clear how to create the final product. This book is like that cooking show, but for wicked cool After Effects tricks instead of food.

Now, where possible, I've tried to just stuff this book full of extra tidbits of information. In the right column of most of the right hand pages, I've included extra bonus tips with optional methods to achieve a result, additional insight or information on related concepts, or ways that you could expand the current cheat and make it even better.

At the end of most chapters, you'll also find a little break from the hot, non-stop cheat action of the rest of the book. We call this break an "interlude". And the interludes are filled with tons of extra information to help you get more out of the After Effects experience. These interludes cover topics from how to shoot better green screen video so that it's easier to key, to the story behind HDR (High Dynamic Range) color and bit depth, and much, much more.

As far as difficulty goes, the book is pretty simple and easy to follow, but it's meant for people with a little bit of After Effects knowledge already. There just isn't time enough to explain basics like how to apply an effect, or what a solid layer is, or how to create a new composition, or the difference between importing and opening, and so on. These are basics that After Effects users in all disciplines should be familiar with. But I realize that if you've spent your time as a compositor and now want to perfect the craft of animation, there may be some new terms there. So, I try to explain core concepts where possible. Don't let your pride be offended. This is still an intermediate book. But not everyone is intermediate in everything. Still, I won't be able to explain all concepts from scratch as much you'd like, or might need. To that end, I've created an interlude at the end of Chapter 1 to help you find your own solutions if I refer a feature that you're unfamiliar with and would like to learn more about.

Because users are often slow to upgrade, I should also point out that this book was made with After Effects CS5. You're welcome to use the book with any version of After Effects, but know that After Effects will not open up future projects. So if you're using CS4, you won't be able to open the projects from the book. You'll still be able to import the assets (e.g. video, audio, images, etc.), just not the projects. This is the way Adobe made their software, and there's not much I can do about it. But for those of you that do have CS5, you'll be happy to know that many CS5 features are covered in cheats here, including Roto Brush, Mocha Shape, applying color look up tables, and Freeform AE.

The moral of the story is that this cheat format is ridiculously fun. You can jump around where you'd like to, and only in a few instances are cheats predicated upon knowledge from previous cheats (and those instances are clearly noted in the text). For the most part, these are little bite-sized tidbits of sweet tips and tricks that will enhance your workflow, get you out of sticky situations, and spark your creativity. You're gonna love this.

# Acknowledgments

This book is dedicated to Heather, Mikey, Natty, and Lizzie, who have been so infinitely patient as I've been laboring away at this book. I love you all so much.

I'm also really grateful to the following peeps:

Dennis and the entire crew at Focal Press. The experience of writing with Focal Press has been incredible. I feel like I've missed every deadline, and they're always very professional when telling me how much I suck. I've written books with other publishers, but Focal is my favorite. They also make most of the filmmaking books I like to read as well. Way to go, team.

Steve Caplin. He has been an incredible resource. I'm not sure that a more helpful person exists on this planet. This book would have looked worse than the local high school newspaper had he not coached me through the page layout process for this template. He's also created a brilliant system with this book.

B-dub and the seminary kids. You guys had to deal with a lot of instability from me because of this process, and I'm so sorry for that. But we still had an amazing year, right?

The models on the front cover. The cover was a last minute thing, and a few friends/models showed up at the last second, did what they were supposed to, when they were supposed to, and looked freaking awesome doing it. And thus this book has a unique and visually interesting cover. And having beautiful people on the front cover creates the illusion that I'm beautiful, too (well, in the minds of those that have never seen me in real life).

I've been able to use some incredible art from some great artists and content providers. Thanks to Daniel Johnson for the incredible matte paintings. Thanks to Dan Grady for dropping everything and creating some sweet vector art for me. Thanks to uberstock for providing great high quality stock video to my (picky) specifications.

Aharon Rabinowitz and Red Giant Software. I desperately wanted to show off some of your amazing products in this book, and you guys were so willing to participate. I'm in awe of the plugins you put out there, and the whole After Effects world is benefited by them as well.

# How to use this book

As mentioned, feel free to jump around as you please. You certainly don't need to go in order.

As you do go through this book, be aware that the project that accompanies each cheat can be found in the corresponding folder of the current chapter in the Exercise Files folder on the book's DVD. Because that was the most confusing sentence in the book, here's an example - if you're learning about how to make molten gold in Chapter 8, then you'll find the accompanying project (surprisingly called Molten Gold.aep) in the Chapter 08 folder in the Exercise Files folder on the DVD. In most cases, you don't really need to use the project file or even follow along to get the most out of this book. I think the screenshots are sufficient enough to see what's going on. So feel free to take this book with you on the subway, or some other public place where potential book buyers are found. That was a joke. There will be many of those. Fortunately, they will get better as we go along (in most cases).

For this book, I've used a Mac, but that really doesn't matter. Adobe made After Effects look almost exactly the same on both platforms. When keyboard shortcuts are used, I have provided both the Mac version (color coded red) and the Windows version (color coded blue). Shortcuts that are the same on both platforms (such as Shift or a letter on your keyboard) are shown in black.

This book has also been tremendously blessed by a very generous and helpful supply of high quality stock video provided to us by uberstock. com. Because they've provided so many clips for us to use, they have been watermarked, and their quality and resolution is a little different than what is seen in the screenshots. But I've adjusted the projects so that the difference is as minimal as possible.

■ This chapter is going to be the proverbial stretching of the legs, as we learn some sweet tricks in preparation for the rest of the cheats in the book.

# 1 Cool Tricks Appetizer!

WE'VE GOT A LOT OF JUICY STUFF TO COVER IN THIS BOOK. So let's get warmed up by just getting the sampler platter of sweet After Effects tricks at the outset.

This chapter will be a great warm-up for the rest of the book, and we'll even conclude this chapter with a small section about getting extra help in case you find yourself stuck as you go through the cheats.

# Fireball

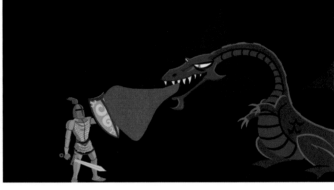

**1** We'll start in the Fireball START comp in the Fireball.aep project in the Chapter 01 folder in the Exercise Files folder. In this cheat, we're going to take a simple animated shape layer (discussed in Chapter 7), and apply fire from the Fractal Noise effect (discussed in Chapter 10), and then roughen it up. Note that we learn how to make the pretty background from scratch in Chapter 10.

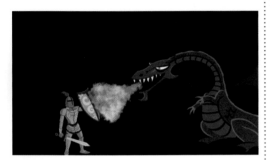

**W**HAT BETTER START TO A BOOK COULD YOU HAVE than a fire breathing dragon? In this cheat, we're going to be turning a plain red blob into this glowing fireball above.

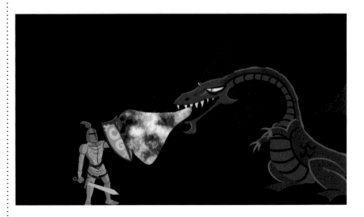

**3** Now apply the Colorama effect to the Fire layer. In the Colorama effect controls, open the Output Cycle area, and from the Use Preset Palette drop down, choose Fire.

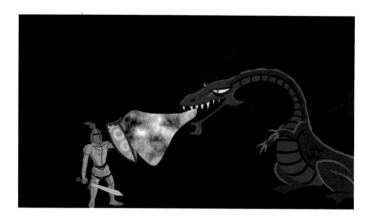

2  Apply the Fractal Noise effect to the Fire layer. In the Fractal Noise settings in
   the Effect Controls panel, increase Contrast to 150, and in the Transform area,
decrease Scale to 80.

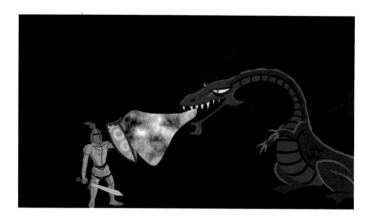

4  To make this blob look like a fireball, apply the Roughen Edges effect to the
   Fire layer. In its effect controls, take Border to 75, Edge Sharpness to 0.5,
Scale to 80, and Complexity to 3. It's looking pretty good, but perhaps we could
get a better final result by playing with the Fractal Noise and Roughen Edges
settings?

**HOT TIP**

To animate the
fireball, animate
the Evolution
value in the
Fractal Noise
effect, and the
Offset and/or
Evolution values
in the Roughen
Edges effect.

# Cool Tricks Appetizer!

# Growing Vines

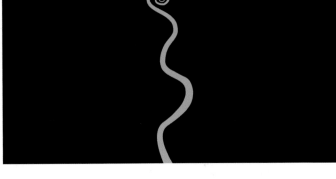

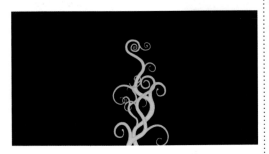

**1** Start out in the Growing Vines START comp in the Growing Vines.aep project in the Chapter 01 folder of the exercise files. This contains a few vine layers from Adobe Illustrator. It's very important for this trick that the vines are cut up into separate components like this. I'm going to solo just the Main Vine layer and work on it first.

**T**HIS CHEAT IS A LITTLE MORE INVOLVED and takes a bit more time than the others in this chapter. But nevertheless, having vines or filigree grow is a very common trick. It's a great way to draw a viewer's attention to something important.

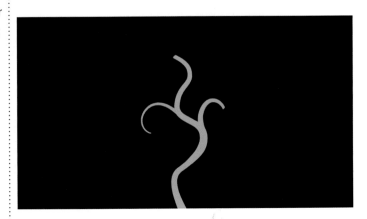

**3** Once you've completed painting the vine, go back to the Write-on effect controls and change the Paint Style to Reveal Original Image. Now, there's no more paint. Your "paint" is just unmasking your layer. This is how the growing vines effect is created. You then repeat this for each vine and time their reveals so that it appears that they are growing together.

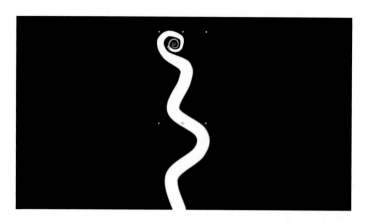

**2** Apply the Write-on effect to this. In its effect controls, increase the Brush Size to about 30 so you can see it. Change the Brush Time Properties value to Size, so that you can animate the size of the brush along the path if you need to. Adjust the Brush Position value so that the brush is at the bottom, then animate it painting the vine as above. Also animate Brush Size as the vine gets more narrow. Trying to paint the spiral at the top is the biggest challenge.

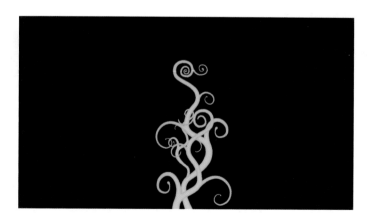

**4** After doing this for each layer, I selected all of these layers and pressed ⌘ Shift C ctrl Shift C to precompose them. I then added some glow and a gradient background. But another secret to this trick is duplication. I pressed ⌘ D ctrl D to duplicate this precomp, then rotated and scaled the duplicates and shifted them in time. This creates the illusion that your project is far more complex and intricate than it actually is, and the result is beautiful.

# Tracked Text

**1** Start in the Tracked Text START comp in the Tracked Text.aep project. Double click the cool bird.mov layer to open it in the Layer panel. In Chapter 4, we'll look at Mocha, which is a better way to track motion. For now, let's use the native motion tracking in After Effects by choosing Tracker from the Window menu at the top of the interface. In the Tracker panel, click the Track Motion button.

**E**VERY EPISODE OF THE NOW-DEFUNCT *HEROES* TV SHOW had this really cool effect that people always wanted to duplicate. It basically featured 3D text that moved with the scene. I still see this effect everywhere from TV commercials to movie trailers. It's actually a pretty easy trick in After Effects.

**3** In the Tracker panel, click the Edit Target button, and choose the text layer (TALKING Bird4) as the target. Then click the Apply button, and OK to choose X and Y dimensions, and that's it! Our text is tracked to the background, and now moves with it realistically.

**2** Now we need to figure out what to track, and we don't have many options. We can't track the bird because the bird moves. That leaves the background. The only area of contrast I see is on the light and shadow between the two fence posts. Drag the tracking point over there, and expand the feature and search regions to include the edges of the posts. Believe it or not, this gave me a near-perfect track.

**4** I've applied some color correction to make this look more intense (we'll cover color correction in Chapter 9). And, to heighten the realism, I've created a spotlight and created shadows (both discussed in Chapter 2). I've created some 3D distance between the bird layer and the text so that the shadows make the text look farther away. Looking at this again, I'm wondering if I shouldn't have reduced the scale on the text and increased the distance even more to increase the apparent distance. What do you think?

# Cool Tricks Appetizer!

# Blooming Flower

**B**ECAUSE OF THE STATIC NATURE OF BOOKS, we aren't going to look at a lot of tricks that need motion in order to be demonstrated. These include the transition effects.

However, these transition effects can often be used in unconventional ways. We'll look at the power of the Card Wipe transition in Chapter 3 when we talk about 3D objects. In this cheat, we'll look at a simple transition that can be used to reveal content like a blooming flower.

1 We're going to be using the Blooming Flower.aep project, where I've created this flower scene using shape layers (discussed in Chapter 7).

3 When the Radial Wipe effect is applied to the video clip, and the Transition Completion value is increased, a transition occurs as above and you can see the blue background layer behind the main clip.

2 We're going to be using the Radial Wipe effect, which is intended to transition between two clips like a clock wipe. Here is one clip from the stock video company uberstock, that has donated a lot of great video clips for this book.

4 Apply the Radial Wipe effect to the flower petals layer. As you animate the Transition Completion property, the flower will seem to disappear. To animate it blooming, animate it from 100% to 0%. This is a great trick for flowers, plus all circular motion graphics as well.

# Tilt Shift

TILT SHIFT IS A TRICK IN PHOTOGRAPHY USUALLY USED TO SIMULATE MINIATURES. I'm actually seeing this effect more and more in commercials these days, as entire cities appear to be tiny miniatures. It's a pretty cool trick and it's easy to do.

**1** Open the Tilt Shift.aep project. This photo comes courtesy of Angela McInroe, one of the photographers at Zombie Crush Photography (they did the photography on the cover of the book). I love their stuff.

**3** In the Lens Blur effect controls, check the Repeat Edge Pixels option so that we don't get feathered edges. Then, with the layer selected, create a mask as shown above.

2 When miniatures are photographed, the depth of field is so shallow that only a small area is in focus. When we recreate that same, small area of focus on a regular photo, it creates the illusion of miniature footage. Press ⌘ ⌥ Y ctrl alt Y to create a new adjustment layer and apply the Lens Blur effect to it.

## HOT TIP

If you are currently reading this book while in the bookstore in the image (in the Southcenter Mall in Tukwila, WA), I apologize if this is a really Twilight Zone-esque creepy experience for you.

4 In the Timeline, change the mask mode from Add to Subtract. Press the letter F and increase the Mask Feather value to 70. And now this looks like a tiny miniature model of a mall.

# Ink Spatter

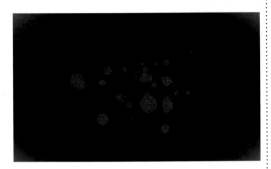

T HE GRUNGY LOOK OF INK SPATTER SEEMS TO BE SOMETHING that is always sought after. Computer graphics usually look too clean and perfect, and a little noise, grain, or ink spatter can sometimes make things (like backgrounds) look much more organic and engaging.

The problem is that ink spatter can be time consuming to create, assuming you create actual ink spatter, scan it, convert it, blah, blah, blah. It's a lot of work. Here's a way that you can fake that in After Effects.

1 Start with a brand new comp at 1280 x 720. Create a new solid of the same size, and change the color to whatever color you want your ink spatter to be. Apply the CC Particle Systems II effect to this solid. We'll talk a lot about this effect and many other particle systems in Chapter 8.

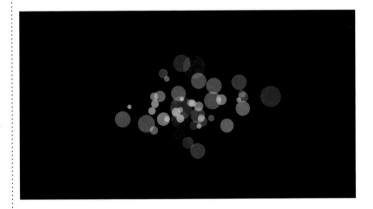

3 In the Producer area, take Radius X to 30 and Radius Y to 7. In the Physics area, take Velocity to 0.7, and Gravity to 0. And to make this begin to look like something decent, take the Particle Type drop down in the Particle area from Line to Lens Convex. We're getting closer to ink spatter, but this little system looks pretty sweet in its own right.

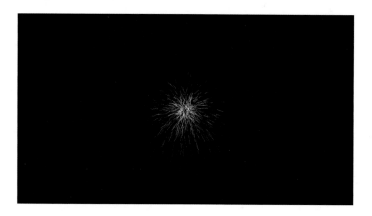

2 In the CC Particle Systems II effect controls, change the Birth Rate to 0.6 and the Longevity (sec) value to 0.4. It's still looking more like fireworks and less like ink, but just stay with it.

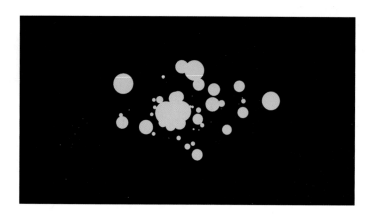

4 For the final touches, go to the Particle area in the Effect Controls panel. Change Birth Size to 0.01, Death Size to 0.5, Size Variation to 100%, Max Opacity to 100%, and change the Opacity Map drop down to Constant. Now, this will change every frame, so you'll probably want to render this out as a still image, then re-import it back into After Effects to use. You might also want to try the Roughen Edges effect to roughen the edges of the ink spatter.

# Damaged Film

W E SPEND SO MUCH MONEY PERFECTING THE QUALITY OF FOOTAGE. The world is adopting HD and the quality of video cameras seems to be improving on a daily basis. But for some reason, people still love the look of bad film and video. It can give our footage some character, add a nostalgic style, or make it feel more edgy and raw. Here are a few solutions for creating that damaged film look.

1 Start in the Damaged Film START comp in the Damaged Film.aep project. This contains a stock video clip from uberstock.com.

3 Now apply the Fractal Noise effect. In its effect controls, change Fractal Type to Smeary, Contrast to 320, Brightness to 300, Complexity to 1, and change the Blending Mode to Multiply. Then open the Transform area, uncheck Uniform Scaling, and increase Scale Height to 6000. This creates those dark vertical lines seen in old film.

2 As we'll learn in Chapter 9, color is the secret to everything. Apply the Curves effect to this layer. Take the bottom left corner of the curve up just a little bit; about halfway up to the first line. This will lighten the shadows, creating a faded look. Then change the Channel drop down to Blue, then take the upper right point down to the first line. This will add a vintage yellowness.

4 Now apply the CC Burn Film effect and take its Burn value to 38. You might also want to adjust its Center value to get the burn in the right spot. Now you have damaged film! See if you can trick a coworker into believing that you have old bootleg footage of your favorite classic rock band!

**HOT TIP**

If you're looking to create a damaged TV footage look, there are several animation presets that ship with After Effects that will instantly help you create that look as well. Animation presets are covered in Chapter 10.

# The Master Solid

1 We'll start with this comp in the Master Solid.aep project. This is a composition that only contains solid layers, a light, a camera, and a background.

THIS MIGHT NOT BE THE COOLEST TRICK to everyone in the world, but this is one of my favorite little tricks. There are several times when I have used this and it just makes me happy, honestly.

I use solid layers all the time. And when you create a solid layer, and then duplicate, After Effects quietly maintains a link between those solids in case you need to make changes.

3 Select any one of the green solid layers (note that they appear red because of a hidden adjustment layer). Press ⌘ *Shift* *Y* *ctrl* *Shift* *Y* to open the Solid Settings dialog box. As long as you check the option that says Affect all layers that use this solid, whatever changes you make will be instantly reflected in all solids that are duplicates. And you don't have to select the original solid – any duplicate will do. I took the Height down to 20 and the Width up to 300, and I also changed the color.

2   As you can see, there are loads of solid layers here. If we wanted to make a
    global change to every solid, it would take a very long time. Thankfully, all of
these solids are duplicates from a single solid.

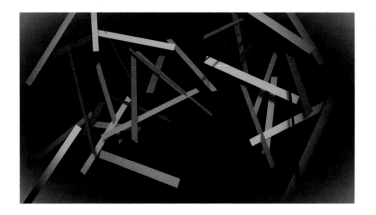

4   In one fell swoop, all solids reflect the changes. Isn't that incredible?

# Using the Help

AS WE BEGIN THIS ADVENTURE together into the rest of this book, I wanted to have this little interlude to mention the incredible help system that comes with After Effects, and all Adobe apps. For the last few versions, the help has only been available in an online system. I'm very happy that there is also a local version now, and it's better than ever.

Now I realize that the idea of reading a manual sounds like the most boring concept one can imagine. Like you, I've spent hours reading manuals in every category of life, from software applications to cable boxes. It's almost always a frustrating experience. I can hardly find what I'm looking for, and when I do find the answer, it's so poorly written that the manual raises more questions than it answers.

Adobe's help is different, especially with After Effects. Of all the software manuals in all the world, the After Effects documentation is the most well written and helpful that I've ever seen. As a matter of fact, it's one of the best references on After Effects expressions I've ever seen

To access the help, just click in the Search Help field in the upper right corner of the interface, type what After Effects feature you want to learn about and hit Enter. This will automatically launch the Adobe Community Help application. This application will search not only Adobe's help, but it will search through many helpful (and free) online resources as well. As shown in the screenshot on the opposite page, you can choose to search through Adobe's help only if desired. The selections (and search field) show up on the left, and when you choose one, it shows up on the left. The help system is also well integrated with itself, offering hyperlink references that will take you to other places to learn more.

I share this little tidbit of info with you at the outset of this book so that if something isn't explained very clearly, you know where to go to get more information. I've honestly had a little bit of a challenge writing this book. I'm the type of chap that likes to know how and why a thing works, and I usually explain why I'm doing something. I hate just telling you what settings to use and not explaining why I chose that particular number or what that property does. But with the nature of this book, there just isn't space for that. We can't have as many cheats as we want and still explain everything.

I know that this book is not for beginners, but what's a pro? How do you define that? You might work for years on feature films with massive Hollywood budgets, but you might not know how to hide layers or properties in the Timeline panel. Theoretically, someone might learn those things the first day of After Effects class.

So, forgive me if I don't have the space to explain things as much I would like to, and know that if you'd like more detail on a certain subject, that the After Effects help is a great resource.

We're going to look at lighting and camera tricks in this chapter. We'll look at how to use lights to actually remove light from a scene. We'll also get more control over cameras, from creating a narrow depth of field, to animating a camera along a path and much more!

# 2 Lights and Cameras

MOST AFTER EFFECTS USERS KNOW HOW TO CREATE BASIC LIGHTS AND CAMERAS. But what many don't realize is that there's a massive wealth of options that allow you to have a significant amount of control over the look of your final product.

In this chapter, we're going to become virtual cinematographers; working with lights and cameras in new and innovative ways. In some instances, we're going to be mimicking real world cinematography techniques, such as when we create a rack focus effect. But because we're using software, we'll be able to also do many tricks that cinematographers only dream about, such as when we create negative light and exclude objects from casting and receiving shadows. This chapter will help you push cameras and lights to the limit, and your 3D projects will be forever benefited.

# Casting Basic Shadows

**1** Open the Basic Shadows.aep project from the Chapter 02 folder of the exercise files. Go to the Basic Shadow START comp. I've already created a basic light for you in this comp, using the default light settings. This art is by artist Dan Grady.

**O**NE MIGHT THINK THAT SHADOWS WOULD BE EASIER TO CREATE in After Effects. After all, the ubiquitous drop shadow has been overused for over a decade. But as it turns out, creating a real shadow using After Effects' virtual lights is actually quite an involved process. Just so we're clear moving forward, we're going to briefly look at how to create a basic 3D shadow using real 3D lights.

**4** Now, it is conceivable that you've followed the aforementioned steps and you're not seeing a shadow. It's important that your light be in front of the objects you want casting shadows. To double check this, go to the 3D View Popup at the bottom of the Composition panel and change the view from Active Camera to Top so that we can see a top view of our light, as well as our other layers.

2 There are three main steps to make sure your lights are casting shadows. First, make sure that when you are creating your lights, you check Casts Shadows from the Light Settings dialog box. If you've already created your light, you can simply double click on the light layer in the Timeline panel.

3 The second step is that we need to make sure that we set layers to cast shadows. Unfortunately, this is one of those things that you have to do manually for each layer that you want to cast shadows. Select the foreground_ waves layer and press **A A** on your keyboard (that's the letter "a" twice quickly) to reveal its material properties. For the Casts Shadows property, click Off only ONCE to turn on shadow casting for this wave. Now the wave casts shadows onto the layers behind it, like the metallic robot ship.

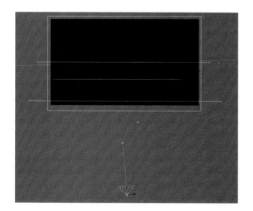

5 In the Top view, the light source (indicated here by the cone because our light is a spot light) should be below the layers you want casting shadows. As you can see here, we're good on this one.

6 And that's really all that it takes to create real, "live" shadows that dynamically respond to changes in light position. This screenshot is from the Basic Shadow DONE comp, where I've also told the Robot_ship layer to cast shadows. Try experimenting with casting shadows. Does it look good to you with all layers casting shadows? Why or why not?

# Stained Glass Shadows

Here's the original image that we're going to use to cast a colored shadow.

**H**ERE'S A QUICK CHEAT FOR CREATING MORE BEAUTIFUL AND REALISTIC SHADOWS. We're essentially going to take a photo of stained glass windows, and transmit that color data in the shadows. For creating shadows from colored, semi-transparent objects (like glass or plastic), this can add an important degree of realism.

**3** Thankfully, the remedy here is a quick and easy one. Select the Stained Glass. psd layer in the Timeline panel. Press **A A** to reveal the Material Options properties. The parameter here that allows colors to pass through into the shadows is called Light Transmission.

2 Open Comp 1 from the Stained Glass.aep project in the Chapter 02 folder of the exercise files. I've already created a 3D scene using our image, a solid (as the floor), and a light that is casting a shadow. Notice how the black shadow looks very unrealistic coming through this colored glass.

4 Increase the Light Transmission value all the way up to 100% (or whatever looks good to your eye). As you increase this value, colors from the object that is casting a shadow will show up in the shadow. This effect is great for stained glass, but also anytime you want light spill. Maybe have a neon sign layer that you want to cast a glow onto a building behind it. Perhaps you want to have a client logo appear first as a shadow, and then reveal the actual logo. This single parameter can add a lot to your 3D projects.

# 2

# Controlling Shadows

IN THE NEXT FEW CHEATS, WE'RE GOING TO EXAMINE THE BENEFITS OF VIRTUAL CINEMATOGRAPHY. We're going to look at several things that we can do with the 3D lights in After Effects that real world cinematographers can only dream of.

In this cheat in particular, we're going to look at how to regulate shadow casting. Sometimes, you might not want a certain object to cast shadows, or to receive shadows. Or maybe you want total control over where that shadow falls. With the simple click of a button or two, After Effects gives you all of these choices and more. This is going to be like three cheats for the price of one!

1 So here's our starting point (which you can find in the Controlling Shadows.aep project in the Chapter 02 folder of the exercise files). Only the front wave and the robot ship layers are casting shadows, but they are still just terrible. They are particularly artificial and distracting on the right side of the image. The shadows fall on the background waves, which is not how real shadows would behave.

3 You can also use the settings in a layer's material options to create a gobo, or "cookie". A gobo is an object placed in front of a light that controls the shape of the light. This is like the professional equivalent of shadow puppets. To make our front waves a gobo, select the foreground_waves layer and press Ⓐ Ⓐ. Click the Casts Shadows value to change it to Only. Now, all we see is this layer's shadow, not the layer itself, which almost makes it look like a sea monster is attacking.

2 If this were a film set that we were lighting, we would have a heck of a time fixing this. We would probably add more lights to the background, which would not only lighten non-shadow areas, but it would also throw off the mood of the lighting we've already created. Instead, select the wave4_silhouette layer, press **A A** and change the Accepts Shadows value to Off. I'm going to do the same thing with the waves3 layer.

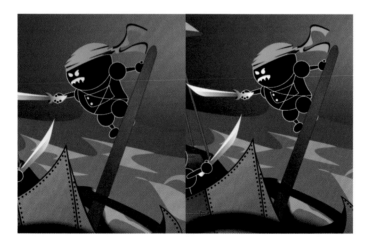

4 This one last trick can also bail you out of a pinch. Every once in a while, you'll light a scene and get everything perfect – except for one, annoying, rebellious object. You can exclude objects from lights, and still keep it 3D. Just press **A A** to reveal its material options, and change the Accepts Lights value to Off. In this case, I can remove the light falloff and make the robot captain and the background waves pop a little more by not allowing lights to fall on them. Falloff is generally good though, so use this trick prudently.

**HOT TIP**

Another great virtual cinematography trick that After Effects provides is that it lets you turn off Accepts Lights and still cast a shadow! Movies would be made in half the time if scenes could be lit with this much flexibility!

SHORTCUTS
MAC WIN BOTH

# Negative Light

**1** We're going to be working with this really impressive Photoshop document by matte painter Daniel Johnson. You'll find this in the Negative Light START comp in the Negative Light.aep project in the Chapter 02 folder of the exercise files. What I want to do here is to add some meaning to this. I want it to have a bright streak down the middle, but I also want it darker on the sides, almost as if to show hope in the midst of all this carnage and devastation.

**A**NOTHER IMPRESSIVE VIRTUAL CINEMATOGRAPHY TRICK that is possible in After Effects but isn't possible in the real world is that of negative light. Essentially what that means is that we can use lights to actually remove light, rather than add it. Although this is a very simple trick, it kind of messes with your mind a little because it's so different than what lights do in the real world. So, swallow that red pill and follow me down the rabbit hole as we discover negative light.

**3** The problem is that now there's too much light generally in the scene. It all looks too happy. Oddly enough, I'm going to create another spotlight and point it at the left side of the layers. But when creating the light, I'm going to take the Intensity of the light to a negative number; negative 66% to be exact. This will actually suck light out of the scene.

2 First, I'm going to add a new spotlight (seen here as the selected light). I'm going to add it pointing at the sun, to exaggerate the brightness in the clouds, and the strip of sunlight coming down the middle portion of the piece.

4 With the light on the left sucked out by the negative light (shown selected on the left), our piece looks much better. I realize that we could get a similar result from using masks on an adjustment layer with color correction effects. However, when your scene is animated, it's much more useful in many cases to have negative lights that actually move in 3D space.

**HOT TIP**

To check out more of Daniel Johnson's incredible work, go to www. danjohnson imagery.com/ portfolio. He also has some free tutorials available that are quite insightful.

# Film Noir Lighting

D ON'T YOU JUST LOVE THOSE OLD FILM
NOIR SUSPENSE MOVIES? I do. Those old
movies always have such incredible lighting. It
was just so dramatic, often only showing the
actor's terrified eyes. Everything else – including
the actor's neck and forehead – were in shadow.

I created a 3D door out of solids in After
Effects, and then lit it in that film noir style. In
this cheat, we're going to recreate that look.

Note that because this 3D door is made out of
solids, it's a little slow to render. If that bothers
you, you can degrade the view quality.

1 In the Film Noir START comp in the Film Noir Lighting.aep project, you'll find
this 3D door made of solids. Without lighting, these solids are just pure white.

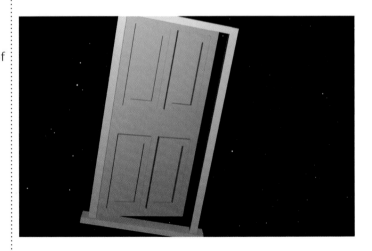

3 The secret to this trick is to get the light close to the subject and then tweak
the settings to create a more narrow strip of light, with shadows on the top
and the bottom of the door. I took the Point of Interest for the light to –95, 2100,
7130, and the Position of the light to 71, 711, 4970. This also puts the Point of
Interest on the other side of the door.

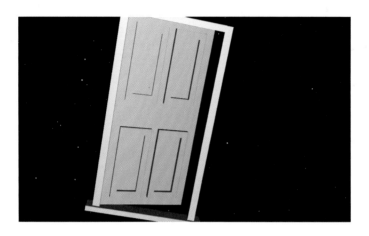

2  Press ⌘ ⌥ Shift L ctrl alt Shift L to create a white spotlight using the
   default settings. Now at least we can see the surface of our door. It's just not
that intense.

4  Double click the Light layer to open the Light Settings dialog box. Change the
   Cone Angle to 20 to create a smaller lighted area. I also reduced the Cone
Feather to 65% so that the edge of the shadows would be a little harder.

# Creating Depth of Field

**1** I love this art by Dan Grady. However, like me, it is a little chaotic. Notice how the clouds and stars in the background and the buildings and planes in the foreground are all in sharp focus. Where should the eyes of our viewers go? We can of course alter the colors and composition, but adding focus by creating a shallow depth of field will do better in this case.

PERHAPS THE MOST SOUGHT AFTER CINEMATOGRAPHY (AND PHOTOGRAPHY) TECHNIQUE IS THAT OF DEPTH OF FIELD. Depth of field refers to the area in a shot that is in focus. In movies, depth of field is used to focus your eye. The subject (or wherever the director wants you to look) will be in focus, and everything closer to the camera or farther away from it will be blurry.

One of the telltale signs of video is a very deep depth of field. In other words, everything in the foreground and background of the shot are in focus. Although this was a cinematic marvel when first achieved in the movie Citizen Kane (1941), deep depth of field typically doesn't make for great story telling.

To achieve a shallow depth of field (where only a very small area is in focus) usually requires a 35mm adapter if you're using a video camera, or you can use an HDLSR camera, or you can just click a few buttons in After Effects.

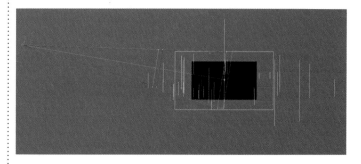

**3** In order to create depth of field, we need a couple things working for us. First of all, we need to make sure that the Focus Distance property is set properly. After enabling Depth of Field, the After Effects camera will get an extra rectangle which represents the Focus Distance. I like to use an orthographic view (such as Right seen above) to make sure that the Focus Distance is lined up with the object we want in focus. This is typically the job of the first assistant camera on a film set.

2 Open up the properties for Camera 1 in the Depth of Field comp in the Depth of Field.aep project in the Chapter 02 folder of the exercise files. In the Camera Options area, click the Depth of Field value to turn this effect on. Hey, what gives? Not much difference so far.

4 With real world cameras, depth of field is enhanced by opening the aperture of the lens. The same is true in After Effects. Increase the Aperture value of the Camera 1 layer to about 200 or so. That looks good to me, but I used an exaggerated value of 400 so that the results would be clearer in this screenshot. Now there's no question of what to look at first. The green monster is obviously on the focal plane. To make objects less or more in focus, move them farther away or closer to the focal plane, respectively.

# Rack Focus

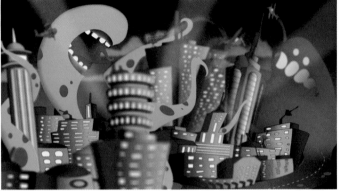

OW THAT WE KNOW HOW TO CREATE DEPTH OF FIELD, WE CAN LOOK AT A COOL TRICK THAT USES IT – RACK FOCUS. Rack focus is a trick where something far away is in focus, and then the focus shifts so that what's far away is out of focus, and something closer is in focus (or vice versa). This trick is quite simple, and can be used to reveal something to your audience, much like the way rack focus is used in the movies.

Be advised that this trick of necessity requires animation. So as you look at the screenshots in this book, you'll kinda have to use your imagination a little bit.

1 We're going to continue on where we left off in the last cheat. If you'd like, follow along with the Rack Focus.aep project in the Chapter 02 folder of the exercise files.

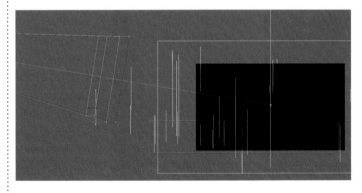

3 Now move out in time and change the Focus Distance value until the guide on the After Effects camera widget is lined up with the frontmost building layer. I used a value of about 2520. Notice that the target of the camera is not changed, only the Focus Distance, shown here on the left side of the image.

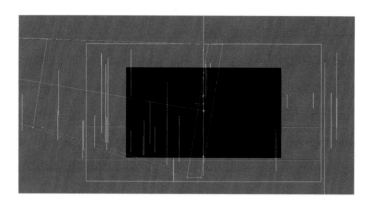

2 The rack focus effect is created by animating the Focus Distance of a camera. Right now, the focus is on the green monster (selected above), which is in the middle of our scene, depth-wise. This is the right view. Click the stopwatch for the Focus Distance property.

4 The final results tell a completely different story. The building in the foreground is now where the viewer expects the story to take place. Perhaps this story started out with monsters attacking, and then we rack focus to the foreground building and find our helpless protagonist stuck on the top floor! Oh no! Oh well. At least our rack focus looked awesome!

# Lens Distortion

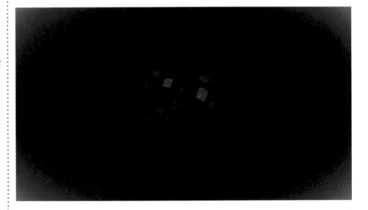

**1** In this 3D scene, we have a bunch of square solids floating around in space. We also have a background, a light, and a camera. As mentioned, the virtual camera lens is set to 50mm, which is very similar to the way human eyes work. So these squares look natural.

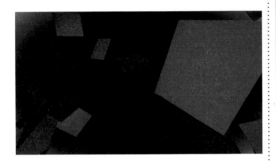

CAMERA LENSES DON'T JUST REGULATE THE AMOUNT OF LIGHT entering into your camera. They also can vary the perspective of a shot, bringing objects seemingly closer together or farther apart. In some cases, they can even add some really intense distortion.

In this cheat, we're going to play the role of virtual cinematographer again as we change the lens on our After Effects camera. We're going to take this from a "standard" lens to a wide angle lens. Wide angle lenses are intended to view wide vistas. But when you bring objects close to them, they have a tendency to distort objects in a really cool way that makes them seem more intense and ominous.

**3** As mentioned in the intro, wide angle lenses are used to capture wide scenes; almost as if you stepped backwards 20 paces when you changed lenses. So just changing the focal length of the lens changes the composition of our scene.

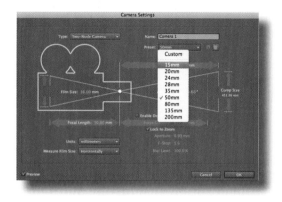

2 Double click the Camera 1 layer in the Lens Distortion comp in the Lens Distortion.aep project in the Chapter 02 folder of the exercise files. This opens the Camera Settings dialog box. Although you can also adjust the focal length of the "lens" by adjusting the Focal Length property here, you can also use the Preset drop down to choose a lens size. Choose the most wide angle lens available here – 15mm.

**HOT TIP**

Another side effect of using a wide angle lens is that Z space depth is exaggerated. Use a wide angle lens to make a background look like it is farther away from the subject than it is.

4 Select the Camera 1 layer and press **P** to reveal its Position property. Change the Z value to bring the camera closer to the solids, and rotate as desired. Notice that when you do, these square solids become distorted and rectangular as they get close to the camera. It's a really cool effect that can make objects feel that they are really coming at you. In horror films, this technique is often used to make viewers feel that something is even more horrific. But it can also be used to make motion graphics and animations more exciting.

SHORTCUTS
MAC WIN BOTH

# Multiple Camera Angles

ONE OF THE TRICKS TO MAKING ANIMATIONS FEEL MORE CINEMATIC is to change camera angles the way they do in movies. We can have a wide angle shot, where we see the big picture. Then we can cut in close to see a particular character, then cut to a reaction shot, and so forth. Using multiple cameras (especially with multiple angles), we can really tell a better story.

With a quick trick in After Effects, we can set up multiple cameras using different angles, and render them out – all in the same comp with just one render!

**1** Again we're going to be using this great art by Dan Grady. For this trick, it's a good idea to use Illustrator files (or other vector objects, like shape layers) so that we can zoom in closely with "long" lenses and still have the objects remain sharp. I've already created a wide angle lens camera for you to use as the establishing shot. You'll find this project in the Multi Camera Render.aep project in the Chapter 02 folder of the exercise files.

**3** Let's make another camera, this one using the 200mm preset so we can really get in there. This makes the plane a much more significant character in this drama.

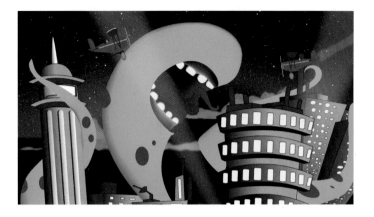

2 Create a new camera by using the keyboard shortcut ⌘ ⌥ Shift C / ctrl alt Shift C and use the 80mm preset. This is a much longer lens than the one in the previous screen shot, which zooms us into the action. Adjust the position of the camera as desired.

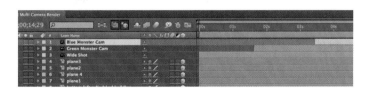

4 Create as many cameras with as many angles as you need to tell your story effectively. The trick then to change cameras within the same comp is to simply trim the length of the camera layers! To do that, simply grab the beginning or end of a layer in the Timeline panel and drag it inwards to make it shorter. Then as one camera layer ends, it will "cut" to the camera angle of the camera layer beneath it. When you render, it will be as if you had rendered multiple shots and edited them together.

SHORTCUTS
MAC WIN BOTH

# 3D Camera Path

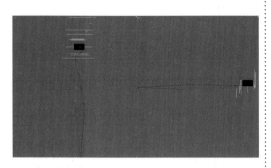

ALTHOUGH AFTER EFFECTS HAS INCREDIBLE 3D FEATURES for an application that was designed to be a 2D app, sometimes those dang cameras are just so hard to control. In this cheat, we're going to look at a way (okay, actually two ways) to control a camera using a path from another layer. This might help you be able to get better control of your camera movement. We're going to look at a way to use a 2D mask to create a camera path, and also how to create a 3D motion path for cameras. An example of this 3D camera path is shown above. Notice the curvature of the camera's path in the two different viewports.

1 Open the 3D Camera Path.aep project from the Chapter 02 folder of the exercise files. I've already got a camera set up for you here. Note that this is one of those new-fangled one-node cameras, new to After Effects CS5. I find that these are easier to use for creating predictable camera paths.

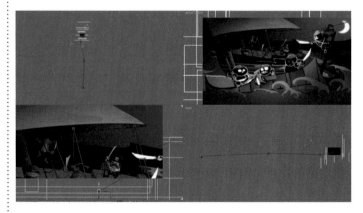

3 The other way to create a camera path isn't as easy to control, but it allows you to create a 3D motion path for your camera. The secret is to create a new null object. Masks reside on layers, and layers are 2D, therefore masks (and the paths created from them) must be 2D. However, we can move this null in 3D space. The screenshot above shows the 3D path that I created for the null object.

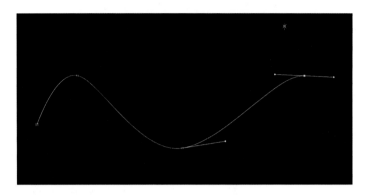

2 To easily create a 2D path for the camera to follow, grab the Pen tool. Create a new solid the size of your comp and create your camera path on it. Then select the new solid you created and press *M* to reveal the Mask Path property. Click Mask Path and then press *⌘ C* *ctrl C* to copy it. Select the camera layer and press *P* to reveal its Position property, and click it to select the property (NOT the layer). Then press *⌘ V* *ctrl V* to paste the mask, and have your camera follow this path! You may need to make small tweaks to Focal Length after pasting.

4 Select the camera layer and press *P* to reveal its Position property. *⌥* *alt* click the stopwatch to add an expression. Click and drag the expression pickwhip to the Position property of your null object. Now your camera navigates through your scene as your null object did! This made it much easier for me to navigate this camera through my 3D scene, and tell an entire story with just this one still graphic.

# Orient to Camera

AFTER EFFECTS HAS A COOL (AND SIMPLE) WAY TO AUTOMATICALLY HAVE OBJECTS POINT AT THE CAMERA, no matter where the camera goes. Although this trick is obviously handy for those times when you animate a camera moving through a room full of people, and you want those people to continually stare at the camera. However, this trick is also really helpful for adding an extra degree of apparent volume.

As the After Effects camera travels by an object, it becomes very apparent that it is only a flat layer. If the object auto-orients (i.e. automatically points) to the camera as it goes by, the object doesn't quite seem so flat.

**1** Here we have the characters and objects in their standard state with the camera looking at them straight on. This is the Orient to Camera.aep project in the Chapter 02 folder of the exercise files. All is well and good thus far...

**3** In the Timeline panel, right click on the layers for the robots (PRECOMP robot 1 and PRECOMP robot 2). Choose Transform>Auto-Orient. In the Auto-Orientation dialog box, change the setting from Off to Orient Towards Camera. This will ensure that this object will automatically point towards the camera at all times.

2 But when we orbit the camera around, they start to skew. We can see that the robots are 2D, and it makes the whole scene look less realistic.

4 With their orientation now automatically set, these two robots look towards the camera, which gives them an increased sense of life. In the screenshot above, contrast their appearance and scale with the robot on the far right with its back turned. The distortion created by the lack of proper orientation is very apparent when viewed side by side with the robots that we've adjusted. The benefit of this feature is even more pronounced when animated.

**HOT TIP**

Note that after changing the camera angle to a degree this extreme and then turning on auto-orientation, you may need to tweak the position of the characters or the Focus Distance parameter of the camera.

# Lighting is the Secret

LIGHTING IS EVERYTHING. NO, SERIOUSLY. As you work in 3D (and even as you work in 2D), it pays to remember that the lighting of a scene makes all the difference. Talk to any director of photography or talented 3D artist and they will no doubt confirm that lighting is in fact the most important ingredient in the recipe of getting a quality looking final result. Look at the werewolf on the opposite page. This is from a werewolf model created for a low poly video game. Without proper lighting, the model looks awful. But with some sweet lighting, it's a significantly improved piece of artwork.

Have you ever gone to a museum or a movie set where they have props from famous movies? If that's your thing, check out the Warner Brothers museum on the VIP Studio Tour in Burbank, CA or the Science Fiction museum in Seattle, WA. It's an incredible experience, mostly because it's not that incredible. The costumes and props that look so cool in the movies look like prizes you'd find in the bottom of your favorite  breakfast cereal when viewed up close. So how come they look so cool on screen? Yep. You guessed it. Lighting.

So then, how do you light a scene properly? Although the answer to that question might take a lifetime of experience to master, there are some good tips that I can give you to at least help you get started.

The first is what they call three point lighting. It's a basic lighting setup where you have one main light (called a "key" light). This is the light that creates your shadows, and it's placed in front of the subject, usually higher in the air and slightly off to the side a bit. The second light is a fill light, to basically lighten the shadows and create more ambient light. The third light is placed behind the subject and is used to highlight the edges around the subject, creating more of a sense of the volume of the object. Check out the shot on the opposite page of this kid that I made (with a little help from my wife, I guess). This is a raw still from a short film I made called *The Young are the Restless*. You can see the shadows under her chin, on the plate, and (unfortunately) on the back wall. The shadows indicate where the key light is. Notice the light underneath her right arm and on her back. This is from the backlight. I'm admittedly not that good at lighting, but I think the backlight here adds a lot of volume and dimension to this shot.

Another tip is to simply observe the real world. Try this: go somewhere where there is an obvious light source coming from above you (e.g. a room with a light, or outside in daylight). Then hover your hand right above the surface (maybe about a half inch or so). Note the shadow – it's opacity, it's color, and the softness of the edges. Now raise your hand away from the surface. What happens to the shadow? Why does it do that? Little tests like this can help you understand more about the way that light works.

Even if you never take on the role of gaffer in a movie production, your job as an After Effects artist will be greatly improved by knowing about lighting, and how to control it to get the results you're looking for.

■ We're going to
be making both
of these scenes
from total scratch
in After Effects,
without the use of
external images or
footage.

# 3

# 3D Objects

TURNING A 2D LAYER INTO A 3D LAYER COULDN'T BE
ANY EASIER – just check the 3D Layer checkbox in the
Timeline panel. Cake. Anyone can do that.

But what we're going to examine in this chapter is a load
of tricks and features in After Effects to create 3D objects,
including some unconventional ones, and some great new
stuff in CS5. We'll even look briefly at a new feature in
Photoshop CS5 Extended that allows you to create and
texture 3D objects from scratch, and then import those
objects (keeping them 3D!) into After Effects. After going
through the tips in this chapter, you will no doubt be able
to create more thrilling 3D objects and environments in
your future After Effects projects.

# The Parallax Effect

PARALLAX IS NOT REALLY AN AFTER EFFECTS-SPECIFIC CHEAT. It's a principle that you should be aware of when working in 3D. Because of the nature of the 3D in After Effects, you're typically just moving flat objects, or "postcards in space" as it's been called. As we rotate around a 3D scene, we see objects that are near to us moving at a different rate of speed than those objects that are distant from us. This is parallax.

This is also the way that you are able to see 3D. Try this experiment. With both eyes open, hold up a finger centered between your eyes, about six inches away from your head. Look at a stationary object off in the distance. Now take turns closing one eye and opening the other. Notice how the difference between the two views. Your finger appears to move in the opposite direction of the background object. Being aware of this phenomenon will help you get the most out of your 3D experience in After Effects.

1 Take this art for example (which you can find in The Parallax Effect.aep project in the Chapter 03 folder of the exercise files). By the way, this fantastic art was created by artist Dan Grady.

3 The reason I keep all that stuff in the background (and foreground) is that these objects provide important background layering necessary to enhance the parallax effect. There really isn't anything behind the green monster's head without the clouds and stars. Notice the first frame of the moving camera when the stars and clouds are visible.

2 One might argue that the art looks much cleaner without all of the stars and clouds in the background, especially when static.

4 Here is the same scene with the camera moving in the opposite direction. Again pay particular attention to the area behind the head of the green monster. What gives you clues that the camera has moved? What if those background objects weren't there? The clouds and stars in the extreme background and the fighter planes in the extreme foreground are what I refer to as "depth cues" – objects that indicate that the camera is moving in 3D space. Can you find any other depth cues in these images? The careful use of depth cues is the key to using the parallax effect, and is what will make your 3D projects in After Effects really come alive.

**HOT TIP**

In most 3D scenes, objects are adjusted in 3D space to exist farther away from the camera, or to be closer to it. Objects that have not had their Z position changed from the default value typically don't move much when the camera is orbited around the scene. For that reason, I refer to this zone as the "focal plane". The focal plane is a good spot to put things that need to be very clear for the duration of the animation, such as text or a client logo. Note that if your camera animation is less orbital and more of a dolly shot, then the focal plane will be irrelevant.

# 3D in Repoussé

OK, SO TECHNICALLY, THIS CHEAT DEALS WITH PHOTOSHOP. But as we'll see in the following cheat, this is a direct benefit for After Effects users. Besides, every After Effects user uses Photoshop, right? Of course.

In Photoshop CS5 Extended, Adobe has added a new module called Repoussé which allows you to create 3D objects from scratch. And it's just so easy! You take practically any object, and Repoussé will extrude it, and/or bevel it, bloat it, texture it, and give you all kinds of interesting creative options.

Here, we'll create a 3D object from scratch and use that object in a real world design. In the next cheat, we'll take this same 3D object into After Effects where we can manipulate it as if it were a true 3D object. Note that using 3D from Photoshop files is the only way to get truly 3D objects natively into After Effects.

1 In Photoshop, open up the Repousse.psd file from the Media folder in the Exercise Files folder. Then ⌥ alt click the eye icon for the flower shape layer in the Layers panel to see only this layer (kind of like the equivalent of soloing the layer in After Effects).

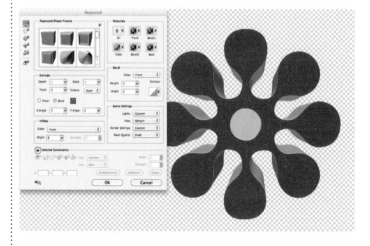

3 Behold Repoussé! Even without adjusting any parameters, we see that Repoussé has made our little flower an extruded 3D object. Even while the Repoussé window is open, we can click and drag around the flower in our document window to rotate it around in 3D.

2 To make this simple layer a 3D object, click on it to select it in the Layers panel, then go to the Window menu at the top of the interface and choose Window>3D, which will open the 3D panel. At the bottom of the 3D panel, in the Create New 3D Object area, select 3D Repoussé Object, and press the Create button. You will get a warning saying that Photoshop will have to rasterize the layer. Choose yes to make it happen.

**HOT TIP**

If you inadvertently close Repoussé, or would like to edit your Repoussé object again after you've created it, go to the 3D menu at the top of the interface and choose 3D> Repoussé>Edit in Repoussé.

4 While we're here, let's play around a bit. In the Extrude area, increase the Depth value to about 3.3. Increase the Twist value to about 110 or so. Decrease Scale to about 0.5. I'm also going to click and drag on my shape to rotate it a little. Not bad, Photoshop!

**continued...**

# 3D in Repoussé (continued)

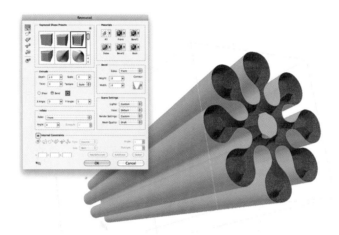

**5** OK. Enough goofing around (for now). Let's get back to the project at hand by going to the Repoussé Shape Presets area at the top, and choosing the preset called Bevel 2. Notice that completely overrides our previous settings for Depth, Scale, and Twist. Let's leave Twist at 0. But take Scale back down to 0.5 and take Depth to 2.5. In the Bevel area, take the Width value down to 15.

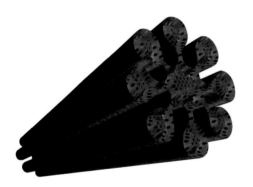

**8** Go ahead and click OK to accept this object. Photoshop will render it with better quality. I like it!

**9** Of course, it gets much better. You can also go to the 3D panel to improve the quality further. At the top of the panel, make sure Filter By: Whole scene is selected. Then, from the Quality drop down, change this from Interactive to Ray Traced Draft. This takes a LONG time, but it improves the quality quite a bit.

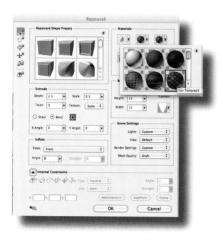

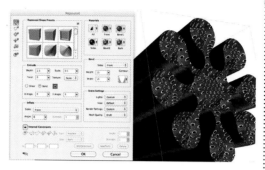

**6** This is looking a little funky. So let's use another great Repoussé feature and texture this object. In the Materials area, click the Front texture and from the popup library, choose Fun Textured3. Yep. Fun Textured 1 and 2 just aren't enough fun for us. Apply the same texture to Bevel1.

**7** Now change the texture for the Sides, but this time choose Satin Black as the texture. I realize the red "fun" texture still looks a little rough. Photoshop will fix that for us automatically once we exit Repoussé.

**HOT TIP**

Adobe has generously created loads of additional materials libraries that you can download and install for free. Just go to the 3D menu in Photoshop and choose Browse 3D Content Online. And they're actually really GOOD libraries, too. There's a library of glass textures, a library of metal textures, and several more.

**10** Select the Object Rotate Tool in the Tools panel to rotate this object in 3D space if you like. From there, you can arrange these 3D objects into a design like this. And remember that these are live 3D objects. So if you wanted to change the red or black texture, or if you wanted to adjust the light source, or if you wanted to change the bevel or extrusion settings, you can do that. Ahhh... I just love 3D.

# Photoshop 3D in After Effects

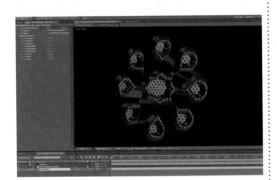

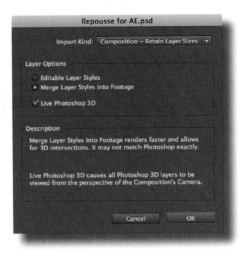

N OW THAT WE KNOW HOW TO CREATE 3D
OBJECTS from scratch in Photoshop, it's
time to look at importing those 3D objects into
After Effects. There are a few tricks to this, so
here's hoping that this cheat is helpful for you.

I should also point out that not only does
this technique work for importing 3D objects
created in Repoussé, but it also works with any
other 3D object in a PSD file. As mentioned
previously, this is the only way natively to bring
a truly 3D dimensional object into After Effects
and manipulate it in 3D space.

**1** In After Effects, import the Repousse for AE.psd file from Exercise
Files>Media>PSDs. Be sure to choose to import this as a composition. Here,
we'll go ahead and choose Composition – Retain Layer Sizes. In the dialog box that
follows, be sure to choose Live Photoshop 3D so that 3D layers from Photoshop
maintain their 3D-ness. Click OK to import.

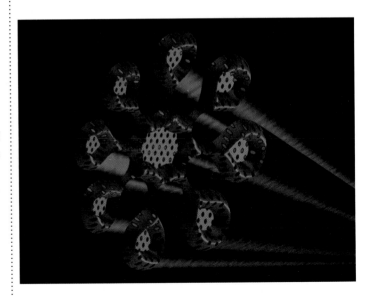

**3** Right about now, you might be looking at this 3D object and wondering about
the quality, or rather the lack thereof. Here's the deal – this object used the
Interactive quality mode in Photoshop. If that's the case, it will never get better
than that here in After Effects. Select one of the layers of this PSD from the
Repousse for AE Layers folder in the Project panel. Press ⌘ E ctrl E to open it
in Photoshop.

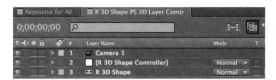

2 Notice our layers in the Timeline panel. Layers 3 and 4 are our 3D layers. Upon import, After Effects turned these 3D layers into their own nested compositions. Double click layer 3 to open it up. You'll find that After Effects has actually created a null object and a camera for each of the 3D objects. Use the camera to navigate around the 3D object. Use the null to transform the 3D object instead of using the 3D layer's layer transforms.

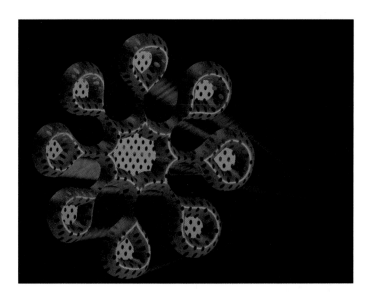

4 In the 3D panel in Photoshop, change the Quality drop down to Ray Traced Draft and then go get yourself a sandwich. It takes quite a while to render. After that's done, save the file and go back to After Effects. Right click on a layer from the Photoshop document in the Project panel and choose Reload Footage. Now, this will make things look better, but render slower in After Effects. To remedy this, change the 3D layer's quality switch in the Timeline panel from Best to Draft while you're working. Then change it back to Best for your final render.

**HOT TIP**

Although 3D objects from Photoshop are truly 3D, and therefore can respond to lights, they do not respond to the lights in After Effects. So, if you want to customize the lighting on your 3D object, you must do so in Photoshop.

# 3

# 3D Shatter Scenes

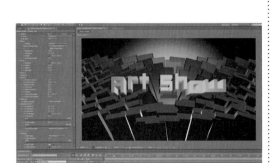

S O THE 3D IN THE ABOVE SCREENSHOT IS KINDA COOL, YES? Can you guess what program it was made in? Was it 3DS Max? Cinema 4D? Perhaps Maya?

Actually, the 3D in the project shown above was created entirely in After Effects, without the help of additional plugins. And both the text and the background were not only created from scratch in After Effects, but they are completely editable in 3D. You can adjust the 3D lighting and the 3D camera angle.

What might be even more surprising is that these objects were created by playing around with the Shatter effect. Created many, many years ago by After Effects legend Brian Maffitt, this effect was originally intended to just blow stuff up (as it says in its description in the Effects Control panel if you press the "About" button). But this effect was years ahead of its time. As we'll see, Shatter is capable of much more than just shattering, thanks to the 3D environment that it creates.

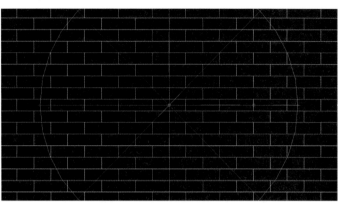

**1** In the Shatter.aep project in the Chapter 03 folder of the exercise files, open up the Shatter START comp (which is actually blank). Press ⌘ Y / ctrl Y to create a new solid layer. Make it white. Apply the Shatter effect, which isn't much to look at in its default state. This view is a working view. The Shatter effect breaks your layer up into pieces. The wireframe shows the pieces. The blue lines show you the force that blows up your layer.

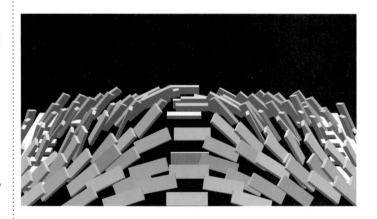

**3** As mentioned, the real amazing thing (to me) about Shatter is that it creates a three dimensional shatter. In its effect controls, scroll down to the Camera Position area and open that up. This is the virtual camera that controls Shatter. Take X Rotation to about −70 degrees. Take Y position down to about 230 or so.

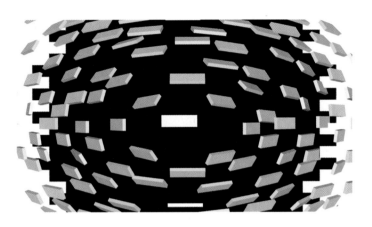

**2** In the Shatter effect controls (in the Effect Controls panel), change the View drop down from Wireframe + Forces to Rendered. If, after changing the View value, you only see white, go out a few frames in time. Shatter is an auto-animating effect, and the shattering effect doesn't start until the layer's second frame. This shot is from 0;00;00;08 in my comp.

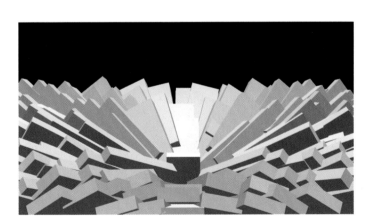

**4** So, as you can see, these are real 3D bricks we're dealing with here! Let's make these bricks look more like buildings by going to the Shape area in the Shatter effect controls and increasing the Extrusion Depth value to about 5 or so. That's kinda cool, but now you can see that the edges aren't blowing up. In the Force 1 area, increase the Radius value to about 0.6 to blow up those pesky edges. You may want to increase the Y position of the camera after that.

continued...

**HOT TIP**

In addition to controlling Shatter with the Camera Position controls, you can also change the Camera System drop down to control Shatter with either corner pins, or the first camera in your composition.

SHORTCUTS
MAC WIN BOTH

# 3D Shatter Scenes (continued)

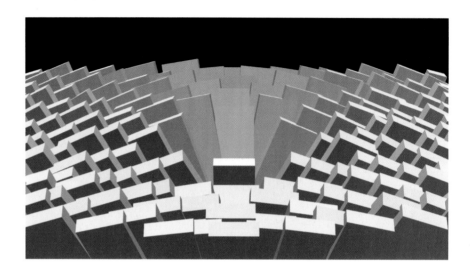

**5** One of the benefits of Shatter is that it auto-animates. One of the problems of Shatter is that it auto-animates. If you preview a frame later on in the timeline, you'll notice that your design just falls apart (well, it technically shatters). In the Physics area, make the "air" thicker by increasing the Viscosity value to 1.0 and take the Gravity value down to 0. Wait a minute! What happened?!? To fix this, let's increase the Force 1>Strength value to 13.

**7** As part of the "real" 3D environment that Shatter creates, a light is created for you. Adjusting the light can help you create significantly more realism in your 3D Shatter scene. Change the Lighting>Light Type value to Point Source to create a more dramatic effect. Then take Light Depth to –0.1, and increase the Light Intensity to 1.5.

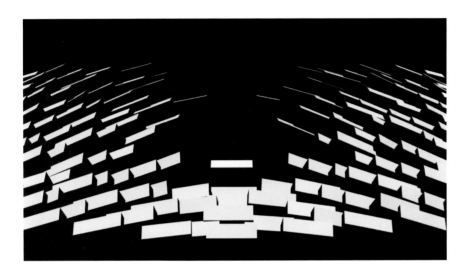

6 I think I've gone without color for about as long as I can stand. Thankfully, Shatter allows you to add textures to the front, side, and back of these 3D pieces. When we texture a side, we basically have two choices – we can texture it with the color in the Textures>Color swatch, or we can use a layer. Click that color swatch and change the color to a deep red. Change the Textures>Side Mode drop down to Color.

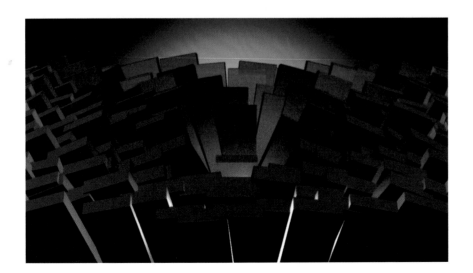

8 For the finishing touches, I boosted contrast with the Levels effect and the Glow effect, then added a gradient background. I also fiddled around with the Materials settings in the Shatter effect to change how the light reacts when it hits the shattered pieces. Keep in mind that this scene is still 3D, and can be navigated with cameras in 3D space.

# 3 3D Objects
# 3D Text

O NE OF THE BIGGEST REASONS THAT
MANY AFTER EFFECTS USERS LEARN a
dedicated 3D modeling application is just to be
able to create three dimensional extruded text.
In the last cheat, we used Shatter to create a 3D
environment. Here, we're going to take things
to an entirely new level. We're going to use
Shatter to create our own custom 3D objects –
3D text, in this case.

1 In the 3D Text.aep project in the Chapter 03 folder of
the exercise files, go to the 3D Text START comp. This
comp contains some background layers (which are currently
shy), and some shapes created from a text layer. It's the text
shapes that we're going to be converting into 3D objects.

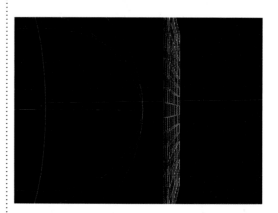

4 So that Shatter doesn't blow up our text, open the
Force 1 area and increase the Depth value until the blue
force doesn't touch the wireframe shattering wall. A value
of about 0.5 should do it. Now that the blue force never
touches the text, it will never shatter.

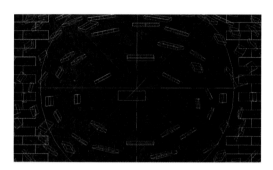

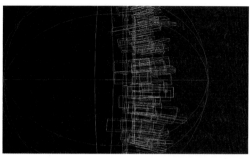

**2** Press ⌘Y ctrl Y to create a new solid. Make it the same size as the comp and name the layer Shatter Text. Apply the Shatter effect to this solid layer (NOT the layer with the text shapes on it). In the Timeline, click the layer's solo switch so we're only seeing this layer.

**3** As it stands now, Shatter is just going to blow up our solid layer. Unlike the previous cheat, we don't want anything blowing up here; we just want to use Shatter to make our text three dimensional. Open the Camera Position controls and take the Y Rotation value to –88 degrees. Now we can see the side view of our explosion.

**5** The last step is perhaps most important. In the Shatter effect controls, go to the Shape area. Change the Pattern drop down to Custom. Then, from the Custom Shatter Map drop down, choose the Art Show Outlines layer. Now you have 3D text! To see it, change the View drop down from Wireframe + Forces to Rendered. Change the Y Rotation value of the camera in Shatter back to 0. Increase the 3D extrusion by increasing the Extrusion Depth value in the Shape area. Here, I also changed the color of the light to a cyan color to match the background that we created in the last cheat.

# 3D Postcards

W HEN PEOPLE SPEAK OF THE 3D IN AFTER EFFECTS and the lack thereof, they often deride it be referring to it as "postcards in space." Well, there might be occasions where that's exactly the look that you are going for.

After Effects actually has a couple of tools for creating instant distribution and animation of 3D postcards, including what is seen on the back of the virtual cards. This can be helpful for creating an instant array of playing cards, or for creating the look that an entire stadium of people is holding up and flipping posters, or for simply creating a massive, three dimensional array of photographs, as we'll do in this cheat.

1 We're going to start with the 3D Postcards START comp in the 3D Postcards.aep project in the Chapter 03 folder of the exercise files. I've created this very large PSD file to use. This is a bunch of animal photos I've taken that have been arranged in a 6 x 6 grid.

4 Now let's play with this! Apply the Card Wipe effect to the Photos.psd layer in the 3D Postcards START comp. The cards don't quite match our photos. So in the Card Wipe effect controls, make the Rows and Columns values both 6, because that corresponds to how many rows and columns our photo grid has.

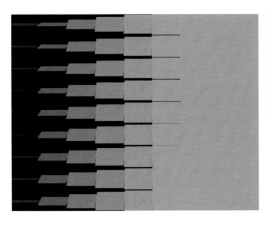

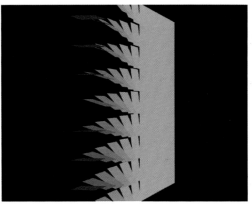

**2** We're going to bring this to life with the Card Wipe effect. But before we do that, I want to demonstrate what this effect does using a simple solid. This is what the solid looks like after Card Wipe has been applied with its default settings.

**3** At first, it's really not clear (to me, anyway) what Card Wipe is doing exactly. It's actually creating a series of 3D cards and is flipping them to reveal the content underneath. To see the "3D-ness" of the cards, I can adjust the Y rotation of the virtual camera, similar to what we did with Shatter. Ah, now it's easier to see what Card Wipe is doing.

**5** Another cool trick with Card Wipe is that you can put stuff on the back of the cards! In the 3D Postcards DONE comp, you'll see this Animal Discoveries logo layer. We're going to put this on the back of the cards, so that they flip to reveal it. To do that, simply choose the layer from the Back Layer drop down in the Card Wipe effect controls.

**6** At the bottom of the Card Wipe effect controls, open the Position Jitter controls. Increase one of the jitter amount controls to distribute the cards along that axis. Then animate Transition Completion to flip the cards and you're done!

**HOT TIP**

Animating these cards is easy, but a little confusing. In both the Position Jitter and Rotation Jitter areas, you'll find that each dimension has an amount value and a speed value. Once you increase the amount value to anything besides 0, that property of the cards will auto-animate (wiggle) using the amount value and the speed value. To transform them without the wiggle, take the speed value to 0.

# 3D Objects from Solids

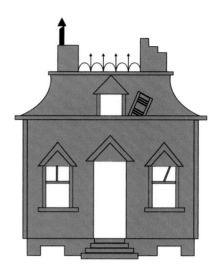

ALTHOUGH NOT IDEAL, IT IS POSSIBLE in a pinch to create simple three dimensional objects entirely out of solid layers. The screenshot above was taken from a video tutorial that I created, demonstrating ways to create 3D in After Effects. The entire door – including the door jamb paneling on the door – was created using solids in After Effects. The group of solids that make up the door was then parented to a null object so that the door can open and close. Sexy 1940's era film noir lighting was added, and there you have it.

In this cheat, I'm going to walk you through the steps of how I created a more elaborate 3D object with solids. Again, this method is not preferable to creating a 3D object in a 3D program. However, it is a good reminder that solids can be oh so much more than just flat objects.

1 For this particular project, I started in Adobe Illustrator. Man, I love Illustrator. I find that it's often a lot easier to sketch out ideas in Illustrator than After Effects. So this is what I drew there. And actually, this is based on the art of Ed Emberley, who makes these really fun drawing books that I've been a big fan of since I was a kid.

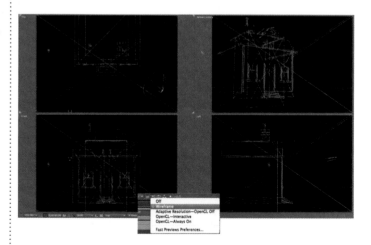

3 After I had assembled the rough template, I went to work making solids for every side of everything – a solid for each side of each post of the door frame, each side of each step, and so on. So that I could align each layer a little easier in 3D, and so that these layers would render a little faster, I used the Wireframe view from the Fast Previews drop down at the bottom of the Composition panel. This had the added benefit of making me feel like an architect, which I enjoyed.

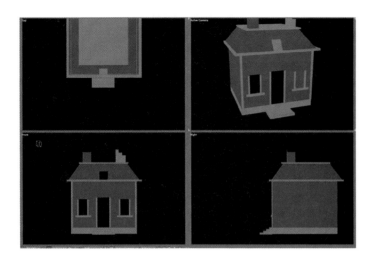

2 I then imported this AI file into After Effects so that I could use this as a template for creating my 3D house. Once imported, I locked the Illustrator file so that I couldn't mess it up on accident. I then used this as a reference to assemble a rough 3D structure using solids.

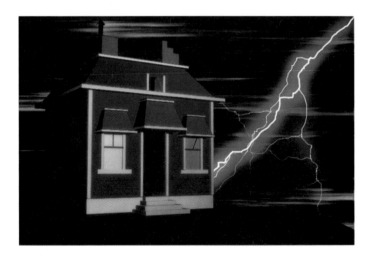

4 For the final house scene, I added some lighting, some lightning, and a cool fractal noise cloud background. Now again, it's not the most impressive thing you've ever seen, but it is 3D. I can move lights around it, and pilot a camera through it if needed. Having objects with three dimensions gives you a lot more control over their animation and lighting.

# 3D Distortion

THERE ARE SEVERAL TOOLS FOR WARPING OBJECTS IN AFTER EFFECTS. Heck, there's even an entire effects category devoted to warping, stretching, bending, and otherwise fiddling with your layers.

But most of these effects only distort in two dimensions. Using included 3rd party effects, however, we can absolutely warp objects in all three dimensions. In this cheat, we're going to get more familiar with two effects that can be used to create 3D distortion. We're going to use these effects to create a three dimensional circus tent. We might even learn a few extra tricks along the way!

1 First, we're going to make the bottom part of the tent. You can open up the 3D Distortion.aep project in the Chapter 03 folder of the exercise files if you'd like to use that as a reference. Create a 1280 x 720 comp. Create a white solid and make it the same width as the comp (1280 pixels), but make it half of the height (360 pixels).

3 Now we need to precompose these layers. Select the Timeline panel and press ⌘ A ctrl A to select all layers, then press ⌘ Shift C ctrl Shift C to precompose these layers. Name the precomp Tent. Now we can edit them as one. To this nested precomp layer, apply the CC Cylinder effect, which will wrap this layer around a 3D cylinder. This is the base of our tent. Using the CC Cylinder effect controls, we can rotate, move, and change the lighting of this cylinder.

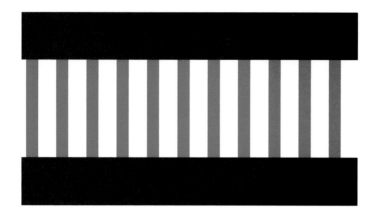

2 Select this solid and press ⌘ D ctrl D to duplicate the layer. Select the top copy and press ⌘ Shift Y ctrl Shift Y to adjust the settings of this solid. Making sure that the "Affect all layers that use this solid" option is turned OFF, change the color of this solid to red. Then apply the Venetian Blinds effect to the red solid layer. In the Venetian Blinds effect controls, increase the Transition Completion value to 60% and the Width value to 115.

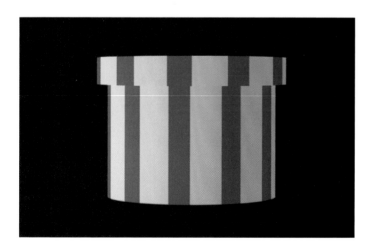

4 Select the Tent layer and duplicate the layer using the shortcut from step 2. Name this copy Tent Overhang. Adjust the Y scale and the Radius value in the CC Cylinder effect controls for each layer to create a tent with an overhang.

continued...

**HOT TIP**

So this is probably the most depressing "Hot Tip" of all time. The CC Cylinder does have 3D camera and 3D lighting controls. Unfortunately, however, the CC Cylinder effect does not respond to After Effects cameras or lights.

SHORTCUTS

# 3D Distortion (continued)

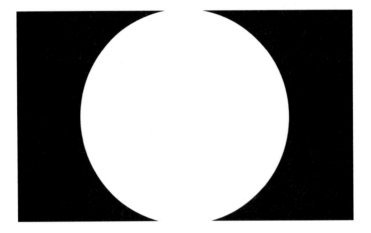

**5** Temporarily turn off the visibility for the Tent and Tent Overhang layers. Press F2 to deselect all layers. Then select the Ellipse tool in the Tool bar and create an ellipse in the center of the comp. Hold *Shift* while creating it to make it a perfect circle. Give it a white fill and no stroke.

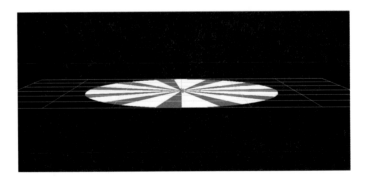

**8** In the DE_FreeFormAE effect controls, change the Rotation X value (found in the 3D Mesh Controls area) to –82 degrees so that we can see what we're doing. Click a point in the center of the mesh to highlight it.

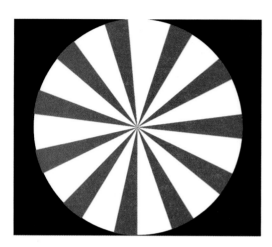

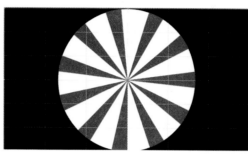

**6** This step is fun. Make a red solid the size of the comp. Apply the Venetian Blinds effect to this layer. In the Venetian Blinds effect controls, change the Transition Completion value to 60% and the Width value to 115. Now apply the Polar Coordinates effect, and adjust its Type of Conversion to Rect to Polar and increase Interpolation to 100%.

**7** Now select both of these new layers using the **Shift** key and precompose as we did in step 3 and call this nested comp Tent Top. Then apply the DE_FreeFormAE effect to the Tent Top layer. This is a 3rd party effect that now comes with After Effects CS5. In the Grid area in its effect controls, increase both the Rows and Columns values to 6.

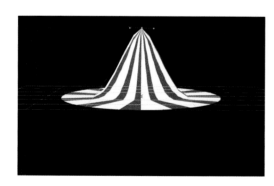

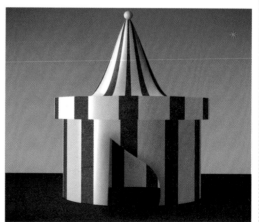

**9** Drag it upwards to deform this mesh in 3D, creating a point to the top of the tent. Unlike CC Cylinder, FreeFormAE responds to After Effects lights (but not After Effects cameras). In the 3D Mesh Quality area, change the Antialiasing value to High to increase the quality (if desired).

**10** Here is the final image after arranging the Tent Top layer in 3D space, adding lights, adding a background, adding a ball at the top (using CC Sphere) and creating a mask for the front part of the door. Each component of this tent is 3D!

SHORTCUTS
MAC WIN BOTH

# 3D Planetscape

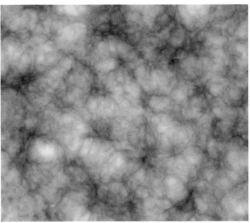

S IMILAR TO THE PREVIOUS CHEAT, WE'RE GOING TO MAKE A 3D SCENE using FreeformAE and a Cycore 3D effect. This time we're going to be creating a 3D planet scene. But this time, when we use the FreeformAE effect, we're going to use fractal noise as a displacement map to create 3D displacement on a regular old solid layer.

**1** If you'd like to dissect a finished version of this project, I've created one called 3D Planet.aep which you'll find in the Chapter 03 folder of the exercise files. The first step is to create a 1280 x 720 comp. Then create a new solid layer and apply the Fractal Noise effect to it. In its effect controls, change the Fractal Type to Dynamic. For more info on Fractal Noise, check out the cheats in Chapter 10.

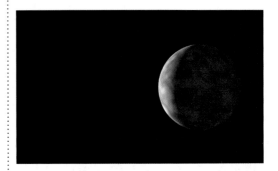

**4** To make this beautiful planet match our scene a bit more, in the CC Sphere effect controls, change the Light Intensity to 225, the Light Height to −40, the Shading>Ambient value to 20, and increase the X value of the Offset property to about 925 or so to move our planet over to the right. Note that you can make the planet rotate in 3D by adjusting Rotation>Rotation Y

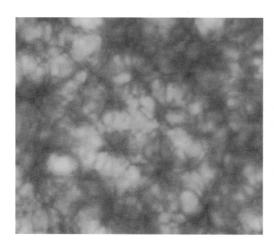

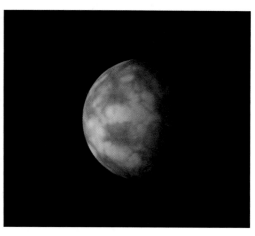

**2** This pattern will be the texture for our planet. To me, there's too much contrast here. So change the Overflow drop down to Soft Clamp to make sure that our highlights and shadows are more dull. Adjust Complexity, Scale, Brightness, and Contrast to your liking. I also created a yellowish solid above this layer and put it into the Soft Light blend mode in order to colorize this.

**3** Press ⌘ A ctrl A to select all layers and then press ⌘ Shift C ctrl Shift C to precompose these layers. Call this new composition planet. Apply the CC Sphere effect to the nested precomp.

**5** Press ⌘ Y ctrl Y to create a new white solid. Make it the size of the comp, and apply the CC Star Burst effect to it. It's important that the solid is white because the CC Star Burst effect creates stars that are the same color as the layer it's applied to. Drag this layer beneath the planet layer.

**6** OK, so the stars look terrible. Let's fix them. In the effect controls for CC Star Burst, take the Scatter value to 200, and the Size value to 30. I also added the Fast Blur effect with a very low Blurriness value (0.5), just to soften the edges.

continued...

SHORTCUTS
MAC WIN BOTH

# 3 3D Planetscape (continued)

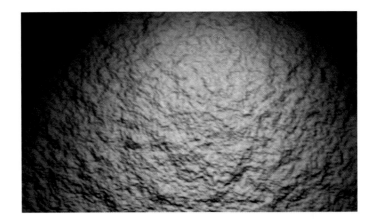

**7** Make a solid and apply Fractal Noise. The default settings will be fine. Select this layer and precompose it as we did in step 3. Choose the "Move all attributes..." option and call it foreground texture. Create a new light yellow solid layer (or whatever color you'd like your foreground planet soil to be). Apply the DE_FreeformAE effect to this new solid. In the Displacement Controls area in its effect controls, choose the foreground texture layer from the Displace Layer drop down. Change the 3D Mesh Quality>Mesh Subdivision property to 300 and Displacement Controls>Displace Height to 50. Create a light.

**9** One of the things that the eyes really love is contrast. Right now, we're looking at two planets in shadow. In space. And as expected, it's dark. Press F2 to make sure all layers are deselected, then select the Ellipse tool in the tool bar. Click and drag to make a light yellow-orange ellipse about the size of the foreground surface. Then deselect all again and make another ellipse about the size of the planet and drag these below their corresponding layers in the layer stack in the Timeline panel.

**8** The cool thing about this displacement is that it's actually three dimensional. In the 3D Mesh Controls area of the FreeformAE effect controls, adjust the Rotation X value to about −70. Adjust the position and rotation values, and the settings of the light as desired. For a more controlled way to displace a layer, check out the cheats in Chapter 5.

**10** For the final touches, I applied the Fast Blur effect to both of the shape layers and increased the Blurriness value to taste. For additional sexiness, I then applied the Optical Flares effect from Video Copilot. Note that if you do not have this effect installed on your machine, you will not be able to see these layers in the project file, but they are not essential to the scene. Also keep in mind that although these objects can't be controlled by an After Effects camera, they are volumetric 3D objects that can be moved in 3D space!

# 3
# Echospace

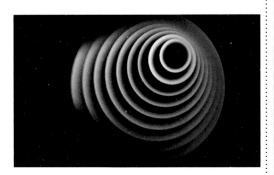

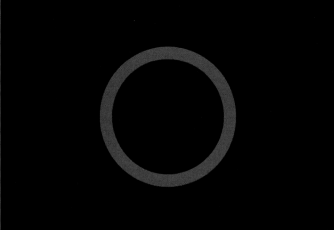

RAPCODE'S ECHOSPACE IS A GREAT LITTLE PLUGIN EFFECT that duplicates and distributes layers in 3D space, and provides a handy way to control all of these layers as well.

The screenshot above is taken from a (free) tutorial that I created for Red Giant Software. I used Echospace to create a psychedelic spiral in the style of the old *Twilight Zone* television show intros. The copies created by Echospace are just regular layers, and as such, respond to lights, as seen in the film noir style lighting above. We're going to be creating something similar, but slightly more colorful than that.

For creating motion graphics or even abstract animated art, I find Echospace a helpful and creativity-inspiring plugin. If you don't own Echospace, you can get a free trial download of it from redgiantsoftware.com.

1 Create a new 1280 x 720 comp, and a new black solid of the same size. Apply the somewhat rare Circle effect. In the Effect Controls panel, take the Radius to 122, the Edge drop down to Thickness*Radius, and the Thickness to 20. Click the Color swatch and replace it with something more colorful. I chose purple.

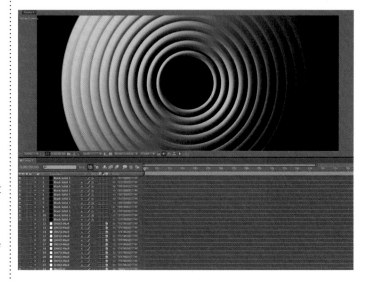

3 Echospace creates multiple copies of your layer. The Setup>Instances value determines the number of copies. This is similar to the repeater operator with shape layers. In the Repeater area, increase the Z Offset value to 300, and the Scale value to 30. Then click the Setup>Commands>Repeat button to generate the copies.

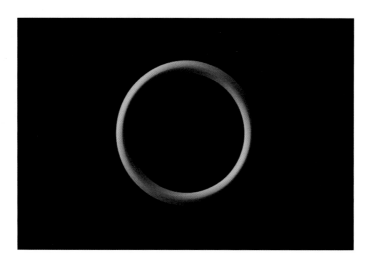

2 Next, apply another oft-used effect – the Bevel Alpha effect. In its effect controls, take the Edge Thickness value to 12 and the Light Intensity value to 0.6. Then apply the Echospace effect.

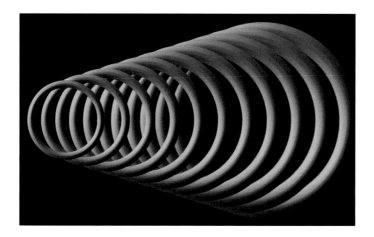

4 So that's pretty convenient, but the real magic of this effect is that you can still make adjustments, either to the master null (called "Main[14]" here) or to the Echospace effect on the original layer. In this case, I increased the Repeater>X Offset value of the Echospace effect on the original solid to about 70, and I decided to reduce the Scale value to about 15.

**HOT TIP**

Echospace automatically creates multiple null objects to control each duplicate, and a master null is created that is the parent to all of those nulls. Additionally, it makes all layers it creates (except the master null) shy. So all you have to do is to click the master shy switch at the top of the Timeline panel to hide all layers except the original layer with Echospace and the master null.

77

# 3D in Nested Compositions

**W**ORKING WITH 3D LAYERS IS PRETTY STRAIGHT FORWARD. However, once those layers are precomposed, it's a different story. It can be a challenge accessing 3D data in nested compositions. So in this cheat, we're going to look at how to save your sanity in those cases where you have 3D in nested comp layers.

1 We're going to start with this little promo video that I made. You'll find this project in the Chad Show Bumper Final.aep project in the Chapter 03 folder of the exercise files. I had all of these layers, and I wanted to precompose them so that I can move them together, and mask them as one object as well. These layers can be found in the PRECOMP left stuff composition. I added a white background so it would be easier to see what is happening.

3 The cheat here is that the three dimensions of the original layers CAN in fact be accessed in the parent comp! Instead of clicking the 3D switch for the nested precomp layer, enable Collapse Transformations (which is also the switch used to continuously rasterize Illustrator files). Then create a new camera. Now when we rotate around with the camera, we can see that the layers are 3D again!

2 These layers have been arranged at different places in 3D space (along the Z axis). If we precompose these layers, the resultant nested comp will be a regular old 2D layer. If we enable the 3D switch for this layer, we can move and rotate it in 3D space, but we've lost all of the depth of the original layers! Boo!

4 With the Collapse Transformations switch enabled, we can now access the 3D depth from the original layers using cameras, lights, or nulls that the nested comp is parented to. Additionally, this switch will allow blend modes from the nested layers to be respected as well.

**HOT TIP**

I learned from Aharon Rabinowitz from All Bets Are Off Productions that you can increase the Z scale value on the nested precomp layer to increase the 3D distance between the layers in the precomp!

# 3 INTERLUDE

# Picking a 3D App

FOR MANY USERS OF AFTER EFFECTS, THESE COOL 3D TRICKS JUST AREN'T
ENOUGH. They need a dedicated 3D application. And hey, I can relate to that. I
got into 3DS Max many years ago, and totally fell in love with the world of 3D.
I've since switched computer platforms (from PC to Mac), and unfortunately,
they don't make 3DS Max for the Mac. So, I've switched over to Cinema 4D,
which I really love. No 3D application integrates better with After Effects than
does Cinema 4D, which can actually output your 3D scene as an After Effects
project file. It also has many features dedicated just to creating incredible
motion graphics.

But do you need a 3D application, and if so, which one? Notice the text on
the opposite page. This was created in Cinema 4D. I took some basic splines (i.e.
paths) from Illustrator and then extruded them and beveled them in Cinema
4D. Although Photoshop CS5 Extended is getting close to this, it's much
more awkward and clunky doing it in Photoshop than it is in a dedicated 3D
program like this. Notice the beveled edges on the front, and the way that the
light interacts with them. That type of thing is just so much easier in a 3D app.
Also, if you wanted something with roundness (like a humanoid character)
or something to deform and animate in 3D, or if you just want to create a
complex structure (like a skyscraper), you're probably better off learning a 3D
app.

But which one? For many, price is a huge consideration. The big 3D apps
(e.g. Maya, 3DS Max, Cinema 4D, Lightwave, Softimage, etc.) all carry a hefty
price tag, starting around $1000, and averaging around $3000. If price is a
big concern for you, fear not! Check out Blender from Blender.org. It is a high
quality 3D app with most of the features of the big guys, but it's completely
free! Although I find the interface and workflow less intuitive and the learning
curve much steeper, you can't beat the price tag!

For those wanting to work in the video game industry, you should know
that most video games are created in 3DS Max. For the film industry, Maya is

probably still the champion in that arena. And Cinema 4D is perhaps the most common software out there for broadcast graphics. Be advised however, that any 3D app can be used in almost any setting because the core features are very similar between 3D apps.

While it's definitely not essential to learn a 3D program to create phenomenal 3D art, I find that it helps a lot. It's also great for sparking creative ideas that I had never thought of while working only in 2D. As another side benefit (that might not apply to you), I found that learning a dedicated 3D app really helped me in the 3D environment in After Effects. I've always found AE's 3D environment really awkward, like the program wasn't really designed to do 3D stuff (which it wasn't). Seeing how 3D is SUPPOSED to work with cameras and lights and viewports that are much easier to control, has really helped my 3D in the relatively scaled down world of After Effects 3D.

■ Blowing up houses? Making a fake subway? Toy monsters destroying a peaceful suburban neighborhood? A pretty girl flirting with me? All of these seeming impossibilities will be made real in this chapter!

# 4

# Compositing

COMBINING MULTIPLE OBJECTS INTO ONE is surely one of the most common purposes of using After Effects. In this chapter, we're going to cover everything from near-automatic rotoscoping with Roto Brush to motion tracking with Mocha, and the basics of compositing and removing a green screen background, and tons of stuff in between. We'll also look at a few little tips and tricks that help me when I'm working in the world of compositing.

Compositing is just one of those things that makes people's mouths hang open in disbelief when done properly. And this is a great time to make this course of study, as most of the new features in After Effects CS5 were geared towards the compositing workflow. So, much of this chapter is going to be cutting edge stuff. This is going to be a blast.

# Making a Garbage Matte

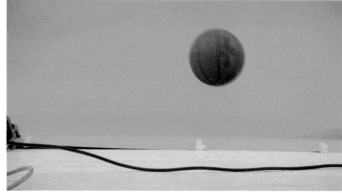

1 Import the IHB ball 01.mp4 clip from Exercise Files>Media>Video. This is some footage we shot for the short film *I Hate Basketball* by Jef Faulkner. The film is about these basketballs that come to life. We only want the basketball here so that it can be composited in with the actual footage with the actors later.

**B**EFORE WE LOOK AT HOW TO REMOVE GREEN SCREEN BACKGROUNDS FROM FOOTAGE and other compositing tricks, we need to first look at creating a garbage matte. A garbage matte is used to remove the excess junk areas from footage, making it easier to pull a good key.

Honestly, I've fought the whole garbage matte thing before. When no one was looking, I tried to just muscle through and to key the footage as is. Let me tell you, that was a mistake! I always end up punching myself in the face for being so stubborn. The garbage matte is intended to be a very rough, very quick outline around only the stuff you want to keep, and I swear on my Mom that it really helps the keying process.

Note that this may include the shadows from the green screen as well, as these can often help the object look more believable when composited.

3 Create a complete shape by clicking on the first point that you clicked to start the mask. You want to make sure that your subject (the thing that you're trying to isolate by keying) is never cut off by the garbage matte at any point in time, as shown above.

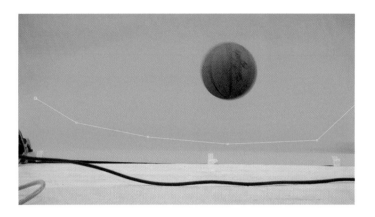

2 The problem is that there is a bunch of junk around the basketball. This is typically the case when keying; you'll have equipment or the end of the green screen around the edges of the frame. This makes it more challenging for the keying tool to do its job efficiently. To create a garbage matte, select the layer, and using the Pen tool, click an area around where the basketball bounces.

**HOT TIP**

For more information on creating the perfect mask for your garbage mattes, check out Chapter 7. It's full of cheats pertaining to masks, including how to animate them.

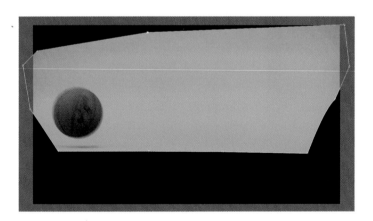

4 Click on a point to move it if necessary so that your subject is not accidentally masked out. In some cases where your subject gets too close to the "garbage" areas, you may need to animate the garbage matte. In the final result, you can already see how much easier it will be to key out this basketball because the background is much more clean and solid.

## Compositing

# Removing a Green Screen

**1** In the Keying.aep project in the Chapter 04 folder of the exercise files, you'll find this green screen footage. Here I am, your humble author, waiting to get keyed. Although there are many keying solutions in After Effects, Keylight is definitely the best one that ships with the program. Apply the Keylight effect to this footage.

**O**NE OF THE MOST COMMON USES OF AFTER EFFECTS IS TO REMOVE A GREEN SCREEN background from footage. This allows for all kinds of visual chicanery. I once saw a brilliant Conan O'Brien bit where he put circles of green screen fabric on his body and they were digitally removed to make it appear that he had these giant, gaping bullet wounds. Genius.

More commonly, however, a green screen is used so that subjects can be put into a different environment; one that might not be feasible to create in real life. Some environments might be created with computers (such as Mount Doom in *The Lord of the Rings* trilogy), or they might be too expensive to recreate (such as Superman flying through the sky), or they might not be safe (such as someone standing on the top of a building, or drinking Southern California tap water). There's really no end to what can be done with a green screen and a healthy dose of creativity.

**4** Sometimes, you can get an improved key by simply pressing ⌘ Z / ctrl Z to undo and picking a different color. But we're going to just fix this. In the Screen Matte area, increase the Clip Black value to make the background completely transparent. Decrease Clip White to make the subject fully opaque. Be careful that you don't create little pockets of transparency in the subject (as seen above).

**2** Our first order of business is to let Keylight know which color we want removed. To do that, click the eyedropper for the Screen Colour property in Keylight's effect controls. Then click on a spot on the green screen that is a good representation of the green colors in the background. I picked a spot right in front of my chest.

**3** So our instant results are not too bad, right? Well, it may seem that way. To see what's really going on, take the View drop down from Final Result to Status. The white areas indicate opaque areas. Black indicates transparent areas. Gray indicates partially transparent areas. Yikes!

**5** Ideally, our subject should be completely white (in the areas that they SHOULD be completely opaque, of course), and the background should be completely black. A little gray around the edges is not only acceptable, it's actually preferred so that the edges are a little softer, and so the subject can be composited a little easier.

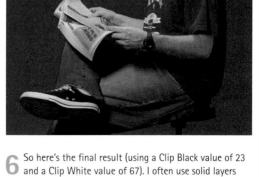

**6** So here's the final result (using a Clip Black value of 23 and a Clip White value of 67). I often use solid layers as a background to check my key, as above. There are a few yucky spots that are driving me crazy (such as the spot under my nose), but we'll talk about improving our key in the next cheat.

**HOT TIP**

Although Keylight is a fantastic effect, an industry standard, and a great addition to After Effects, my favorite keying tool is Primatte Keyer Pro by Red Giant Software. It has a very intelligent and intuitive way to remove a green screen, and I'm almost always able to get better results with it than I can get with Keylight. But that's just been my experience.

**SHORTCUTS**

# 4 Compositing

# Pulling a Luma Key

I N SOME CASES, THE BACKGROUND THAT YOU NEED TO REMOVE ISN'T GREEN OR BLUE – IT'S WHITE OR BLACK. In many cases, this is because the footage wasn't intended to be keyed. In other cases, the subject has blue or green in it, making it nigh unto impossible to get a good key.

Now, to be honest, the end of this cheat is going to leave you feeling unfulfilled a little bit. To pull a luma key, we're going to use the Luma Key effect, which is a keying tool that our forefathers used when establishing civilization. Seriously though, it's really old and outdated. In the next cheat, we'll look at a new effect in After Effects CS5 that will help us make the most of our luma key.

**1** We're going to start with this footage from uberstock.com of a kid dancing in front of a white background. In the Luma Key.aep project in the Chapter 04 folder of the exercise files, I've added this file to a comp and created a garbage matte for you. Again, the powers of Keylight are useless against this white background. So apply the Luma Key effect to this footage.

**3** We have some stray pixels in the background, but I'm not worried about those because we can just enlarge our garbage matte to fix them. The excess white around the edges is really the problem here. Increase the Edge Thin value in the Luma Key effect controls to 1.

2 In the Effect Controls panel, change the Key Type drop down from Key Out Darker to Key Out Brighter. Then we need to increase the Threshold value to increase the amount of allowable luminance. I found that a value of about 243 worked pretty good. Any higher than that, and it's going to start eroding the highlights from this poor kid's face, and we just can't be responsible for that.

4 Increasing the Edge Thin value definitely helped, but our key still looks terrible. We can try fiddling with the Edge Thin and Edge Feather values a bit more, but this key is never going to look good. Zoomed in close, we can see some major issues here, including motion blur on the right hand. To make it look awesome and fix these problems, we'll need the help of another effect, discussed in the next cheat.

**HOT TIP**

Using luma to pull a key can also be helpful for sky replacement in video. Often, video doesn't have the dynamic range to capture a bright daytime sky, so it is captured as pure white. This looks awful and amateurish on screen, but it makes it much easier to remove using this method.

# Refining a Matte

W E SAW IN THE PREVIOUS CHEAT THAT
SOME KEYING TOOLS AND SOME
FOOTAGE JUST CAN'T GO WHERE WE WANT
THEM TO. For that, we have a brand new effect
in After Effects CS5 called Refine Matte.

The Refine Matte effect is actually the spawn
of the new Roto Brush tool in CS5 (which we'll
look at later in this chapter). When the good
folks in charge of After Effects saw how helpful
some of the matte refining controls in Roto
Brush were, they decided that they should make
those controls its own effect. Hence, the Refine
Matte effect was born.

The Refine Matte effect is pretty incredible
in its own right. Its purpose is not to create a
key or a matte, but to refine what has already
been created. It even allows you to significantly
improve footage that has motion blur! I've
found it to be a big help in fine tuning mattes.

1 I know it's painful to look at, but we're going to start where we left off in
the last cheat. This is uberstock.com footage that we have keyed using only
the Luma Key effect. You can see how that didn't work out all that great. The
edges still have white in them, they are disgustingly blocky, and there's also some
obvious motion blur from the dancing. You can find this in the Refine Matte START
comp in the Refine Matte.aep project.

3 To improve the Refine Matte results, I took its Smooth value to 1, and I took
the Increase Decontamination Radius value to 4. Now check out how much
better this matte looks! Even the motion blur on the subject's right hand looks
great.

2 Apply the new Refine Matte effect to this footage. Even without adjusting any parameters, the matte is really improved! Huzzah! I've zoomed in to 200% so you can see the results more closely.

4 Even when composited on a dark background (the opposite of the white background that we started with), our key looks fantastic thanks to the Refine Matte effect.

# Compositing

# Using Multiple Mattes

1 In this simple example, found in the Multiple Mattes.aep project, we have an elephant grabbing some munchies out of a tree, courtesy of uberstock.com. There are three different textures here: that of the leaves and branches, the trunk, and the hair on the elephant's head. Here, I tried to key out everything with one effort. The trunk looks great, but the elephant's hair and the branches are being eroded.

I N A PERFECT WORLD, EVERY KEYING JOB COULD BE FIXED WITH JUST A FEW ADJUSTMENTS OF AN EFFECT. In reality however, most matte jobs need multiple mattes in order to get the job done. In some areas of your matte, you might want more hard edges, such as around a subject's clothing. In some areas, such as with wispy hair or partially transparent fabric, you'll want completely different settings. Trying to use one set of settings for an entire image with different aspects like this is a good way to drive yourself crazy with frustration, or create a lower quality matte.

The solution is to break up your footage using masks. That way, you can give each component of the key individual treatment and attention. The final result of this extra effort is a greatly improved final product, not to mention an added measure of sanity for yourself.

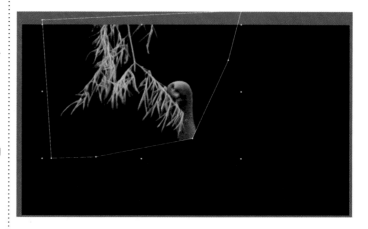

3 Then apply Keylight (or your keying tool of choice) to key out just that one component. Here, I took the Clip Black value to 8 and Clip White to 60. These settings aren't ideal on the trunk or on the head, but they're perfect for the branches.

2 The secret is to press ⌘ D ctrl D twice to make it so that there are three
duplicates of this layer, making sure to name them branches, trunk, and head.
Then, on each, make a mask that surrounds that component. For example, on
the branches layer, make a mask that only surrounds the branches. It's OK (and
actually preferable) if the masks overlap a little bit.

**HOT TIP**

For more cheats
and information
about creating
and using
masks, check
out Chapter 07!

4 After applying Keylight and adjusting its settings for each individual
component of this matte, our finished product looks much better. Shown here
with a dark red gradient background. Considering how compressed this footage is,
the results from using multiple keyed pieces is quite impressive. The hair on the
head of the elephant and the edges of the branches have benefited the most.

SHORTCUTS
MAC WIN BOTH

# Intro to Compositing

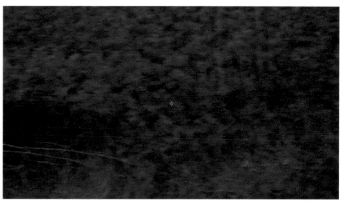

I N THE WORLD OF AFTER EFFECTS, WE ALL COME FROM DIFFERENT BACKGROUNDS. To make sure that all readers of this book are on the same page for the remainder of this chapter, I wanted to give you an intro to the concept of compositing. Sometimes, when we are working on a project, be it a short film or a commercial, we are too quick to say that something is impossible, or that we don't have the resources. However, with some good old fashioned creativity and some compositing know how, we really can create entire worlds from scratch.

**1** If you'd like to follow along, you'll find this project in the Intro to Compositin. aep file. The backmost layer of this composition is some footage actually shot by my wife. On a drive up the Oregon Coast, she just hung the video camera out the window and shot the greenery as we drove past. It's interlaced and looks terrible, but it still works great as the stuff in the window of the subway.

**3** The next layer we've seen before. It's just me with the green screen background that we removed earlier in this chapter.

**2** The next layer is a still image. It's a render from a 3D program by Kymnbel Bywater of Spilled Ink Animation. Without lighting, it doesn't look completely realistic. But again, that's OK. We'll fix it when we smoosh it all together.

**4** Once you have the pieces, all you have to do is layer them, add some animation, lighting, unifying color correction, some shadows (underneath me), and a reflection (in the window), and you have a somewhat believable scene. Shown here is the orthographic front view, and a view from the side to see the stacking of the layers.

# Blending Away Dark

SOMETIMES, THE BEST WAY TO ISOLATE A SUBJECT ISN'T TO PULL A KEY AT ALL. In some cases, when we have bright or dark areas that we want to remove, they can be removed in an instant with blend modes. In many cases, the results even look much better when compared to keying.

In the case of blending away dark colors, this becomes especially helpful when creating light effects, as we'll look at in Chapter 6.

**1** For this cheat, we're going to be using the Blending Away Dark.aep project. This is footage starring my son, from the short film that we made together. Hey, it's what nerdy fathers and sons do.

**3** We put this on a black solid layer because it's the opposite of the bright flare we added. But how do we get rid of the black around the flare? Simple. With blend modes. Click the Toggle Switches/Modes button at the bottom of the Timeline panel if you're not seeing the blend modes drop down. Change the blend mode from Normal to Add. The black is instantly removed!

2 This shot needs some help. The lightning looks like it's just appearing out of nothing, and the shot is just too dark. So, I've created a new black solid layer for you to apply the Lens Flare effect to. Don't forget to turn back on the visibility of the lens flare layer.

4 In the Lens Flare effect controls, adjust the Flare Center value until the flare is lined up with the end of the boy's wizard staff. If desired, you can create a mask to remove some of the extra junk from the lens flare, as shown here. Note that in the original image at the beginning of this cheat, I used a 3rd party plugin called Optical Flares by Video CoPilot to create that sweet flare.

# Blending Away Light

N SOME CASES, WE HAVE BLACK OBJECTS ON A WHITE BACKGROUND THAT NEED TO BE REMOVED. Similar to the previous cheat, we can use blend modes to instantly remove the white background to blend the dark objects into our scene.

In this cheat, we're going to take a simple photograph of a quiet suburban neighborhood and apply some stock effects footage from the great Detonation Films library.

The screenshot above is after applying some additional compositing tricks to give this scene the appearance that it was shot with a handheld cell phone camera.

**1** In the START comp in the Blending Away Light.aep project, you'll find this project. The explosion footage from the very inexpensive Detonation Films (detonationfilms.com) is of a dark explosion cloud on a white background. I've pretty much just put it in the right place for you. Images in this cheat are shown at 200% size so you can see detail, so they might appear a little soft or pixelated here.

**3** Now we could just end it there. But in professional compositing, there are typically many components that add to the realism. We could add debris, shadows, flames, or other elements. In this case, we're going to make this look like bad video footage. Create an adjustment layer at the top of the layer stack and apply the Noise effect to it. I used an Amount of Noise value of 12%, and I deselected Use Color Noise.

2 To composite this explosion, all you have to do is go down to the modes area of the Timeline panel, and change the blend mode of the BlackMushroom01 layer from Normal to Multiply. That will remove the white background, and also darken the cloud and realistically blend it into the background. This makes it look as if there has been an explosion on this house, or immediately behind it.

4 The photo of this neighborhood was taken with a pretty good quality DSLR camera. The homes and other objects in this scene are just too sharp for the look we're trying to achieve. So apply the Fast Blur effect to the adjustment layer you created. A little Blurriness goes a long way in this case – probably no more than 1.5 (I used 1.2). What else would make this composite more believable?

**HOT TIP**

As you'll probably see me say over and over again in this chapter, any element shared by all of the components of your composite will help to create the illusion that they actually belong in the same scene.

99

# Compositing

# Compositing Textures

**B**LEND MODES ARE NOT ONLY GREAT FOR REMOVING LIGHT AND DARK AREAS, but they're also really great for compositing textures onto a surface.

In the same way that we can use Add (and other blend modes in that area, like Screen) to remove dark areas and brighten colors, and Multiply (and other blend modes in that area, like Color Burn) to remove light and darken colors, we can use the overlay category of blend modes to composite textures. Most of these blend modes remove 50% gray, and then brighten bright areas and darken dark areas.

Although this example is simple, there are several lessons to be learned here. One is that this text looks like it is part of this rocky surface. This can be helpful if you want to create the illusion that text or a logo has been painted on a surface.

The other lesson is that even a simple solid can look like a real wall with the proper texture applied. And again, using these blend modes, that can be done in a single click.

**1** In the Compositing Textures.aep project, you'll find a comp with three simple layers. The top layer (and most important here) is a concrete surface. It's important that it is down the middle of the road luminance-wise, with some highlights and shadows. It's a great texture for the overlay modes.

**4** Take the blend mode of the top layer to Overlay. Again, this removes midtone gray, and brightens the areas of the layers beneath where there were highlights, and darkens them where it had darker areas.

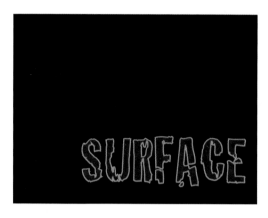

2 The next layer below the concrete photo is some simple text with the Opacity value set to about 76%.

3 The bottom layer is a simple solid layer with a gradient overlay layer style applied to create that sort of vignette look.

5 If this look is too intense, try using the Soft Light blend mode. It does the same basic thing as Overlay, but it doesn't brighten and darken quite so much. Other than Add, this is probably the blend mode that I use most often.

6 In this case, I actually want this way more intense. I changed the blend mode to Hard Light here, which is a much more gritty and intense effect. In the image at the beginning of this cheat, I used the Linear Light blend mode. I just love the way that looks.

**HOT TIP**

Because the "overlay" modes increase contrast, you can often make any layer look much more intense by duplicating it, and putting the top copy of the layer in one of the overlay blend modes, such as Soft Light.

# Temporal Alignment

THIS CHEAT IS GOING TO LOOK AT A MORE UTILITARIAN USE OF A BLEND MODE. Here we're going to look at how to align layers. Now I know that we have an Align panel for that very purpose. It's even been upgraded in CS5 to allow you to align objects to a composition.

But if you have to align layers that have the same content, but are at different sizes (such as with an SD clip and an HD version), or if you have layers that must be aligned in time, the Align panel can't help you. However, there is a blend mode that I've found to be very useful in such cases. This is one of those tricks that you won't use everyday, but it can really save your sanity when you need it.

1 We're going to work with the Temporal Alignment.aep project. This contains a video clip from uberstock.com. There are two copies of this layer, and I want to align them in time.

3 The trick is to use the Difference blend mode. Usually, the Difference blend mode creates really psychedelic effects, as seen above.

2 The challenge with this particular clip is that it's very similar throughout the clip. The previous screenshot was from about 9 seconds in. This screenshot is from about 28 seconds in, almost 20 seconds later. It's impressive how still this actress can remain, but it makes it really hard to align this footage in time.

4 But the Difference blend mode has a special trick. When you blend a layer using Difference, pixels that are the same as the colors beneath will turn black. As you can see above, two frames that seemed almost identical are now discernibly different. Now, simply move the top layer in time until your image is completely black. Then your layers will be perfectly aligned, in space and time.

# Compositing with Color

**1** Here are the two objects we'll be compositing together: a toy and a photo of a neighborhood. You'll find these in the Compositing with Color.aep project.

T HE NEXT FEW CHEATS ARE GOING TO LOOK AT A FEW CONCEPTS THAT WILL HELP OUR COMPOSITES LOOK BETTER. They will be less hands on, and more concept-driven and principle-based.

The overriding idea will be that if we can make objects share more common properties and attributes, then it will be easier for our audience to believe that these objects really were photographed together.

In the first of these concept based cheats, we're going to take a toy from my son's vast toy arsenal, and try to make it look like a monster is attacking. We're going to use blend modes, and then color enhancements to add to the believability of the effect.

**3** The monster still looks too vibrant for my liking. If we can't see the bottom of his legs, then we assume he is far away. Notice the hills between his legs, and how hazy they are. I hesitate to even share this with you, but I lowered the toy's opacity to 80%. It's not an ideal fix in all cases, but this makes it look farther away.

2 I initially created this composite as part of a short film competition that I was in. The project was timed, and I was in a hurry. To composite these quickly, I dragged the toy layer beneath the photo, and put the photo into the Multiply blend mode since the toy was darker than most of the photo. I then added a mask to mask out the toy's legs. This mask has been added for you, just change the mode of the mask from None to Add.

4 To combine these together more, I added an adjustment layer above the toy and the photo, and adjusted the colors with the Color Balance effect. Mostly, I took red out of the image to give it a more sinister cyan tint. I also added a quick vignette to pull attention more to the center of the image. Because these adjustments are applied to the entire image, it makes a more realistic composite.

# Compositing with Animation

**M**OVEMENT IS ANOTHER WAY THAT WE CAN MAKE OUR COMPOSITES LOOK MORE BELIEVABLE. If two objects move in tandem, there appears to us to be more of a connection. Continuing with our toy monster scene from the previous cheat, we're going to add a camera and some random movement to those elements to give the illusion that this was shot with a handheld camera.

1 Start in the START comp in the Compositing with Animation.aep project. In the Timeline panel, make the toy monster layer and the houses background layer into 3D layers by enabling the 3D switch for each layer.

3 Hold ⌥ *alt* while clicking the stopwatch for the Point of Interest property on the camera you just created. This will create an expression field. In that new text field, type wiggle(2,10) to create some random animation for the camera.

2 Press ⌘ ⌥ *Shift* C *ctrl* *alt* *Shift* C to create a new camera. Go ahead and use the default settings. Then decrease the Z position value for the houses background layer to bring it closer to the camera. I used a value of –300. I increased the Z position of the toy monster layer to about 300 to move it farther away. This will add a little more perspective when our camera moves.

4 OK, so if you're just reading this, you'll just have to use your imagination, but the scene now has subtle but random movement, which is shared by both the toy monster and the background. This again adds more to the believability of the composite.

# Compositing with Focus

OUR FINAL CHEAT IN OUR MINI-SERIES OF COMPOSITING HELPS IS BASED ON DEPTH OF FIELD BLUR. We've looked before at how things look better when composited if they share common properties, like a similar movement or color temperature.

Likewise, if we use a shallow depth of field, we can really heighten the realism of our composite. In this cheat we'll borrow from the rack focus cheat in Chapter 2 to focus on the houses in the foreground, and then we'll shift focus to the monster in the background.

**1** Starting where we left off in the previous cheat, you can find this project in the START comp in the Compositing with Focus.aep project.

**3** When switching back to the Active Camera view, the depth of field isn't quite blurry enough, so I've increased the Aperture value to 1000. This is a little too much blur, honestly, but I wanted to make sure that you could see the difference in these screenshots. A value close to about 600 would probably be more appropriate.

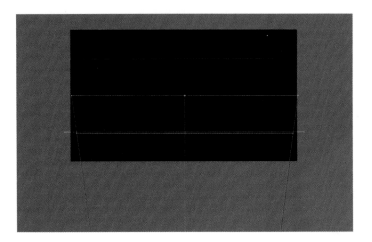

2 In the camera layer, turn Depth of Field on. Adjust the Focus Distance value while looking at the Top view. Fiddle with that property until the focal plane of the camera lines up with the houses background layer. A value of about 6810 worked for me, but I've offset this just a bit in the screenshot so that you see the camera's focal plane.

4 We can then animate the Focus Distance property of the camera to get the toy monster in focus, almost as if the camera person was caught unprepared and had to adjust focus. This not only adds believability, but it's also good visual storytelling, building anticipation as we take our time to guide the eye of the viewer to the scary monster. I used a Focus Distance value of about 7410.

**HOT TIP**

For more control over the depth of field on flat layers like this houses background that appear to cross many depth planes, try the Lens Blur effect. With that effect, you can use a map to control which part of the layer has blur applied to it, as if the blur was created by the lens.

# Motion Blur

WHILE WE'RE ON THE SUBJECT OF BLURRING IN COMPOSITING, let's take a look at using (and adjusting) the motion blur in After Effects.

Motion blur is an important part of the visual experience of watching movies. This started a while back with film cameras. Due to the shutter of the camera, when subjects (or the camera) moved quickly, the shutter wasn't open long enough to capture a full, crisp frame of that action, so the result was a little blurry.

Seems like a problem, right? Well, our eyes have grown so accustomed to the look of motion blur that motion doesn't quite look right without it! In some cases, such as with intense fight scenes, or sporting events filmed in HD, the shutter of the camera will intentionally be adjusted so that the motion is not blurred and is very crisp. But typically, especially when compositing graphics or 3D renders into live action footage, adding motion blur can do a lot for the realism of the shot.

**1** We're going to use the Motion Blur.aep project for this, which contains a matte painting by artist Daniel Johnson, and a UFO that I created in Cinema 4D. This is already animated so that the UFO takes off very quickly upwards through the hangar opening at the top of the image.

**3** This looks much better! It's important to note that motion blur is not applied as an effect because it's automatic. This means that the faster your layer moves, the more that After Effects automatically blurs it for you. Like late night infomercial TV slogan fodder, you set it and forget it!

2 Without motion blur, this animation looks distinctly artificial. Just atrocious. To turn on motion blur, we must enable it both for the composition, and for the UFO layer. The icon looks like a little stack of circles.

4 To adjust this blur, press ⌘ K ctrl K to get to your composition settings. Go to the Advanced tab. Increase or decrease the Shutter Angle value to respectively increase or decrease the motion blur in your comp. A little secret is that you can adjust the Shutter Angle value on a per layer basis using the oft neglected Transform effect!

# Matching Color

ANOTHER ONE OF THE MOST COMMON COMPOSITING TASKS is matching the color of two layers. After all, this is compositing at it's most basic level.

So here we're going to look at an amazing trick from After Effects wizard Mark Christiansen. This trick will help you analyze the separate components, and tweak their color channels to make objects seem like they belong in the same scene.

1 In this example from the Matching Color.aep project, we again have a piece of art by matte painter Daniel Johnson and one of my 3D renderings from Cinema 4D. I chose these two pieces because they couldn't be more different, thematically and from a color perspective. If we can make this believable, we're doing alright!

3 The trick is to go through each channel, and match the Output Black, Output White, and Gamma values in the Levels effect with the appearance of each channel in the background you're trying to match. If you put your cursor over the darkest and lightest spots of the image, the Info panel will tell you the light output for that channel, so you can match values accordingly. For example, here I put my cursor over a shadow area, and the Info panel tells me that the value is 25, so then I changed my Red Output Black value to 25. I additionally, increased the Red Gamma value to match the brightness of the rest of the red channel.

2 Apply the Levels effect to the robot layer. The key here is that we want to analyze each channel independently. So, click the Show Channel and Color Management Settings, and change the channel to Red, so that we're only viewing the red light used to make this image. In the Levels effect controls, change the Channel drop down to Red.

4 Then, just repeat the same process for each channel. MAKE SURE that you are always viewing the same channel that you are editing in Levels! Once you're done, take the Composition panel view back to RGB to see the finished product. Although we could do further tweaking, this is a fairly believable composite.

# Premultiplied Alpha Channels

**A**LPHA CHANNELS COME IN TWO FLAVORS: STRAIGHT AND PREMULTIPLIED. Because alpha channels play such a big role in compositing, it's important to know the difference between the two and how to address them.

Straight alpha channels are certainly easier to deal with. These alpha channels are black and white (no pun intended) – the transparency is all in the alpha channel, and the colors of the object are not in the alpha channel. Pretty straightforward (OK, that pun was kind of intended).

Premultiplied alphas are a little different in that the transparency information is also kind of blended (or "premultiplied") into the color data as well. If not interpreted correctly when imported, premultiplied alphas will create a halo as we'll see (and fix).

The reason that premultiplied alphas exist is that they can create a more believable composite because the edges are partially transparent. This makes them blend into a background more easily – provided, of course, that the correct color is premultiplied into the alpha channel. Premultiplied alpha channels are also compatible with more older systems, although I've never personally run into a situation where I couldn't use a straight alpha channel.

**1** Here's this UFO again that I created against a white background. You can find this project in the Premultiplied.aep project in the Chapter 04 folder of the exercise files.

**3** Select the UFO premult file in the Project panel and press ⌘ ⌥ G / ctrl alt G to open the Interpret Footage dialog box. You can also open this by pressing the leftmost button at the bottom of the Project panel. Here, you can change the interpretation of the alpha channel. Click Premultiplied – Matted With Color. If this UFO had been premultiplied with a color other than black, it would be very important to choose that color in the swatch next to this option.

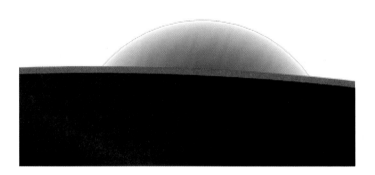

2 When we zoom in closely (shown here at 300%), we can see an ugly black halo caused by the incorrect interpretation of this alpha as a straight alpha channel. If we were compositing against black, this would look great. But in this case, it's icky.

4 Once the alpha channel has been correctly interpreted, the ugly halo disappears, and our alpha is fixed.

**HOT TIP**

Another new feature in After Effects CS5 is that you can preview just about anything. This applies to dialog boxes with lights, cameras, solids, composition settings, and you can also preview interpretation settings before applying them.

SHORTCUTS

# Tracking with Mocha

ONE OF THE BEST FEATURES OF AFTER EFFECTS ISN'T ACTUALLY A FEATURE OF AFTER EFFECTS – it's Mocha. Mocha is a standalone motion tracking application that comes for free with After Effects CS5.

It is far superior to the native motion tracking system in After Effects. The motion tracking in After Effects tracks individual points, making it unreliable. Mocha actually tracks features. So, instead of tracking a highlighted pixel (that might change as the light or camera position changes), you could track an entire object or surface.

In this introduction to Mocha (before we dig a bit deeper into it in the next cheat), we're going to create a track using a blurry background surface. This could be a disaster with the native After Effects tracker, but it's a piece of cake in Mocha. We'll also use this track to composite a photo of me to create the illusion that a beautiful girl is flirting with me. No visual effects have ever tackled such a challenging task.

1 Open the Mocha application on your computer (it can't be launched from After Effects). From the title screen press Start. In the upper left corner of the screen, click the Create a new project button. In the upper right corner, click the Choose button to navigate to the file you want to track. In this case, go to Exercise Files>Media>Uberstock>barwoma n_w.mp4 and press OK.

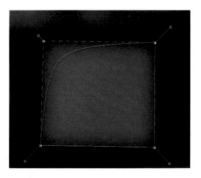

4 Now it doesn't really help in this project, but in some cases, you might want tighter or even pointed corners. To adjust the angle of a point, simply click and pull its handle. Drag the handle inwards to create a more round point.

2 This sweet stock video clip from uberstock.com depicts a woman flirting at a bar. The first part of the video is just a white screen, though. So, right below the big white screen, you'll find a timeline with a tiny black vertical line. Drag the current time to about frame 731.

3 Now we need to tell Mocha what area to track. Click the Create X-Spline Layer Tool. Then click a point in each of the corners of that rounded rectangle at the right of the image as shown above. Right click to finish the spline. Click and drag on a point to adjust it after you've created it.

5 If needed, adjust the handles so that the default tension is used. Underneath the timeline, click the Track Forwards button. Mocha will begin tracking the footage, but be really careful. As soon as you see the first sign of Mocha drifting, click the stop button and make fixes to the points to get Mocha back on track. Mocha will even track stuff when part of it is off screen! When this shape is completely off screen, stop the track (assuming Mocha doesn't stop it automatically).

6 A great help with the problem of "drift" is the little widgets that Mocha provides for you that show you an extreme close up of the currently selected point – both at the current time, and what you set it as last. That way you can tell sooner when Mocha starts to get off track. Above, I have the upper left corner of the shape selected. Note the guides in the upper left corner of the frame.

**continued...**

# Tracking with Mocha (continued)

**7** The frame that we started tracking on actually wasn't the first frame we wanted to track. It was just the frame where the subject we wanted to track was the most clear. Go back to frame 731. Then click the Track Backwards button and track the motion until the tracked object is off screen again. When you are satisfied with the track, click the Export Tracking Data button at the bottom of the interface.

**9** We created a solid layer to store this tracking data because we don't want to fiddle with our original layer. This Mocha data also creates a keyframe for every single frame of Position, Anchor Point, Scale, and Rotation. Import an image to apply the tracking data to (I used a photo of myself). Select that object and press **P** to reveal its Position property. **⌥** *alt* click its stopwatch to create an expression, then drag the expression pickwhip to the Position property of the solid layer.

**8** From the Format drop down, choose After Effects Transform Data. Then go back to After Effects. Import the same clip we've been tracking, and make a new comp that has the EXACT same dimensions as the clip by dragging the clip to the Create a new Composition button at the bottom of the Project panel. Then create a new solid with the same size and duration, and press ⌘ V ctrl V to paste the Mocha tracking data on to this solid layer. Note that the solid layer doesn't need to be visible.

**10** Because we used an expression instead of pasting directly, the Anchor Point and Scale properties of the tracked object are still available for adjusting and animating, if needed. I animated Anchor Point to make it appear that I'm coming in to frame. It's actually really amusing, and I recommend checking it out. I've also applied some color correction here. My new lady friend and I wish you luck with this tutorial.

**HOT TIP**

Hold down the Z key and drag with the mouse to zoom in and out in Mocha. Hold down the X key and drag with the mouse to pan around.

# Mocha Shapes

**1** In Mocha, select File>Open Project. Then navigate to Exercise Files>Chapter 04>Mocha Projects>handheld sunset.mocha. This image of a sunset was shot from inside my house looking out. There's a bit of wall between the two window panes, and also a house in the distance. I've already created a mask to track these in Mocha using the same techniques we covered in the previous cheat. It's certainly not a perfect track, but I mainly wanted to mask out the middle black bar so that we can add a UFO in the background, as if it were flying around outside.

T HE NEW VERSION OF MOCHA THAT SHIPS WITH AFTER EFFECTS CS5 HAS A POWERFUL NEW FEATURE. It allows you to create and track shapes, and then export that shape data back to After Effects.

Since we've already gone through the Mocha tracking process in depth, and because the process of tracking shapes is identical to tracking motion, we're going to go through this rather quickly. But it's easy to see how significant this one feature is when you're trying to composite objects together.

**3** When you paste this data, it first appears as if nothing has happened. This is because it has created a hole where our tracking mask was. I've added a green solid layer below this to show you what I mean. To fix this, go to the new mocha shape effect that has been added to this layer. Click the Invert checkbox. Now you have a layer of just the mask area.

**2** In Mocha, with Layer 1 selected in the Layer Controls area in the upper left area of the interface, click on the Export Shape Data button at the bottom of the interface. Then click Copy to Clipboard. Then go to After Effects, and in the Mocha Shapes START in the Shapes from Mocha.aep file, select the handheld sunset layer and press ⌘ V ctrl V to paste in this shape data.

**4** The trick is to duplicate this layer and have the top copy be just the mask, and then the bottom copy be just the regular old layer. Then you can stick stuff in between them (like a layer sandwich) and the objects – such as this UFO – will appear to exist behind the front object but in front of the bottom object. When you play this UFO animation, it actually looks pretty cool the way it zips through the scene, which is actually just one video clip.

# Using Roto Brush

**R**OTO BRUSH IS CERTAINLY THE KEY NEW FEATURE IN AFTER EFFECTS CS5. It's the one thing that everyone has been talking about.

Roto Brush is a very intelligent tool that helps you extract stuff from a clip. Its name comes from the traditional process called rotoscoping, where frames are manually fixed by hand, frame-by-frame. To put it bluntly, rotoscoping sucks. It is perhaps the most monotonous and frustrating job in the entire After Effects world.

Although Roto Brush isn't an instant fix (as it appears to be at first glance), it is instead a tremendous help and timesaver in the rotoscoping process. Take, for example, the screenshot above. Big deal, right? But it is, in fact, a pretty big deal. Look at the motion blur on the right leg. That kind of thing is nearly impossible to remove. Not only that, I got this result in a matter of seconds. And going even further, Roto Brush almost instantly and automatically gave me similar results from all of the surrounding frames. Although it's not perfect, it's an incredible start.

1 We're going to start by importing another sweet stock video clip from uberstock.com. Found in Exercise Files>Media>Uberstock, open the crosswalk_w.mp4 clip and make a comp with the same settings and add it to it. Then double click this layer to open it in the Layer panel. Then select the Roto Brush from the Tools panel at the top of the interface. Move in time to 0;00;13;05. Click and drag the Roto Brush tool down the leg as shown above.

3 At the bottom of the Layer panel, click the new Toggle Alpha view to see just our matte.

4 In the Roto Brush effect controls, click the Use Motion Blur check box (as we did earlier in this chapter with Refine Matte), check Higher Quality, and take Samples Per Frame to 20. Check out how intelligently it removes the background from our motion-blurred leg!

**2** Once you let go of the mouse, Roto Brush goes to work trying to guess what you want selected. The purple outline represents the foreground that Roto Brush has selected. If Roto Brush selects something in the background, hold the ⌥ alt key while you drag on it, as shown above. Continue selecting and deselecting until all of the legs are selected (and none of the background is).

**5** One of the absolute best parts of Roto Brush is that it automatically guesses what the matte on the next frame is going to be! Simply advance to the next frame, and this is what you get without any extra effort on your part! It's not perfect, but it's certainly a great leg up (pun intended, because the leg is actually up. That amuses me quite a bit).

**6** When we switch back to the Composition panel, we can see that a pretty decent matte has been pulled for us by the Roto Brush. I still can't get over how magically that background was removed from the motion blur!

SHORTCUTS

123

# Compositing

# Restoring Opacity

OCCASIONALLY I'LL RUN INTO THIS PROBLEM THAT WILL FREAK ME OUT for a split second. Then I'll remember that there's a quick fix.

The problem is that an object will have a slightly lowered opacity. Normally, this wouldn't be a problem because we can just increase the Opacity value of the layer, right? But what happens when a layer (or part) of it already has reduced transparency, and the Opacity value for the layer is at 100%?

I actually ran into this problem a few times in this book already. In Chapters 2 and 3, the robots vs. pirates art contains a mast on the pirate ship that has lowered opacity. And then, in this chapter, in the cheat on tracking in Mocha, I noticed that my Photoshop work was crappy, and I left some partial transparency above my head. In this quick cheat, we're going to look at a quick fix for this dilemma.

**1** In the Restoring Opacity.aep project, we see this same annoying picture of me (sorry about that). Even against a white background, it appears like the background has been completely removed.

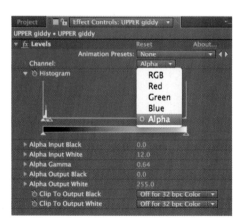

**3** The solution is to apply the Levels effect to this layer. Change the Channel drop down to Alpha. Then we can process just the alpha channel, making the opaque areas less opaque, or the transparent areas more transparent, or vice versa.

2 But when I exaggerate this alpha channel, you can see some definite problem
areas. The gray above my head indicates semi-transparency, and in this case, I
only want transparent and opaque pixels, and nothing but.

4 I increased the Alpha Input Black value to about 7, which was enough to
remove all of the extra junk and compensate for my Photoshop blunder. Even
the delicate matte of my hair on the top of my head remains as it should be. Pretty
cool trick.

## HOT TIP

Another way
to tell that
this is an alpha
channel fail is
by using the
Info panel. As
you put your
cursor over
areas that are
completely
transparent,
the A value
in the Info
panel should
be 0. Anything
higher means
that something
is there, and
that area is
not completely
transparent.

# Manual Shadow

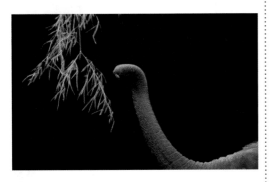

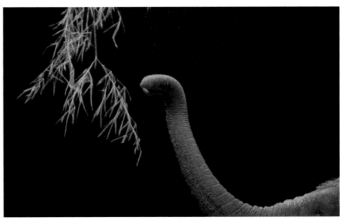

**1** Open the Manual Shadow.aep project from the Chapter 04 folder of the exercise files. This contains the project we looked at earlier in this chapter when we covered creating multiple mattes. I've precomped our 3 masks, and duplicated that nested comp.

IDEALLY, WE SHOULD BE CREATING SHADOWS WITH AFTER EFFECTS LIGHTS. However, sometimes, it's tough to get shadows to look exactly the way we want them to in a timely fashion.

This cheat is a true cheat in every sense of the word. Again, we *should* be using real 3D shadows. I can already hear the After Effects gurus and professors of the world whining about how unprofessional this is. And they're probably right. There's much less control over this method of creating shadows, especially in 3D. But sometimes we know exactly where we want a shadow to go and exactly what we want it to look like. Trying to position the light in 3D space to achieve that look is another story altogether. So, this cheat is for those times when you're completely desperate and want to create a "fake" 3D shadow in a hurry.

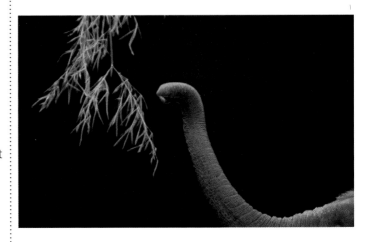

**3** Turn back on the top copy of the layer, and adjust the shadow layer as desired. We can adjust its opacity and blurriness using the controls in the Drop Shadow effect, and we can use its layer transforms, such as Position and Scale, to control it further.

**2** Turn off the top copy, and apply the Drop Shadow effect to the bottom copy. The trick to this effect is to check the Shadow Only property in the Effect Controls panel. This removes the regular content of the layer and leaves only the shadow, and therein lies the power.

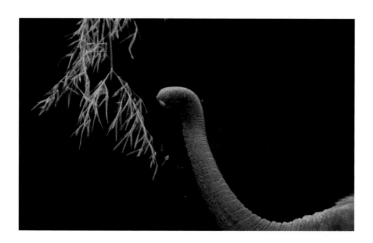

**4** Remember that this shadow is now its own layer, so we can even make it a 3D layer and move and transform it in 3D space if desired. Here, I've also adjusted the solid background in 3D as well.

**HOT TIP**

I realize that the shadow here doesn't match the lighting of the scene. But the gradient on the background gives the illusion of a light source coming from the direction of the camera, so I created a shadow from that imaginary light source. It might not have been the best choice. Don't judge me.

# Guide Layers

G UIDE LAYERS AREN'T THE MOST INTERESTING SUBJECT IN THE WORLD. I'll give you that. But they really can make life easier if you know how to use them.

How many times have you created a layer just to test something out? Maybe you've created a temporary solid layer as a background to check a key. Or maybe you've created a temporary adjustment layer to brighten a layer to make sure you're seeing all the details. Or maybe you created a layer to display timecode, or some other type of helpful text. You probably don't want any of things to render, or even show up in a parent composition – EVER. After Effects understands your situation, and has created guide layers for this very purpose.

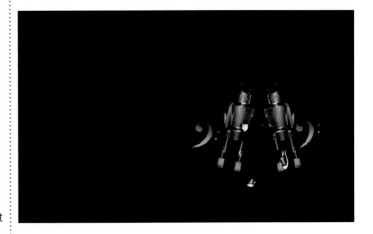

1 Here's this project I made with some sweet motion graphics. We'll be working in the GUIDE LAYERS START composition in the Guide Layers.aep project. Be aware that this is a fairly complex comp, which has been nested in an even more complex parent comp.

3 The problem is that when we go up in the chain to the parent composition, the white solid shows up and ruins the art. What to do, what to do?

2 It's hard to see what's going on, so I added a white solid background. It's much clearer to see what's going on here with the bright background.

4 The solution is to simply right click on the white solid layer and choose Guide Layer. This will make it show up in the current comp, but when you go to render, or even when you go up to a parent composition, you don't see it! Isn't that brilliant? I use guide layers all the time, especially when testing mattes.

# Shooting Better Green Screen Footage

BECAUSE KEYING OUT GREEN SCREEN FOOTAGE IS SUCH A HUGE PART OF COMPOSITING, I wanted to take this interlude to share with you some tips for shooting green screen footage properly. I realize that many times, a client might provide footage to you that has already been shot, and you've got to get to work pulling a key. But if you can help it at all, you can pass some of these tidbits on to clients so that they can create footage that is much easier for you to work on. Even some really talented directors of photography that I've worked with don't understand what can ruin an otherwise great green screen shot. Help them help you.

First and foremost is lighting. It's important that footage is lit well. When video cameras record footage that is underexposed, the footage gets grainy. Trying to key grainy footage is next to impossible, as the keying tool is thrown off by the grain around the edges of the subject changing every single frame. This usually results in a subject with "dancing" edges, which looks horrible. In those cases, you might be forced to apply a choking effect (such as the new Refine Matte or Matte Choker), which erodes the edges of the subject, and that's not good either.

The green screen not only has to be lit well, but the screen should be lit evenly as well. Uneven lighting will create multiple shades of green, making it challenging to key out. Wrinkles in a green screen will also provide this icky unevenness. It's also best if the subject is standing a few feet away from the green screen so that they don't get light from the green screen spilling on them. This is referred to as spill, and it can be a pain in the hind quarters to remove in post. I've seen some directors of photography put a backlight on the subject, just to avoid any accidental spill from the green screen.

Another problem that I've seen amateurs make is that they let the movement of the subject go out of frame. If you were shooting a movie, this isn't that big of a deal. But if you're shooting cheerleaders against a green screen to composite them in a field really far away, and their hands go off screen, then they'll be cut off when they're composited really far away.

It kind of goes without saying, but make sure that you're subject isn't the same color as the screen behind them. Green is typically used for video because it's the most unlike flesh tones, so it's easiest to remove. But if you're shooting a green alien against a green screen, good luck trying to isolate it! In that case, you might want a maroon screen. Sometimes directors and producers don't realize that allowing an actor to wear a green tie in front of a green screen will mean that the actor will have a tie-shaped hole in him in post.

Be sure to use the highest quality video when shooting green screen as well, especially when it comes to color. Use as many colors as your camera has. Typically, HD cameras can capture more colors than DV cameras, which will help you when removing the green screen.

This isn't really a tip for removing green screen, but if you are shooting a talking head against a green screen (say for an interview, or a host for a video podcast), you can actually get HD footage from an SD shot. Turn your camera sideways to record the host. This will create a frame that is 480 pixels wide by 720 pixels tall. In 720p HD video, the height of the frame is only 720 pixels, and your host will only be a narrow part of the frame anyway. It works. And it's cool. Trust me.

The final tip is probably the one that I've seen ruin more keying tasks than anything else. As an After Effects trainer, I'm constantly compressing videos to distribute to people so y'all can practice with them as exercise files. Videos get big, so I try to compress them as much as possible. Problem is, compression causes artifacts in many cases, even if you can't see them. You'll probably get a taste of this when you try using Roto Brush and Keylight on some of the provided footage from uberstock.com. It might look pretty good, but when you try to pull a key from it, it's literally impossible. And you can actually see the huge blocky edges in the matte resulting from the compression. So, try to shoot with video as high quality as possible, and try to get it as uncompressed and pristine as you can get it.

You might feel that shooting green screen footage isn't your job, and your client should worry about that. But if this footage is coming to you eventually, then you're going to be inheriting a big headache. It's much better to offer to help with advice and feedback if you can, even if you have to volunteer. It only takes a tiny amount of effort to save loads of time in post, and to create a much better final product.

■ Creating simple
animation is easy.
Bringing a photo
or graphics from
Illustrator to life
is a completely
different story. We'll
look at some great
cheats for creating
organic movement
in this chapter.

# 5

# Animation

THE ACT OF PLAYING DR. FRANKENSTEIN and bringing stuff to life has always been one of the best things about After Effects to me. Taking a still illustration from Illustrator and making moving characters out of static lines and shapes is just incredible, and it never gets old.

In this chapter, we're going to look at some great tricks for imbuing objects with a sense of life and organic movement. Included in these tricks is what it takes to animate a still image and bring it to life.

I'm well aware that this is a book, and that I'm using a static medium to talk about a topic that is inherently non-static. So we're not going to get into perfecting motion and movement. Instead we're going to focus on HOW to bring a variety of objects to life in a variety of different ways.

# The Puppet Pin Tool

THE PUPPET TOOL IS ONE OF THE GREAT MIRACLES OF MODERN SCIENCE. OK, maybe that's a tad hyperbolic, but maybe not. It certainly is one of the greatest animation tools I've ever had the privilege of playing with. It's the best way to bring a still image to life. It uses the paradigm of a puppeteer, controlling pins like a marionette to deform a layer. It's fantastic for animating elements from a photo or a graphic from Illustrator, or even making photo adjustments. Is it any wonder that the Photoshop team has borrowed this technology, now that Photoshop CS5 has a Puppet Warp feature as well?

In this cheat, and in the few to follow, we're going to be looking at this amazing tool (it's actually a series of 3 tools) and all that it offers. It has saved my neck on many occasions, and it is just a joy to use. In this cheat, we'll have a brief overview of the main feature of the Puppet tool. And in the next few cheats, we'll look at the other, lesser-known Puppet tool features.

1 Open The Puppet Tool.aep and go to the Puppet Tool comp. We're going to be moving the crazy tongue of this green monster around.

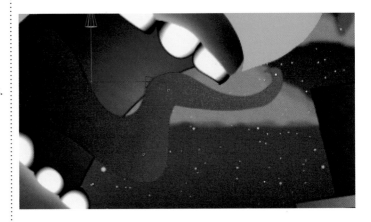

3 Click on one of these pins to organically deform the layer. The Puppet Pin tool automatically creates keyframes for you at the current frame when you apply the pins. As you move in time and change the location of the pins, animation is created.

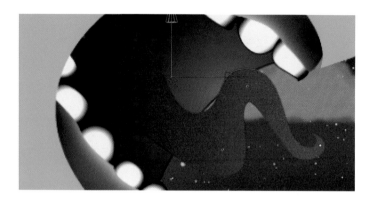

**2** Select the Puppet Pin tool in the tool bar at the top of the After Effects interface. As we'll look at in the next cheat, the Puppet "tool" is actually 3 tools. The Puppet Pin tool is the main tool used for deformations. Select the tongue layer and click a point on the back of the tongue (as an anchor of sorts), and on each curve of the tongue, and on the tip of the tongue as shown above. The above is zoomed in 400% to show detail.

**4** Continue to adjust other points as desired. Note that if you accidentally deselect the layer, the pins will become invisible. You can see them again by selecting the Puppet effect in the Effect Controls panel.

# Puppet Overlap

W HEN YOU USE THE PUPPET TOOL, you're basically folding a single layer. But what happens when that flat layer folds over on itself?

Another one of the Puppet tools – the Puppet Overlap tool – allows you to have control over what happens when Puppet pins overlap one another.

**1** Open the Puppet Overlap comp in the project with the same name. This contains the same art from Dan Grady that we saw in the last cheat. I've added deformation pins for you on the tentacle middle layer.

**3** In the Tools panel at the top of the interface, choose the Puppet Overlap tool. Now place new Puppet Overlap pins over the layer. Note that you're given an outline of the original shape of the layer to use as a guide. I put my pins about where I put my original pins. Whenever possible, apply Puppet Overlap pins before deforming a layer with the Puppet Pin tool. Also, with each Puppet Overlap pin selected, increase the Extent value in the Tools panel. This controls the area of influence of the pin.

2 Grab these Puppet pins and move them around so that the layer overlaps itself. What we want is for the tip of the tentacle to go behind the rest of the tentacle. And we also don't want it to look terrible, which is what mine looks like now.

4 And now, just select each overlap pin and change its In Front value. Whatever area has a higher In Front value goes in front of the area with a lower In Front value. I put the In Front value of the overlap pin at the bottom of the tentacle higher than the In Front value of the tip of the tentacle. And now order is restored.

**HOT TIP**

The third Puppet tool is the Puppet Starch tool. Use this tool if there are areas of your layer that are getting deformed that you don't want to deform. Thankfully, all of these pins are different colors so they don't get confusing. Deformation pins are yellow, overlap pins are blue, and starch pins are red.

137

# 5

# Puppet Animation

1 Open the Puppet Animation START comp in the project of the same name. I have this duck graphic that I've already applied Puppet deform pins to.

A S IF THE PUPPET TOOLS THEMSELVES WEREN'T COOL ENOUGH, there is also a built-in method for doing motion sketch animation. It's a little hidden because it needs to be accessed by a keyboard shortcut. But this is an incredible feature of the Puppet tools that just can't be missed.

3 You can see that After Effects has created keyframes for you as you moved that Puppet pin around.

2 Put your cursor over the Puppet pin on the beak of the duck. Hold the ⌘ ctrl key. Notice how your cursor turns into a stopwatch. Now drag that point around. After Effects will capture your movements in real time! Be aware that in order to capture your movements in real time, you will only be able to deform a yellow outline of your object.

4 This duck now animates in a very organic way, and it took me no time at all to create this complex and lifelike animation.

**HOT TIP**

As your object animates with the Puppet tools, you may notice some undesirable blocky edges. If that happens, select your object and select the Puppet Pin tool, and then increase the Triangles value. This will increase the resolution of the mesh that After Effects is using to deform your object.

SHORTCUTS
MAC WIN BOTH

139

# Animation

# Bouncing Ball

T HIS IS SO COMMON IN ANIMATION CLASSES THAT IT'S FAIRLY CLICHÉ BY THIS POINT. But that doesn't change the fact that knowing how to bounce a ball is an extremely educational experience.

As beginners in After Effects, we were all introduced to easing. But easing just isn't enough. We need the ultimate animation control and power of the Graph Editor.

1 Open the Bouncing Ball START comp in the Bouncing Ball.aep project. Since our focus here is on advanced animation, I've already animated the ball doing a simple bounce. The keyframes are linear. The animation looks awful.

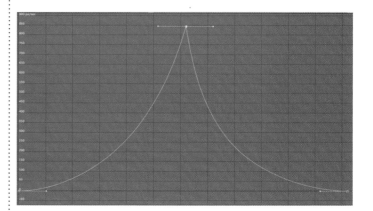

3 This graph represents the velocity of our object. The higher the line goes, the faster the object is traveling at that frame. The lower, the slower. This graph is totally wrong for a bouncing ball. We want it to start slow as it drops, then pick up speed, and hit full speed as it hits the ground, and then slow at the top again. Click the center points and drag them upwards as shown above.

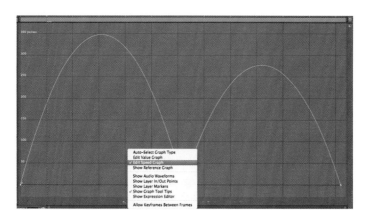

2 Select the ball layer. Press **P** to reveal its Position property. Then click the
word Position in the Timeline panel and press the F9 key to add easing to
these keyframes. That will do almost nothing for us here, but it will add some
curves in the Graph Editor. Click the Graph Editor button in the Timeline panel
to open the Graph Editor. From the Choose graph type and options menu at the
bottom, make sure Edit Speed Graph is chosen.

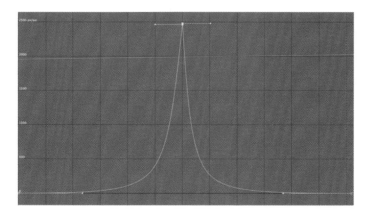

4 This is already looking much better! But to add some fine tuning, drag the
outer handles inwards a little bit. You may need to drag the center points
upward more to maintain the shape of the curves. Note that our work in this cheat
didn't change any keyframe values, only velocity. The Graph Editor is where real
masterful animation takes place, and it's important for all users of the program to
be comfortable with what you can do here.

**HOT TIP**

Be aware as
you're dragging
speed points
higher to make
things faster
that the graph
automatically
re-scales itself
to include all
points. This is a
very convenient
feature, but it
also makes it
easy to create
animation
that is way too
fast. Just be
cognizant of the
speed values (in
px/sec) on the
left side of the
graph.

SHORTCUTS
MAC WIN BOTH

141

# Parenting

1 Open the Parenting.aep project and the comp of the same name. This is some sweet Illustrator art work by Dan Grady. Because we set this up with layers in Illustrator, each component of the robot captain (above) is a separate layer. We want to animate his right arm coming up, and then down to rally the troops. Because each component of the arm is a separate layer, this can be really challenging. Well it would be, if it weren't for parenting.

PARENTING IS A BRILLIANT WAY TO CONNECT LAYERS. When layers are connected through the parenting relationship, you can animate or adjust the parent object, and the child object will automatically follow suit. While this is useful in a host of circumstances, this is especially helpful when animating characters.

3 We want the torso to be like the granddaddy of all of these layers. So grab the pickwhip on the shoulder layer (always grab the pickwhip of the child) and drag it to the torso layer. Parent the hand to the arm, and the sword and fingers to the hand.

**2** In the Timeline panel, create a parenting relationship by dragging the pickwhip on the robot captain R arm layer to the robot captain R shoulder layer as shown above.

**4** Now when we adjust Position, Rotation, Anchor Point, or Scale (and ONLY those four properties!) of a parent, the child also changes in the same way, using the anchor point of the parent. Note that the child can still be adjusted independently. Adjust the Z Rotation of the robot captain R hand layer to 75 degrees, and the Z Rotation of the robot captain R arm layer to 30 degrees. You can now see the relationship created in the arm, and it's so much easier to animate this character!

# Waving Sail

THERE ARE SOME ANIMATION TRICKS THAT EVEN THE PUPPET TOOL CAN'T HANDLE. Taking a flat surface and making it look like it's waving fabric is one of them.

Thankfully, there are other tools. One of my favorites is an effect called Turbulent Displace. The Turbulent Displace effect has a slightly intimidating name, but it's purpose is just to turn a layer into a wavy surface. It will work perfectly for breathing life into the sail of this pirate ship, and it's surprisingly easy to use.

1 Open the Waving Sail.aep project. I want the ship's sail here to wave. Thankfully, it's on its own layer.

3 We want this to look like big gusts of wind are flying through this. To make the size of the turbulence bigger, increase the Size value to 175. Then take the Amount value to 30 to it's not as intense.

2 Apply the Turbulent Displace effect to the pirate ship sail layer. And instantly, we see a difference. But we can make this look even better.

4 Finally, take the Pinning drop down to Pin All Locked to pin the corners of the sail to the mast a little bit more. Then all you need to do is animate the Evolution property, and this sail will come to life in all of its simulated windblown glory.

**HOT TIP**

Sometimes, Turbulent Displace creates ugly, blocky edges. If that happens to you, you can usually fix that by either increasing the Complexity value or by taking the Antialising for Best Quality drop down from Low to High.

# Animation

# Animating the Blob

URBULENT DISPLACE IS GREAT, DON'T GET ME WRONG. But there are times when I want more control over edges and Turbulent Displace just doesn't get me where I want to go.

Enter: the Wave Warp effect. The Wave Warp effect is an auto-animating, wave-based distortion effect. I don't think I've ever actually used it on waves, but it works great for distorting the edges of objects. Because it auto-animates, it's great for those times when you want a slender object to look like it's waving in the breeze.

**1** Open the Animating the Blob.aep project. We want to animate the edges of this blob in a blobby way. OK. The spellchecker is freaking out with "blobby". We'll animate it in a blobbish way. Nope. That's not a word, either. Whatever. You know what I mean.

**3** In the Wave Warp effect controls, change Wave Height to 3, Wave Width to 70, and Wave Speed to 0.4. Now the blob animates in an organic way.

**2** Apply the Wave Warp (NOT the Wave World!) effect to the blob body layer. Play this comp back and you'll notice that this blob animates automatically. It doesn't look very blob-like yet, though.

**4** As another example of this effect, I also used it with the Parenting.aep project to animate the tails of the bandanna of the robot captain.

# Animation

# Animating a Photo: Part 1

ONE OF THE MOST COMMON TRICKS IN AFTER EFFECTS is to animate the elements of a photograph. I've heard many After Effects users question how this is done.

Like many tricks in After Effects, this effect is achieved through the clever use of Photoshop and After Effects together. So we're going to break from the standard path here, and go over into Photoshop a bit over the next few cheats as we dig deep into this project. Because this is a bigger project and it's quite involved, we'll be doing a high level overview of what this effect entails, rather than going step-by-step.

Because this is an After Effects book and not a Photoshop book, I'm going to assume some basic Photoshop knowledge here. For more information on Photoshop techniques, I heartily recommend my brother book, *How to Cheat in Photoshop*.

1 We're going to animate this image of the Tacoma, WA rock band You Yell You Kick. Photo courtesy of Zombie Crush Photography. We're starting with the file Exercise Files>Media>PSDs>YYYK Cut Up START.psd, but I've provided a final version of this PSD for you in the file YYYK Cut Up FINISH.psd.

3 Do this for each person, the pool table, each of the billiard balls, the lights, and anything else you want to animate in After Effects. The downside is that this leaves a bunch of holes in our background (and yes, it also takes FOREVER!).

2  Our task here is to isolate each person. Using your selection tool(s) of
choice, select the girl on the pool table. If you give up, I've stored a selection
for you. Just choose Select>Load Selection and click OK. Once selected, press
⌘ Shift J / ctrl Shift J to cut this out of the background and make it a new
layer.

4  Now comes the time consuming part. We have to use Photoshop's Clone
Stamp tool to sample from the background that still exists, and fill in the
blank space in the background. That way, when we move our characters, we will
see the background. Above is my completed background. It's not perfect, but it will
be good enough for the animating that I want to do.

SHORTCUTS
MAC WIN BOTH

# Animation
# Animating a Photo: Part 2

1 Import the YYYK Cut Up FINISH.psd file that we discussed in the last cheat. Make sure that you import this as a composition, and in the Import As drop down, I recommend choosing Composition – Retain Layer Sizes. This will make sure that your anchor points are in the center of each layer, and not in the center of the entire composition.

CONTINUING ON FROM THE LAST CHEAT, we're now going to bring this to life in After Effects. I think you'll agree that the magic of this trick really is in Photoshop. Once you have it your Photoshop document cut up into layers, the steps in After Effects are a piece of cake.

As with the last cheat, this won't be a step-by-step cheat, it will be more of a high level overview of some things you can do to bring an image to life.

3 When I was working in Photoshop, I also isolated the cue stick and the finger on top of the cue stick so that I could animate it in After Effects. And animate it, I did. I actually used the Puppet tool to deform the guy and make it look like he was hitting the ball. I also animated the position of the cue stick and the white pool ball as seen in the before/after above.

**2** The first thing that I did was to distribute these layers in 3D space and create a camera. That way, I could navigate a camera through this scene or pan around it. That's really what makes animating a photo look cool – when you rotate a camera around it or zoom into it with all of the layers staggered in 3D space. Contrast this image with step 1 and note the camera movement. I also applied the Glow effect to the lights with a wiggle expression on the Glow Threshold property. That makes them flicker and creates the feeling that you're watching a video instead of a still image.

**4** After some color correction and some displacement (which we'll look at in the next cheat), I called it a day on this piece. To get the full effect, you really have to animate the layers in 3D and watch it for yourself.

# Animation

# Displacement Mapping

W E CAN'T LEAVE THE SUBJECT OF BRINGING STILLS TO LIFE without first taking a brief look at displacement mapping. Displacement is just what it sounds like – movement. We are going to use a luminance map to tell After Effects how to move pixels around. If we do this craftily, and we will, then we can create some 3D roundness to our still images.

This will be our last look at the You Yell You Kick image that we've been looking at in the last few cheats. But this trick will give a large amount of additional realism.

**1** This trick also has its roots in Photoshop. Open the YYYK Displace FINISH.psd file from the PSDs folder in Exercise Files>Media. Let's take the Marian layer for instance.

**3** Import this PSD into After Effects as a composition. Turn off the visibility of the displacement (DIS) layers. Restore opacity to the other layers as needed. Apply the Displacement Map effect to the Marian layer. In the Effect Controls panel, choose DIS Marian as the Displacement Map Layer. From Use For Horizontal Displacement, choose Luminance, and choose Off for Use For Vertical Displacement. Take Max Vertical Displacement to 0 and Max Horizontal Displacement to –25.

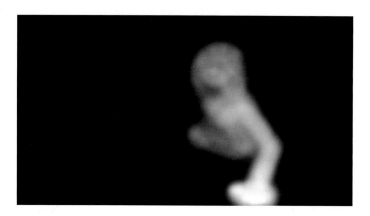

**2** Now this is an art not a science, and it took me many attempts before I could create a decent displacement map. But I create displacement maps by pressing ⌘ J ctrl J to duplicate the layer, then I lock the top copy, lower its opacity, and then fill the bottom copy with black. I then paint with white the areas that I want closest to the camera, and then I paint on the subject, with darker tones where the subject is farther away from the camera. As you can see, it should not have hard edges.

**4** Then animate the Max Horizontal Displacement to change over time to a positive value of 15. Look at the length of her arm, and its relation to her body, as well as her hair. These values may seem extreme, but it will look great when animated. It's just amazing how you can bring people and images to life by using this technique! Now try it on the pool table!

**HOT TIP**

Displacement maps are also really good for objects that cross depth planes (like the girl in steps 1 and 2). Or in other words, objects that come towards you. Those are the objects that typically don't animate very believably in After Effects' normal 3D environment. So I also created a displacement map for the pool table.

SHORTCUTS
MAC WIN BOTH

# 5 Animation

# Resizing Animation

1 Open the Resizing Animation.aep project. Here, I've animated this UFO from Cinema 4D. It starts off at the bottom and zig zags its way to the top (see the motion path above), scaling down as it goes up. We want this scaling to be larger and take more time, and we also want the trip to the top to take longer as well.

I OFTEN FIND MYSELF WISHING MY ANIMATIONS WERE JUST A BIT LONGER OR SHORTER. If you only have two keyframes, this is not a big deal – just drag them farther apart. But what happens when you have a complex animation and you want everything to stay in proportion? Well, the Graph Editor has a quick fix for us. And we're not going to look at how to just resize our animations proportionally in time, we're also going to look how to take a group of keyframes and exaggerate the animation! So, it's kinda 2 cheats for the page count of 1.

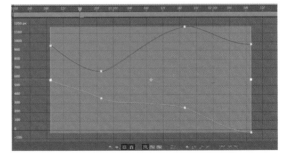

3 Click the Position property in the Timeline panel to select all of its keyframes. In the Graph Editor, you'll see a transform box around the keyframes. Click the white square on the right side and drag it to the right to proportionally scale your animation in time and increase its duration.

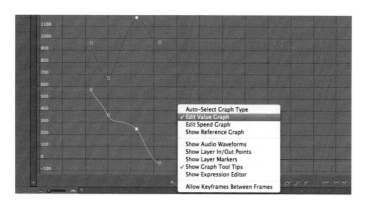

**2** Open the Graph Editor. From the bottom, choose to Edit Value Graph. Enable the option next to that one – Show Transform Box when multiple keys are selected.

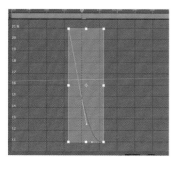

**4** Click the Scale property in the Timeline panel to see its keyframes in the Graph Editor. Click and drag a marquee to select both keyframes. Notice the values on the left.

**5** This time, drag it to the right to lengthen it in time, AND drag it upwards to proportionally increase the amount of scaling. Quick. Easy.

# Text Messaged Animation

THIS LAST CHEAT IS GOING TO BE LESS OF A CHEAT, and more of just a fun trick. We are going to send text message data via a text message.

When you copy keyframes, it's actually copying text data. This data can then be pasted inside of a text document, emailed, or even sent in a text message. After this text has been passed around, it can then be pasted back into After Effects to create an animation.

1 We're going to be starting in a project similar to what we saw in the last cheat, using the Text Messaged Animation.aep project. Select the UFO layer and press **P** to reveal its Position property. Select the Position property and press **⌘ C** **ctrl C** to copy its keyframe data.

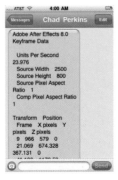

3 Here is the keyframe data in a text message. Also notice my dedication here. I've sent my wife a text message of After Effects keyframe data at 4am so that I could get this one screenshot, thereby ensuring that I sleep on the couch for the next week. That probably deserves a 5 star review on Amazon, right?

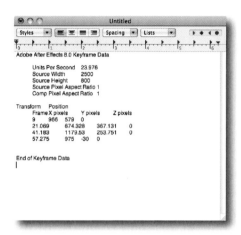

**2** Go to a text editor and press ⌘ V ctrl V to paste the data. See – it's just text! You can now copy this in an email, or text message, or any other text application that can copy and paste.

**4** Back in our project, we can turn the visibility on for the yellow solid. After selecting the text from the email or text message or whatever it is, I can select this layer and press ⌘ V ctrl V to paste it in. Contrast this with the motion path from step 1, and you'll see that only linear data (i.e. not interpolation) is copied in the keyframe data. Still, it's kind of a cool trick.

# Walt's Principles

BACK IN THE DAY, WALT DISNEY AND HIS TEAM OF ANIMATORS created the unofficial rules of animation. These basic principles of animation are still in full effect today, and critics, students, and people hiring animators still use these as the standards by which animation should be judged. I want to share a few of my favorite animation principles here that apply to After Effects users. But if you really want the full story about animation, I strongly urge you to check out the book *The Illusion of Life* by Frank Thomas and Ollie Johnston (two of Walt's most important animators). This book is still considered the bible of animation, and will help you whether you're doing Maya or Flash or After Effects or illustrating characters or motion graphics. It's expensive (and huge), but worth every penny (and second).

The first principle that applies to almost every After Effects user is anticipation. This principle states that in order for an action to have maximum impact, there needs to be something to build anticipation; a warm-up act, of sorts. If you were going to do a high jump, you would first squat down and cock your arms back. This is anticipation. Try this in motion graphics. Before you zoom that text in, try scaling it back a little first, then zooming. It is incredible how much more emotional impact an action has when there is proper preparation for it.

The next idea is that of exaggeration. Exaggeration in animation was really exemplified by Chuck Jones and the old Warner Brothers cartoons (e.g. *Bugs Bunny, Daffy Duck*, etc.). The principle here is to make sure that the key action is clear and obvious. It doesn't have to be Chuck Jones/broadway musical/over the top obvious. But it should be obvious and appear deliberate. In the case of motion graphics, this may actually mean creating sparkles or an additional element to call greater attention to the key action.

When an object is animating, it's important that we as animators are aware of the concept of weight, another Disney principle of animation. Especially as it pertains to computer animation, there is no set weight for any object. If we don't imbue objects with a sense of weight, our audience won't sense it either. Now, many objects in After Effects (like text, for example) might not have an inherent weight to them. But if we are aware of this concept, we can apply fake weight by the way we animate objects. Even if you're just aware of this idea, it will make a difference in your final results. For example, you may want that text to feel a little heavier. So it might take a little longer to start animating, and a little longer to slow down and come to a full stop. Other objects around it might move as if influenced by its gravitational pull.

It's also important that action happens on a smooth curve. One of the things that is very clear from Da Vinci's Vitruvian Man is that oftentimes, even when we move things in a seemingly linear way (such as moving your arm from straight down to straight outwards), the movement is curved. Be aware as you create animation that very few things in the real world move in straight lines.

Easing is big in the world of After Effects; in other words, starting out slow and then ending slow. This is also one of Walt's principles. Like most of the principles of animation, if you want to do this right, you really need to be working in the Graph Editor. However, this is one that After Effects can do on a basic level right out of the gate. Just right click on a keyframe in the Timeline panel and choose Keyframe Assistant>Easy Ease In/Out.

Once an action has been performed, it's important that there is follow through. If you threw a ball, it wouldn't just land on the ground and stop. Depending on the surface and the ball, it will probably bounce and continue rolling a bit. In this case, the throwing would be the key action, and the bouncing/rolling afterwards would be the follow through, another principle of animation. So perhaps, after your text zips off of the screen, there is a little bit of blurred motion trails, or dust particles, or something else to kind of wind down from the action.

There are many more principles of animation, which can be found online (such as on wikipedia.org). The ones I've shared with you here are the ones that I think are the most helpful to After Effects users, but they're all very good to be aware of. Also, the ones we've just looked at pertain to the building up of the action, then the quality of the action itself, and then what happens after the action. And again, just an awareness of these ideas can make your work better. But mastery of these skills can make your animations significantly more engaging.

Since the beginning of motion graphics, artists have always played with digital lighting tricks. Few things grab our attention more than a powerful light source, and the contrast against black is incredible.

# Light Effects

WE TALKED ABOUT AFTER EFFECTS LIGHTS IN CHAPTER 2, BUT THIS IS DIFFERENT. In this chapter we're going to look at how to make sweet lighting tricks, and we won't be using After Effects lights to do it.

We'll be looking at how to create volumetric light (where you can see the light rays), and we'll also be talking a bit about HDR (High Dynamic Range) color. If you're unfamiliar with that concept, the interlude at the end of the chapter is all about that.

In the same way that color really makes things come alive, light (or simulated light) can do the same thing. Knowing these light tricks can also help save time. Instead of trying to adjust After Effects lights to do exactly what you want, you can just fake it, as is the case with the sheen effect in this chapter.

# HDR

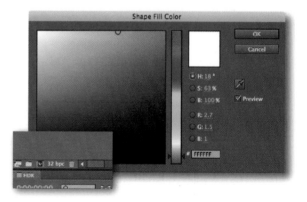

1 In the HDR.aep project, you'll find this shape layer full of shapes. It's an intentionally plain layer.

INTRODUCED BACK IN AFTER EFFECTS 7, 32 BIT FLOAT POINT COLOR allows us to create natural lighting effects that are just beautiful. This is also referred to as High Dynamic Range (HDR) color. We'll discuss this in more detail in the interlude at the end of this chapter. But in this cheat, we'll look at the practical side of HDR that everyone can take advantage of, even if you're just starting out with generic white text.

3 Now let's make this HDR. First, go to the bottom of the project panel and ⌥ _alt_ click the bit depth setting at the bottom twice. It should say 8 bpc, then 16 bpc after one click, and then 32 bpc after a second click. Now the project is in HDR mode (32 bits per channel). Now select the shape layer and click the white Fill color swatch at the top of the interface. What's cool about HDR is that we can have tones whiter than white. In 32 bit mode, 1 represents regular white. Take the RGB color values to 2.7, 1.5, 1.

2 Apply the Fast Blur effect to this, and increase the Blurriness to 19. It gets blurry like you probably thought it would, and it doesn't look all that awesome.

4 Once you click OK, the blur has a completely different effect. The lighting burn is a very natural one when we have this much color depth. As we go throughout this chapter, we're going to be sticking to 8 bit mode, but keep in mind what you could do if you took the same cheats into 32 bpc mode!

**HOT TIP**

It's important to remember that we change the bit depth of the project, not the composition. Thus, all comps in your project will have the same bit depth.

**SHORTCUTS**

MAC WIN BOTH

# Volumetric Light

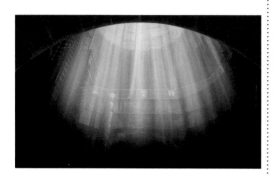

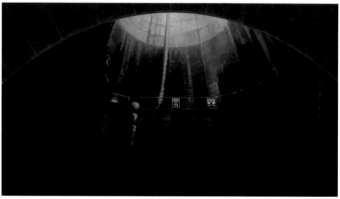

1 We'll start with this matte painting by Daniel Johnson. You can find it in the Volumetric Light START comp in the project of the same name.

**V**OLUMETRIC LIGHT IS LIGHT THAT YOU CAN SEE. These streaks of light are most obvious when light comes through the clouds or through a window. You can see the light because of the particles (dust, smoke, etc.) in the air.

I once did a commercial where I had to show light pouring down from the heavens and this is very similar to the technique that I used. Be aware that this is another one of those techniques that looks sufficient in screenshots, but looks really incredible when animated.

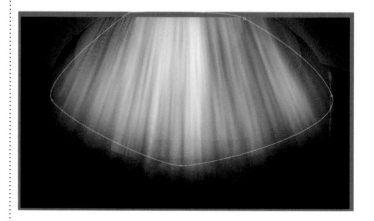

4 We need to create soft feathered edges, so select the solid layer and press ⌘ Shift C / ctrl Shift C to precompose this layer (choosing the "Move all attributes..." option). Create a mask around the light rays. With the solid selected, press **F** to reveal the Mask Feather property. Increase this as desired to soften the edges, as shown above.

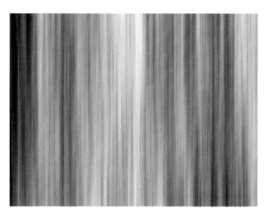

**2** I've already created a solid for you in between the background and the arch. Apply the Fractal Noise effect to this solid layer. In its effect controls, take Contrast to 150. Then open the Transform area, uncheck Uniform Scaling, and take Scale Height to 4000.

**3** To apply some roundness to our light, apply the Warp effect, and take its Bend value down to −100. This will seemingly adjust the placement of the layer. To compensate for this, decrease the Y position value of the solid layer to −267.

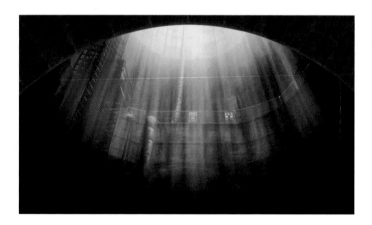

**5** For the final step, I applied the Tint effect, and changed the Map White To value to a slightly warmer color to help the light composite better. I also took the blend mode of the precomp layer to Screen. To bring this to life, double click the precomp to get back to the Fractal Noise effect, and animate the Evolution parameter. If the effect is too intense (or not intense enough), you can adjust the opacity of the layer, or go back to Fractal Noise and adjust the Contrast and Brightness values.

**HOT TIP**

If you're really into this volumetric light effect, I recommend checking out the 3rd party plugin Lux by Trapcode. The purpose of Lux is to create volumetric light from After Effects lights.

SHORTCUTS
MAC WIN BOTH

# Light Effects

## Silhouettes

ALTHOUGH THE OLD IPOD LOOK IS RATHER OUTDATED AT THIS POINT, it's still rather helpful to be able to know how to create silhouettes. It kind of opens the door to new possibilities. Because light tricks are really just about contrast, putting a layer into silhouette can help exaggerate details in a scene.

**1** We're starting in the Silhouettes.aep project and the Silhouettes START comp with a video clip of a kid dancing, from uberstock.com. I've already created a garbage matte for you. We'll also be going through the next steps pretty quick because we've covered these ideas in detail back in Chapter 4.

**3** Let's polish up this matte a bit. Apply the Refine Matte effect. The default settings make this look much better. And silhouettes are very forgiving, so this is good enough.

2 In order to create a silhouette, we have to isolate the subject. Apply the Luma Key effect to the layer with the video clip. Change the Key Type drop down to Key Out Brighter, and change the Threshold to 242. It looks bad, but that's OK for now.

iDo Things

4 Finally, make this a silhouette by applying the Fill effect and changing the Color in the Fill effect to black. Apply cheesy satire text as desired.

**HOT TIP**

You can also fill the layer by right clicking on the layer and applying a Color Overlay layer style. The layer style also gives you the option to blend the color with the original layer by using a blend mode.

# Light Whips

1 Start in the Light Whips START comp in the Light Whips.aep project. Create a new solid at 1280 x 200 pixels. Apply the Fractal Noise effect. In its effect controls, change Contrast to 600, Brightness to –150, and Complexity to 2. In the Transform area, uncheck Uniform Scaling and take Scale Width to 6000 and Scale Height to 5.

YOU'LL SEE LITTLE "WHIPS" OF LIGHT ALL OVER THE PLACE, especially in the world of broadcast. Often, you'll want little animated lines of light to come in and underscore, highlight, or pull your attention towards something in an ad. There are a probably no less than a billion (yes, a billion) different ways to do this, but we're going to look at one of my favorite ways in depth. I'll also mention another way to create this effect as well.

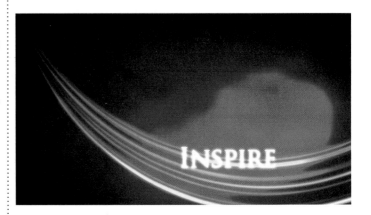

3 Rotate, position, and reorder this layer in the layer stack as desired. Then change the blend mode of the layer. Dragging this layer beneath the adjustment layer makes the whips get all magic and glowy and awesome.

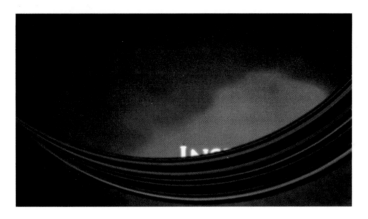

**2** Apply the Warp effect. In its effect controls, change Bend to –50, Horizontal to 50, and Vertical Distortion to –13. Apply the Fast Blur effect to smooth things out a bit. I used a Blurriness value of 6.

**4** At about 1 second into the final version of this animation, you'll see another light whip enter the scene and reveal the INSPIRE text. This light whip was created by using the Vegas effect. Because this effect relies heavily on masks, we'll look briefly at it in the next chapter.

**HOT TIP**

As in most cases with the Fractal Noise effect, create some nice pulsating animation by animating the Evolution value.

# Stage Lights

I'S FAIRLY FEASIBLE TO THINK THAT YOU MIGHT BE CALLED UPON to create stage lights one day. Creating virtual stadiums is becoming increasingly popular, and being able to create the type of lights that they have in stadiums is really helpful. However, that's not really the purpose of this cheat.

The purpose of this cheat is to help us to think creatively about creating light sources. We take tutorials and read books and do all that we can to learn After Effects. But all of that goes out the window when a client asks for something we've never seen made before. At that point, we need to use the tools we have to meet the demand. In many cases in my own experience, thinking creatively about non-traditional tools has saved me on a number of occasions.

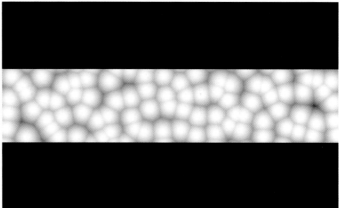

1 Make a new comp at 1280 x 720. Make a new solid at 1280 x 250. Apply the Cell Pattern effect.

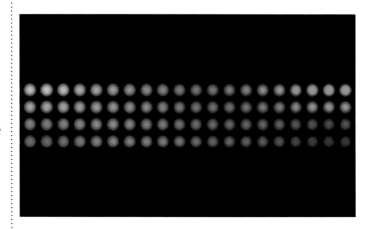

3 Apply the 4-Color Gradient effect. At the bottom of the effect in the Effect Controls panel, change the Blending Mode value to Multiply.

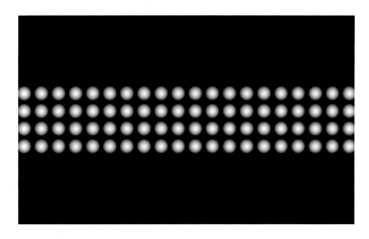

2 In the Cell Pattern effect controls, take the Disperse value down to 0. Increase the Contrast value to 700.

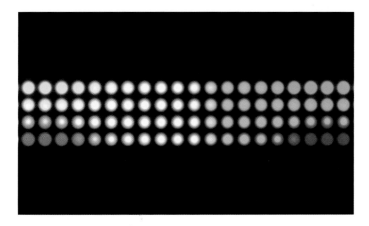

4 To make these dots look like lights, apply the Glow effect. In its effect controls, change Glow Threshold to 30% and Glow Radius to 20. To animate the colors (and location of the colors) of these lights, adjust the Positions & Colors properties in the 4-Color Gradient effect.

# Energy Cube

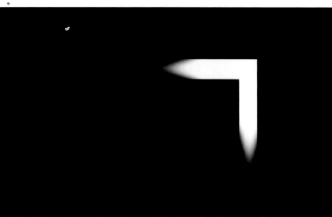

THIS CHEAT PROBABLY HAS ITS ROOTS IN MY LOVE OF SATURDAY MORNING CARTOONS. Before it was turned into its current movie franchise, *Transformers* was perhaps my all-time favorite cartoon growing up.

So this is my take on the energon cubes that were such a staple of those old plots. But there is a more important reason for this cheat here. This again helps us to realize that we can often find answers to problems in unconventional places. This will be less of a hands on cheat, and more of a case study.

I actually created this object on a dare to myself. I created the cheesiest object I could think of in Photoshop (2 rectangular marquee selections filled with white, then smudged with  
challenged myself to  
ects. I really like the  
scores the importance  
d Photoshop together.

**171**

**1** This is the thing that I started out with from Photoshop. Two white rectangles smeared by one of the worst tools in Photoshop.

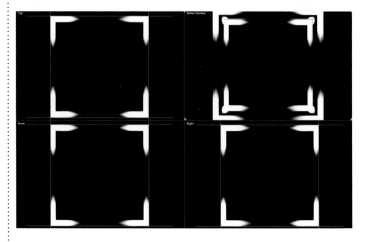

**3** The next part was a little challenging. I selected all of these brackets and precomposed them so that I could adjust all of these brackets at once. I then duplicated that precomp, and arranged them in 3D space to form a cube.

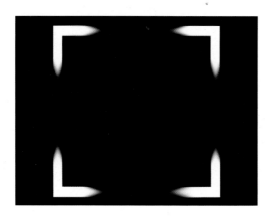

2 I then duplicated it a few times and made it the edges of an imaginary square.

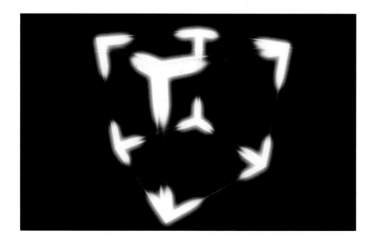

4 At this point, all that was left was to create an adjustment layer and apply a liberal dose of color correction, including a healthy amount of the Glow effect. The project here is included with the exercise files to look at if you're interested.

# Light Effects

# Searchlights

W E'VE ALL SEEN SEARCHLIGHTS, whether they're promoting a large concert, or summoning Batman, or if it's just the local used car dealer trying to move some inventory. Here's a quick way to recreate them in After Effects.

1 Start in the Searchlights START comp in the Searchlights.aep project. All other layers have been hidden and locked for you, so you can concentrate on the task at hand.

3 For a basic searchlight, all that's left is to apply the Fast Blur effect and increase the Blurriness value to taste, put the layer in the Screen or Add blend mode as desired, and reduce opacity to taste. Oh, and you should also probably click the master Shy button in the Timeline panel to see all layers and then reorder this searchlight so it's behind the front buildings (beneath layer 20).

**2** Our searchlight is going to be created by a shape layer. So in the Tools panel, select the Pen tool. Then click 3 times to create a triangle, as shown above. Make sure that the fill is a pale yellow and that there is no stroke.

**4** If you're looking for a little more richness in your searchlight texture, apply the Fractal Noise effect, and change the blend mode (at the bottom of the Fractal Noise effect controls) to Multiply, or another mode of your choosing. This creates the illusion of smoke or dust particles in the air. The noise has been exaggerated so you can see it above. And don't forget to select this layer and press ⌘D ctrl D to make copies so you can put them in other places if needed.

## HOT TIP

To animate these searchlights, hold the **Y** key to temporarily use the Pan Behind tool, so you can drag your anchor point to the bottom of the searchlight. Then when you rotate it, it will move like a searchlight does.

SHORTCUTS
MAC WIN BOTH

# Sheen

SHEEN REFERS TO A SMALL LITTLE STREAK OF LIGHT bouncing off of an object. This effect can be used to create suspense on a dark subject (such as our example in this cheat) to reveal content, or it could be used for the opposite – as a regal highlight on a bright and illuminated subject.

This trick is especially great for those times when the main part of an animation has completed and things aren't supposed to move that much; almost like the aftershock of the animation. The sheen is a perfect thing to maintain interest without being too distracting.

1 In the Sheen START comp in the Sheen.aep project, you'll find this 3D text that I created in Cinema 4D. It's very dark, but I kinda like it like that. It's supposed to be scary. I have a few options here to reveal this text and keep it scary. I could put a faint glow behind it. But we're going to go for the sheen effect.

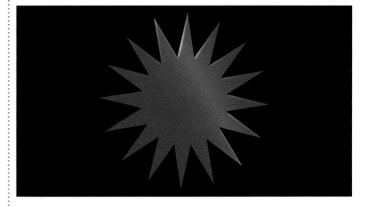

3 One of the things that this effect does is that it appears to create a beveled edge because of its Edge Thickness property. This is shown here above (on a different object so it's easier to see) on a completely flat object. We don't want this fake bevel conflicting with the bevel created in Cinema 4D, so take Edge Thickness down to 2.

2 Apply the CC Light Sweep effect to this layer. Instantly we have a pretty cool light sheen on our subject.

**HOT TIP**

If you want the bevel added by the CC Light Sweep effect to be removed entirely, take the Edge Intensity property down to 0.

4 Adjust the angle of the light sheen using the Direction parameter. Adjust its position using the Center property. Animate the X position of the Center property to have the light sweep go across the object. Here, I created a more subtle effect by increasing Width to 120 and by taking Sweep Intensity down to 12. It's subtle, but it's obvious when compared with the screenshot in step 1.

# The Glow Effect

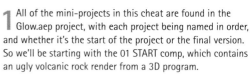

THE GLOW EFFECT IS ONE OF THE MOST USED EFFECTS in the world of motion graphics. It just has a way of making things come alive and look better.

To me, the Glow effect has two main purposes. It can make footage glow, exaggerating the colors that are already there. But it can also be used to colorize graphics as it adds glow. Almost everything looks better with a prudent application of the Glow effect. In this cheat we'll take a mini-tour of Glow being used in a few different circumstances.

1 All of the mini-projects in this cheat are found in the Glow.aep project, with each project being named in order, and whether it's the start of the project or the final version. So we'll be starting with the 01 START comp, which contains an ugly volcanic rock render from a 3D program.

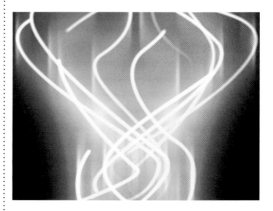

4 Apply the Glow effect to the adjustment layer. At first, it just brightens what is already there. To colorize this, change the Glow Colors drop down to A & B Colors, and then change the white Color A swatch to orange, and the Color B color to red. Then take Glow Threshold, Radius, and Intensity to 10, 400, and 3, respectively.

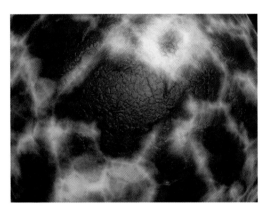

**2** Apply the Glow effect. The main Glow properties are the first 3. Take Glow Threshold (which determines what tones have glow applied to them) to 30%. Take Glow Radius (the size of the glow) to 50. Take Glow Intensity to 0.5. It made this image really come alive.

**3** Move over to the 02 START comp. Because we have multiple layers here, we'll need to create an adjustment layer, which you can do by pressing ⌘ ⌥ Y ctrl alt Y. These layers were created by using the Vegas effect.

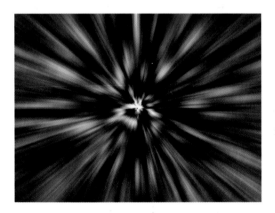

**5** Another example of adding glow color can be found in the 03 START comp. By the way, this was created with the Fractal Noise effect, distorted by the Radial Blur effect.

**6** Apply Glow, and change the Glow Colors drop down to A & B Colors, and then change Color A to the RGB values of 5, 65, 180, and change Color B to 5, 100, 180. Take Glow Threshold to 15 and Glow Radius to 20. Note that in the previous example, we had to increase brightness a lot after using A & B colors, but not in this example. Just something to be aware of.

**HOT TIP**

To use the Glow effect to create a glow on the outside of an object, change the Glow Based On drop down to Alpha Channel, and take the Composite Original drop down to On Top.

**SHORTCUTS**
MAC WIN BOTH

# Laser Beams

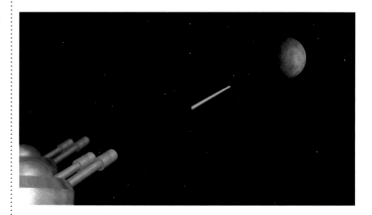

**L**ASER BEAMS AND LIGHT SABERS ARE JUST THE COOLEST. In this cheat, we'll look at a simple way to create those and other effects of that ilk with the Beam effect.

1 In the Laser Beams START comp in the Laser Beams.aep project, you'll find this project set up for you.

3 To shoot this laser beam, all you have to do is animate the Time value. If 3D Perspective is checked (it's on by default), you can have some fun. Here, I took Length to 3%, Time to 5%, Starting Thickness to 24, and Ending Thickness 1. This looks better as a still frame, but when the Time property is animated, the laser appears to shoot into deep space. It's a cool effect.

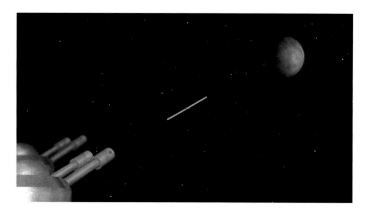

2 Apply the Beam effect to the white solid layer called BEAM. Notice that the while solid layer instantly disappears and is replaced by the beam. With the Beam effect selected in the Effect Controls panel, you can see the effect control points. Put the Starting Point next to the gun turret and put the Ending Point next to the planet.

4 You can also add extra flourishes, like more beams and lens flares. It's a pretty cool result for such little effort.

**HOT TIP**

To use this same effect to create light sabers, just increase the Length value to 100%.

# Trapcode Shine

THE SHINE EFFECT IS SEEN EVERYWHERE, including commercials by McDonald's, Captain Morgan, and other major brands. This effect just won't die. Like lens flares, they were cool for a while, then out of style because the effect was so overused, and then the effect came back in style again.

The Shine effect by Trapcode is perhaps the easiest, fastest, and best looking way to create these awesome light rays that shoot out from behind objects. Because light rays are emitted from behind the subject, it makes the subject seem more important, interesting, and powerful.

The Shine effect is not included with After Effects CS5. If you don't own it, you can download a free trial of it from redgiantsoftware.com. It really is the ultimate effect for light tricks.

1 In the Trapcode Shine.aep project, you won't be able to see anything. This is because this project contains the silhouette we created earlier in this chapter on a black background (I added a temporary white solid background for this screenshot). This will be another cool trick that you can do with silhouettes.

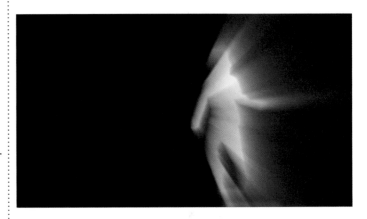

3 There are loads of preset color schemes that you can choose from. In the Colorize area in the Shine effect controls, change the Colorize drop down to Enlightenment.

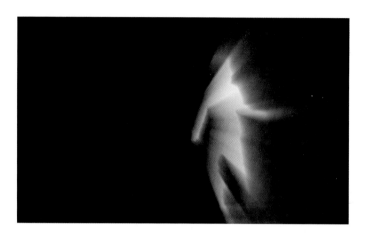

2 Apply the Shine effect to the PRECOMP kid dancing layer. In the Shine effect controls, change the Colorize>Base On drop down to Alpha. Oooooooh......

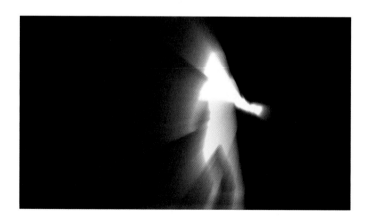

4 In my opinion, the real magic of this effect comes when you adjust the Source Point. Adjust its X value (and Y value, if desired) to the right of the subject. Note that the subject has not moved since step 3. Not only does this look incredible when animated, but notice how quickly it renders! Unbelievable!

**HOT TIP**

If you don't own Shine, you can try checking out the CC Light Rays effect that ships with After Effects. I find that Shine is far superior, but CC Light Rays may work for you.

# High Dynamic Range

THERE'S A LOT OF CONFUSION ABOUT HIGH DYNAMIC RANGE (HDR) COLOR. So I wanted to take these next couple of pages and see if we can't clear some stuff up.

First of all, let's talk about bit depth. HDR color is often referred to as 32 bit color. What does that mean? Well, let's back up a bit. A bit is the most basic level of a computer's understanding, and it has two possible values – a 1 or a 0. Old GIF images (remember those?) were 8 bits of color. If something is 8 bits, the way we express that mathematically is to say $2^8$, which is 256 (where the 2 comes from the bit options – 1 or 0 – and the 8 comes from the bit depth).

Often times, we refer to an image as being 8 bit, when we actually mean that it is 8 bits *per channel*. So, in a standard image or video clip, there are 256 ($2^8$) color variations in the red channel, 256 in the green, and 256 in the blue. We arrive at the total possible RGB color choices by multiplying those together. My calculator tells me that this works out to about 16.7 million colors. That's already more colors than the human eye can see. So why add more?

When we go up to 16 bit per channel images, that's $2^{16}$, or 65,536 color possibilities in each channel. That creates the ability to produce much finer color refinements. I think of this like a toaster. If your toaster had only two settings – raw and burnt – that doesn't leave you much choice in toasting preference satisfaction. If your toaster had 400 different levels of toasting, you would be guaranteed to get your toast the exact way that you wanted it, even though you might not be able to tell the difference between each level of toasting. Having more color choices gives us similar control.

But isn't 16 bit enough, then? Why do we need to jump up to 32 bit? There is a slight but important difference with HDR color. HDR color attempts to simulate the way that light works. On a computer, white is white, right? But that's not the way that white works in real life. If you have a piece of paper, you may say that's white. And you'd be correct. But then if someone shines a flashlight in your face, that would also be white, but that's a much more intense white. Likewise, if we were to then look at the sun: it's a much brighter white. HDR attempts to recreate this by allowing you to create colors that are "superwhite". In the HDR cheat in this chapter, we increased the color levels of some of the channels beyond white. That's why when we added blur, the colors channels that were emitting more light appeared to shine through with more intensity, just like light in real life.

Be aware that HDR is also a big deal in photography, where it also suffers from some confusion. Digital photography (and digital video as well) suffers from having a much smaller dynamic range than film does. It's just impossible to capture bright brights and dark darks simultaneously. Image editing tools like Photoshop allow you to combine multiple exposures of the same image so that you can create full 32 bit, HDR images.

But some people that are using HDR images have created a very distinct visual style with these images. You've probably seen those beautiful shots of celebrity faces in magazines that are very sharp and stylized, and you can see every pore and detail on the face. Well, this isn't necessarily HDR, but it's kind of become equated with it. There's even a new adjustment in Photoshop CS5 called HDR Toning, to simulate the look of HDR images on an 8 bit image. Thus, HDR is further confusing because it's now not only a technical concept (which is really all that it should have ever been), but it's also a style.

Hopefully this helps to clear something up, if there was confusion. Remember that it's never as important to know how something works, as it is to be able to get it to do what you want it to.

■ Masks and mattes allow us to create stencils and cutouts, but they also serve as some great cheat fodder.

# Masks and Shapes

A LOT OF THE MAGIC OF AFTER EFFECTS LIES IN WHAT
YOU DON'T SHOW, as much as it does in what you do
show. So, in this chapter, we're going to look closer at
masks – what makes them tick, and also some cool tricks
that you can do with them.

We'll also spend some time looking at tangential topics,
such as shapes and mattes. After surveying other books
and tutorials online, I find that the real jewels of these
features aren't really discussed that much. So hopefully,
there will be some new tricks in this chapter that allow
you to take your art to the next level.

# Options

**1** Open the Mask Options.aep project and the Mask Options START comp in that project. Then select the Rectangle Tool from the Tools panel at the top of the interface.

I N OTHER PLACES IN THIS BOOK, WE PLAY A LITTLE with mask feathering and mask expansion. But there are several other options for masks, including the ability to animate their shape and position, and blend modes that control how multiple masks interact with each other.

In this cheat, we'll create a frenetic, fragmented look on a sports clip from uberstock using multiple masks and blending them together.

**3** Press **M M** to reveal all mask properties, including the mask modes drop down, and Mask Opacity. It's important to know that the mask modes change how the mask interacts with the masks above it. The top mask affects the alpha channel of the layer. My top mask is the vertical mask over the subject's right eye. As I lower the Mask Opacity to 50%, you can see that only the areas where that mask is have lowered opacity. In the bottom right corner, I change the mask mode to Difference, which creates a hole where other layers overlapped it. Note that Intersect does the opposite.

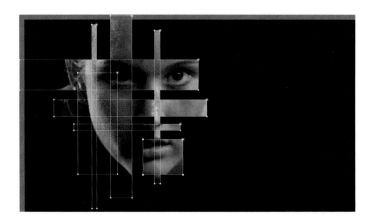

**2** Make sure this layer is selected, and then click and drag to create several rectangular masks. The default mask mode is Add, which will combine the contents of the mask to form the opaque areas of the layer, and anything not masked will become transparent.

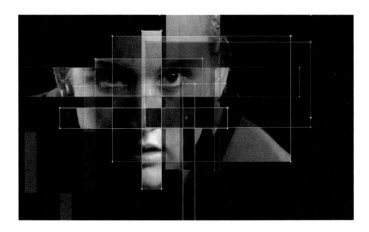

**4** Adjusting these masks can create some pretty cool effects. In the Mask Options FINAL comp, I've played with this a little more. Here I've also added an adjustment layer with some color correction. I've also taken this screenshot with my masks active so you can see what I did here. It's a little time consuming, but a really cool result.

# Instant Vignette

O K, SO IT IS NOT EXACTLY INSTANT, but it's pretty darn close.

Vignettes are just all the rage these days. They help to focus your attention, which is what visual storytelling is really all about.

In this cheat, we'll create a vignette in just a few steps, and we'll look at some cool mask tricks as well.

**1** Start with a video clip or still image. I'm using this clip from the Zen Chemists music video that I did. You'll find this in the Vignette.aep project. It's a cool shot in my opinion, but there's a lot of stuff to look at with all of the textures everywhere. It's a bit distracting from the rap guy who we want to be the focus.

**3** In the Timeline panel, take the mask mode drop down from Add to Subtract. Now this mask will cut an elliptical hole in our layer. Almost there!

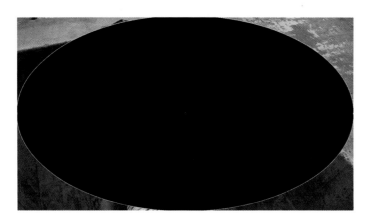

**2** Press ⌘ Y ctrl Y to make a new black solid the same size as the comp. We
want to create an elliptical mask that fills this composition. Select the Ellipse
tool in the Tools panel. Now, we could click and drag an elliptical mask, but there's
an easier way. With the solid layer selected, just double click the Ellipse tool in the
Tools panel. It instantly creates a mask for you that fills the comp. Perfect!

**HOT TIP**

If you're not
seeing the mask
options, just
press M M
(that's the letter
"m" twice) to
reveal its mask
options.

**4** Select the solid layer and press F to reveal the Mask Feather property.
Looks good, but the black is too intrusive. Do we need to manually resize it?
No way! In the mask options area, change the Mask Expansion value to 40. I also
selected the solid layer and pressed T to reveal its Opacity property and took
that down to 80%. This makes the effect very subtle (and probably hard to see in
the screenshots), but that's exactly what we want. We want the vignette to be *felt*
and not *seen*. Turn the visibility of the vignette on and off to compare, and you'll
see that the difference is massive.

SHORTCUTS
MAC WIN BOTH

# Masks and Shapes

# From Video to Shape Layer

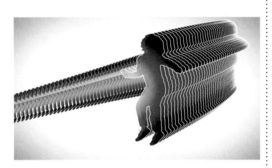

**1** We're going to start with a project very similar to the silhouette project we looked at in the last chapter. It basically contains an uberstock.com video clip of a kid dancing. The background has also been removed.

THIS NEXT CHEAT IS GOING TO BE A LITTLE BIT OF A MIND BLOWER. Here's the deal – I LOVE shape layers, introduced back in After Effects CS3. They are so powerful, and I don't feel like I've really tapped their potential, so I'm always trying to find new ways to use them.

Shape layers have all of these really cool operators that allow you to do very cool things with them, including the ability to wiggle their transform properties and edges, and the ability to create multiple repetitions of objects as well.

I've always thought that it would be cool to have these operators as controls on regular layers, and I just figured out a way to turn video outlines into shape layers. We'll learn a lot about masks and shapes in these few steps!

**3** We need to get this mask data into a shape layer. The way to do this is a little weird and tricky. Deselect all layers by pressing F2. Then press **G** to select the Pen tool. Then click to create a new shape layer. It doesn't matter what you make with the Pen tool. Even a single point will work. If you did it right, the outline will be blue.

**4** Now select Mask 1>Mask Path on the auto-traced layer. Press **⌘ C** **ctrl C** to copy this mask. Now open the shape layer up. Go to Contents>Shape 1>Path 1>Path, and click that Path (the one that has the stopwatch next to it) to select it. Press **⌘ V** **ctrl V** to paste the mask date into the shape layer. If you did it correctly, you'll see the dancing kid with a blue outline.

2 We need to first make a mask around this shape, and we need to do it for every frame. Sound tedious? It's not at all, provided we use the Auto-trace feature. Select the layer, and from the Layer menu at the top of the interface, choose Auto-trace. Make sure the Channel drop down is set to Alpha, and change the Time Span to Work Area, and click OK. Note that this process will take quite a while. But when it's done, you'll have a mask around this layer on every frame!

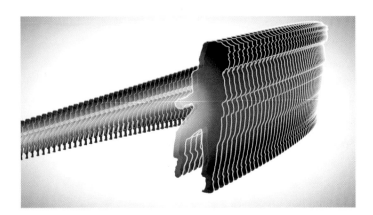

5 Once this is a shape layer, we have all kinds of options, because it's a regular old shape layer. Here I changed the Fill and Stroke, and added some repetition. In the Timeline panel, click the Add flyout and choose Repeater. This allows you to create multiple duplicates of your shape, as seen above. This is after adjusting the number of copies, as well as the Anchor Point and Position properties in the Repeater area. Don't forget that this layer is like video! Shown above is this layer a few frames later in time. Contrast this with the previous screenshots – this is our video!

SHORTCUTS
MAC WIN BOTH

# The Vegas Effect

T HE VEGAS EFFECT WAS CREATED TO SIMULATE THOSE OLD STYLE Vegas marquee lights (as in the example above). But this effect actually has a few more tricks up its proverbial sleeve. In this cheat, we'll look at one of those tricks.

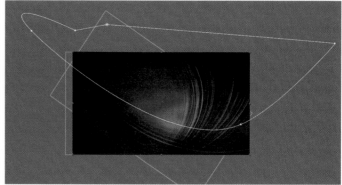

**1** This project is similar to what we saw in the last chapter's cheat on light whips. You'll find this project in the Vegas START comp in the Vegas.aep project. Vegas can use the contours (around the alpha channel) of an image, or a mask. I usually use the mask option because I usually get more predictable results with it. So, I've already created a mask here for you. A big, sloppy mask.

**3** We could shorten the Length value to create the old Vegas style marquee lights, but let's do something different. Take the Segments>Segments value down to just 1. This makes it so that there is only one streak of light traveling around our mask.

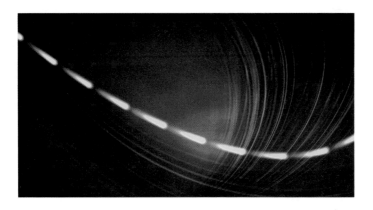

**2** Apply the Vegas effect to the Whip layer. You won't see anything yet. In the Vegas effect controls, change the Stroke drop down from Image Contours to Mask/Path. You still won't be able to see much. That's because Vegas was (unfortunately) designed to have a tiny yellow default stroke, but masks are also yellow! To see what's going on here, take the Rendering>Width value to 15.

**4** Now all that remains is to animate the Segments>Rotation value (from a higher angle to a lower one in this case). I've also reduced Segments>Length to 0.15 to create shorter streaks of light. What's cool about this is that the segment will go all the way around a closed path, which is why I took a wide screenshot of the mask in step 1. Try creating a crazy path and animating multiple segments along it.

**HOT TIP**

If you like this effect, you might want to check out the last cheat in this chapter, where we'll look at the 3rd party plugin Trapcode 3D Stroke. It creates results similar to this, but with some enhanced features.

# Luma Matte

LUMA MATTES ALLOW US TO USE THE BRIGHTNESS OF ANOTHER LAYER AS A MASK for the layer beneath it. In this cheat, and in the next, we're going to look at ways to mask without creating masks – by using mattes. Kind of like blend modes, the downside of this is that there is no manual control over the results. But, also like blend modes, the other side of the coin is that when the setup is right, it works instantly and looks great.

**1** In the Luma Matte.aep project, you'll find two layers in the Luma Matte START comp. One of them is an uberstock clip that shows black ink dripping on a white background. This layer is on top because we want it to be the mask.

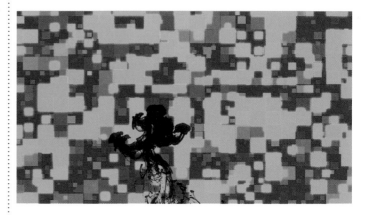

**3** In the Modes area of the Timeline panel, in the drop down in the TrkMat column, change the drop down on the Pattern layer to Luma Matte. If you're like me, you can never remember if white creates the hole or black. Apparently, dark tones make a mask. That's not what we want.

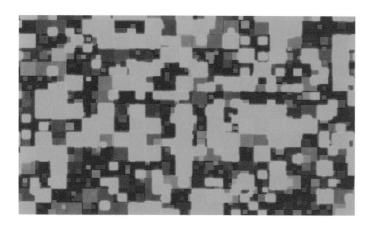

**2** The other layer is a cheesy fractal noise background. This layer is on the bottom because we want it to be the texture that fills the mask.

**4** Not to worry, just change the TrkMat drop down to Luma Inverted Matte, and the white areas will mask out the layer beneath it. This trick is great for creating really intricate and beautiful patterns as motion graphics backgrounds.

# Track Matte

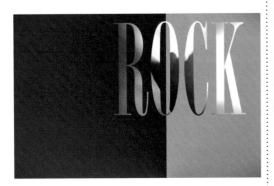

**1** The steps in this trick are really easy, but let's take a look at our layers first. The matte layer on the top of the layer stock is just simple text. Because it's red, it would create a weak luma matte. But its outlines will make for a great alpha matte.

**T**RACK MATTES ARE VERY SIMILAR TO LUMA MATTES, except that instead of using the luminance of the layer above to create a mask, it uses the alpha of the layer.

Because the last cheat was our first look at mattes, we took it kinda easy. In this one we're going to use three layers to show how you can create even more complexity by using a cool background as well. So again, the three components are:

1. The top layer, which is the mask
2. The middle layer, which is the mask fill
3. The bottom layer, which is the background

**3** Remember that when we create our matte, that the video from step 2 will only exist as a fill for the matte in step 1. This leaves the background (everything that isn't the text) as empty. So now we have this third layer on the bottom of the layer stack, and this will serve as the background.

**2** The next layer – the one that will be used to fill the inside of the text mask we'll create – is another video clip from uberstock.com.

**4** On the uberstock video clip layer, in the Modes area of the Timeline panel, go to the TrkMat drop down and choose Alpha Matte. Again, this uses the alpha channel of the layer above it (the ROCK text) to mask out the current layer, allowing the background to show through.

**HOT TIP**

As with luma mattes, the object that is creating the mask can be a video, or it can be an animated layer, or both. Sometimes, you can create the most interesting results by having a traveling (e.g. animated) matte.

# Animating Masks

THE NEXT COUPLE OF CHEATS ARE GOING TO HAVE BONUS INTEGRATION tips built into them. In this cheat, we're going to look at the powerful ability that masks have when animating. We'll then bring in a shape from Photoshop and paste it into After Effects. This will create a shape tween; basically a morph between shapes. We'll then polish the tween using another great After Effects tool. There's a lot of cool stuff in this one.

1 We're going to be working with this fish in the Animating Masks.aep project. This fish is actually an orange solid with a fish-shaped mask applied to it. Select this orange solid layer and press **M** to reveal its mask options. Click the stopwatch for the Mask Path property.

4 Now we're going to paste this shape into our fish layer, but we have to do it carefully. If you select the layer and paste it, it will create a separate mask. That's not what we want. You need to actually select the Mask Path itself, then press **⌘ V** _ctrl_ **V** to paste this shape into the same mask.

2 Move the CTI later in time and adjust some points on the fish. A new keyframe is automatically created for you, and the original fish shape will morph into whatever you just changed it into.

3 Now, hop on over to Photoshop. Open the bird shape.psd file from the Exercise Files>Media>PSDs folder. Click the vector mask thumbnail for the Shape 1 layer. This will select the mask. Press ⌘ C ctrl C to copy this shape. Then head back on over to After Effects, and move a little further in time.

**HOT TIP**

You can hold your cursor over the different options in the Mask Interpolation panel to get a better idea of what they do.

5 If the procedure was done correctly, the fish now morphs into the bird! Isn't that awesome? But there's a problem with the way the fish morphs into the bird. No worries. After Effects provides a fix for that, too. Go to Window>Mask Interpolation to open this panel.

6 Click the Mask Path property in the orange solid layer to select all of its keyframes. In the Mask Interpolation panel, take the Matching Method drop down to Polyline, and click the Apply button. Now we have a much smoother transition between the two shapes.

SHORTCUTS
MAC WIN BOTH

# 7

Masks and Shapes

# Motion Paths from Illustrator

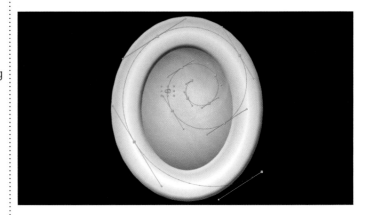

**N**OW WE'LL LOOK AT WHAT ILLUSTRATOR CONTRIBUTES to this whole pasted shape thing. Instead of pasting paths as a mask, we're going to paste a shape as a motion path.

This is one of the biggest reasons to use Illustrator in conjunction with After Effects. You may have noticed that position keyframes in the Timeline panel become anchor points in the motion path in the Composition panel. The converse is true with Illustrator – anchor points from Illustrator paths become keyframes when pasted into After Effects. It's an incredible time saver, and it usually creates much better looking motion paths as well.

I should also point out that even if you've never used Illustrator, you'll be able to follow along here.

**1** We're going to use the Motion Paths.aep project. I love my wife very much, and I've always had this fear that I'm going to flush my wedding ring down the toilet on accident. So while you're learning how to cheat in After Effects, I'll be conquering some longtime fears.

**3** Head back to After Effects. Select the wedding ring layer and press **P** to reveal its Position property, and select it (the Position property, not the entire layer). Press **⌘ V** *ctrl* **V** to paste the shape data from Illustrator into the motion path of the wedding ring. The ring now follows this path, without clicking a single stopwatch or adjusting a single property! The keyframes are also automatically roving keyframes so you can just drag the last one to stretch this animation in time proportionally as desired.

**2** Now go over to Illustrator. Press ⌘ N ctrl N to make a new document of
any size. Then, in the Tools panel on the left of the interface, hold your cursor
down on the Line Segment tool to see the Spiral tool, and select the Spiral tool.
Click and drag to create a spiral. The fill and stroke don't matter in this case.

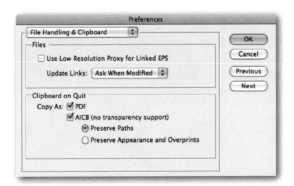

**4** Now – a couple of tips here. There's not an easy way to scale a motion path,
so make sure that your spiral in Illustrator is about the same size as you want
the motion path to be in After Effects. Also, in Illustrator, you'll want to make sure
that your File Handling & Clipboard settings in the preferences are set like the
ones above if you're having problems copying and pasting only the path.

SHORTCUTS
MAC WIN BOTH

# Trapcode 3D Stroke

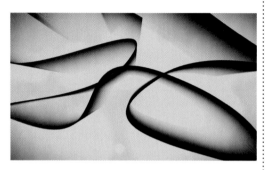

1 In the 3D Stroke.aep project, I've already created a big mask for you to use.

I THINK IT'S PRETTY OBVIOUS FROM THIS BOOK that Trapcode makes my favorite plugins for After Effects. Along with Shine, 3D Stroke is an oldie but a goodie.

The 3D Stroke effect allows you to stroke a mask. Pretty standard, right? But the options – oh, sweet options – are so fantastic that this effect always seduces me into playing with it for way too long. Also, it's completely 3D, allowing you to use a comp camera to navigate its three dimensional shapes. And remember that 3D Stroke is a 3rd party effect that is not included with After Effects, but you can download a free trial version from redgiantsoftware.com.

So, in this cheat, we'll have just a basic introduction to what 3D Stroke can do. Oh, by the way, sorry that the background of my 3D Stroke example kinda clashes with the orange banner at the top of the page.

3 My two favorite areas in this effect are the Taper controls and the Repeater controls. Open each of those categories and check the Enable checkbox to turn them on. Even their default conditions look great.

2 Apply the 3D Stroke effect, and the background of the solid disappears. Click the Color swatch and change the color from white to black.

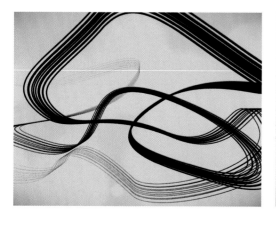

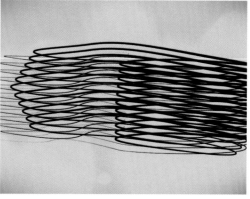

**HOT TIP**

All you have to do to bring 3D Stroke to life is to animate the Offset property.

4 For this shape, I decreased Thickness to 5, increased Start to 9, set Taper>Start Shape and End Shape to 2, and Repeater>Instances to 5, and Repeater>Scale to 96.

5 Remember that this effect is also 3D! Create a new camera. Then, in the camera area, check the Comp Camera checkbox and move the comp camera as desired. This view is the bottom of the shape from step 4.

■ Particles are one of everyone's favorite After Effects topics. I mean, who doesn't want to impersonate divinity for a while and make some elemental magic from scratch, right?

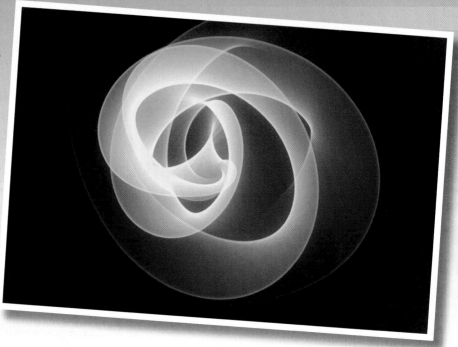

# 8

# Particles

IN THE AFTER EFFECTS WORLD, IT DOESN'T GET MORE FUN THAN PARTICLES. I just love particles. Particle systems allow us to easily control multiple objects. This is almost akin to being the CEO of a very large company, where we just offer some direction, and our underlings do all the hard stuff while we get all the credit!

In this chapter, we're going to start out by looking at what a particle system is exactly, as well as some common controls. That way, we're up to speed for the rest of the chapter. Then we'll make rain, snow, confetti, fireworks, smoke, and much more (even flowing chocolate!) from scratch. We'll also check out some powerful and popular third party effects from Trapcode: Form and Particular. If you don't own these effects, you can get free demos of them from redgiantsoftware.com.

# Particles

# Particle Bootcamp

JUST SO WE'RE ON THE SAME PAGE, I wanted to take these couple of pages to introduce the world of particles. If you're already familiar with particles, or if you just want to jump in and get playing, then feel free to skip ahead.

The thing is that particle systems – whether they're found natively in After Effects or in a 3rd party solution – typically work in the same basic way, and even often use the same verbiage.

The most important thing to realize about particles is that you don't hand animate them. There is a system or multiple systems that create the particles, and we control that system. So if you create a snow storm for example, and you don't like one of the flakes of snow, you typically can't change it manually. You would need to change the settings of the entire system, which would then adjust the individual flakes. Let's look at a few common particle properties and concepts in action.

1 In a new After Effects project, create a new comp that is 1280 x 720, and a new solid (of any color) at the same size. Apply the CC Particle Systems II effect to this solid. This is a basic and yet still powerful particle system that follows many standard conventions. Note that, like most particle systems, particles just start spitting out automatically from frame 1 once applied. No keyframing necessary.

3 Particle systems usually think of particles as living things in the sense that they are "born" when first emitted, and then have a lifespan, and then typically die out at some point. At the top of the effect controls, take Birth Rate down to 0.8 to reduce the amount of particles being emitted.

4 The color at the beginning of the particle's "life" is called the birth color, and the default setting here is that it will fade into its death color as it fades away. Click on the Birth Color swatch and change it to green. Change the Death Color to purple.

**2** Like almost all particle systems, the particles emit from a central point,
typically called the emitter, or in this case, the "producer". The producer
typically emits a bunch of the same thing (the particles), and these usually can be
changed. Right now, it's emitting a bunch of little lines, which creates a fountain
that looks somewhat like fireworks. In the Particle area in the Effect Controls
panel, change the Particle Type from Line to Star. That's a very different result!

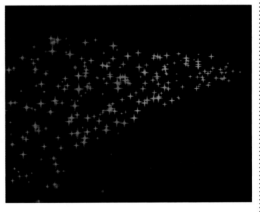

**5** At the current frame, I'm not
seeing any purple. This is because
the lifespan of these particles is set
so long that it's not dying yet. At the
top of the effect controls, reduce
the Longevity (sec) value until you
can see the particles begin to die
and fade to purple. I hope you don't
find me cruel, but I'm really enjoying
watching these particles meet their
maker.

**6** Another cool and common trick with particles is to
animate the producer (emitter). In the Producer area,
I animated the Position property, moving the producer
from left to right over time. This creates a very cool spray
of sparkles going across the screen. In this case, I've also
reduced the size of the particles (Birth Size and Death
Size), and increased the Birth Rate a bit to get these
results. Notice how different this is from our starting
point! And here is the challenge and fun of particles:
just a simple adjustment can produce radically different
results.

**HOT TIP**

If you like your
settings, but
aren't a big fan
of the exact way
the particles
are positioned,
adjust the
Random Seed
value (found in
most particle
systems),
which will give
you another
iteration of
your particles
with the same
settings.

# Sparkles

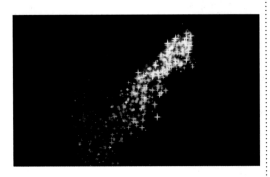

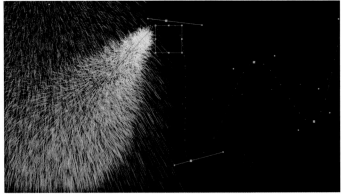

**D**ON'T FIGHT IT. SPARKLES ARE AWESOME. In this cheat, we'll get more familiar with CC Particle Systems II as we create better looking sparkles.

Sparkles are used all the time to spice up logos and text in motion graphics, or to enhance explosions in visual effects. However, notwithstanding their ubiquity, they are remarkably challenging to create using the native tools in After Effects.

Well, I should say that it's hard to make GOOD sparkles using native After Effects tools. We created shabby looking sparkles in just a few seconds in the previous cheat. But to create amazing sparkles is really an art form. Honestly, the particles we're going to create here aren't exactly perfect, either. One of the things that makes sparkles so challenging is that there really isn't a perfect reference in real life. There aren't really fairies that spew pixie dust as they fly around that we can videotape and study. Who really knows what sparkles look like? Hopefully these ideas and tools will get you on the right track to creating more impressive sparkles on your own.

**1** In the Sparkles START comp in the Sparkles.aep project, you'll find a blank solid layer with CC Particle Systems II already applied for you, and a null object that moves around. Open the Producer area of the CC Particle Systems II effect controls. ⎇ *alt* click its stopwatch to create an expression, then drag its expression pickwhip to the Position property of the null object. Now the Producer will follow the path of the null (as shown highlighted in cyan above).

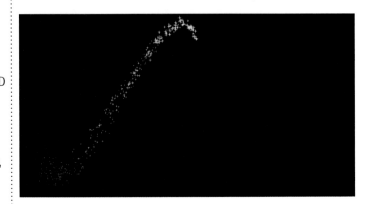

**3** These stars are just way too big. Take the Particle>Birth Size value down to 0.07 and the Death Size down to 0.03. To make them follow the path more closely, reduce the Physics>Velocity value down to 0.1. Ah, that's much better. Let's also create a finer tip to our particles by taking the Producer>Radius X down to 0, and the Radius Y down to 2. These values control the size of our emitter, which we don't want that big. Let's also take the Longevity (sec) value down to 0.8, so that they die out sooner, creating a shorter trail of sparkles, and also so that we can see a bit more of that red Death Color come in.

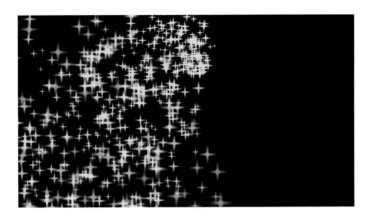

**2** In the Particle area of controls, change the Particle Type drop down from Line to Star. This simple act changes the whole feel of our particles! Particles are everywhere, and we've lost the sense of direction and order that we had.

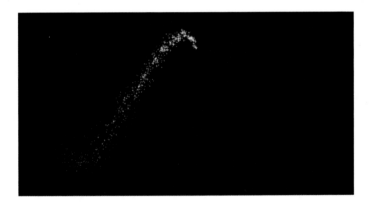

**4** The sparkles already kind of look cool as is, in my opinion. But if you wanted, you could increase or decrease the Birth Rate value to make more or less sparkles, respectively. Another thing that I did, was I duplicated the layer and put it in the Add blend mode, then I adjusted the Particle Type of the duplicate to Shaded Sphere, and changed the Particle>Transfer Mode value to Add. I then slightly increased the Velocity and toyed with the Birth Rate a bit. I duplicated layers a few more times to create the effect in the screenshot at the beginning of this cheat. Playback the animation to get the full effect. Hey, I kinda like this!

SHORTCUTS
MAC WIN BOTH

# Smoke Trail

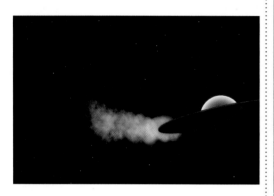

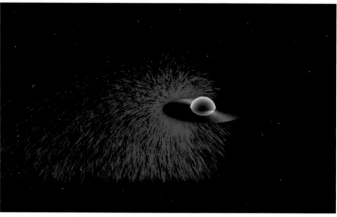

T'S JUST INCREDIBLE HOW YOU CAN CHANGE JUST A FEW SETTINGS, AND END UP WITH A COMPLETELY DIFFERENT RESULT when it comes to particles.

In this cheat, we're going to (intentionally) take the same effect we've been working with – CC Particle Systems II – and tweak just a few parameters to come up with some pretty realistic smoke trails.

In this instance, we're creating smoke trailing out of a UFO. But if you didn't animate the position of the Producer like this, you could add this smoke to a fire to give it increased realism. Or perhaps you could reduce the size of the particles and use it to create cigarette smoke.

**1** In the Smoke Trail START comp in the Smoke Trail.aep project, I've already done some of the tedious setup for you. I've imported the animation of the UFO, created a starry background (which we'll create from scratch later in this chapter), and applied CC Particle Systems II. I've also animated the position of the Producer to follow the backside of the UFO, and I've changed the Birth Color to blue.

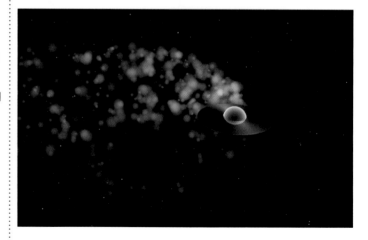

**3** The real "magic" of this trick is found in the Particle>Transfer Mode value. Change this from Composite to Screen (or Add, if desired). This removes the dark outer surface of the particles, and makes this smoky look!

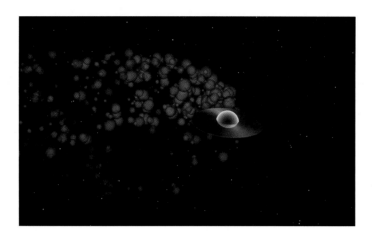

**2** Lines don't look very smoky. Change the Particle>Particle Type drop down from Line to Shaded Sphere. The animation of these particles looks terrible. For now, change the Physics>Animation drop down to Direction Normalized. It doesn't look like smoke, but don't lose faith!

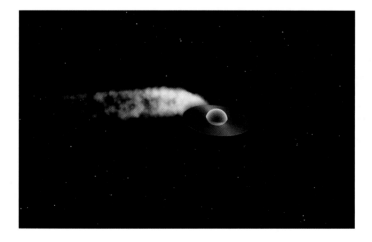

**4** From here, it's just a matter of tweaking to taste. Try increasing Birth Rate, lowering Longevity, reducing the size of Radius X and Radius Y, reducing the Gravity, and adjusting other Physics properties until your smoke looks the way you want it to. Check out my settings in the Smoke Trail FINAL comp to see what I did. Mine is definitely not perfect, but it might be helpful as a reference.

**HOT TIP**

Try fiddling with the Extra property in the Physics area of this effect. It appears to control the circumference of the shape of the emitted particles. A high value can create a three dimensional tube of particles, while a small value can create a single streak of particles. Both can be very helpful in different circumstances.

213

# Foam Basics

I CAN COUNT THE NUMBER OF TIMES I'VE NEEDED TO CREATE DIGITAL BUBBLES PROFESSIONALLY ON ONE FINGER. Many After Effects users have a similar need for bubbles. This is probably the reason that many people shy away from the Foam effect.

However, Foam is actually my personal favorite when it comes to native particle effects in After Effects. It's powerful. It renders quickly. It's intuitive. And it has a few extra features that aren't found in every particle effect, but that really come in handy (such as wind, wobble, and luminance map control over particle flow).

In this cheat, we'll look at how to make Foam do what it does best – bubbles. But later in this chapter, we're going to make Foam spit out everything from snow to music notes. I'm man enough to admit that I have a crush on the Foam effect. I'm confident that if you took the time to get to know it, you'd begin to have feelings for it as well.

**1** Create a new 1280 x 720 comp and create a new solid of any color of the same size. Apply the Foam effect to this solid. The default view is an ugly draft view so it renders faster. This was more important, like, ten years ago. So in the Foam effect controls, change View drop down at the top to Rendered. Move out in time to check out the bubbly awesomeness.

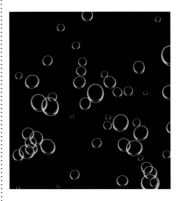

**3** There are also loads of preset bubbles for a variety of circumstances. Change the Rendering>Bubble Texture drop down to Spit.

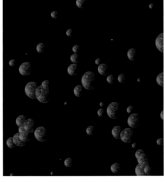

**4** Now change the same drop down from Spit to Magma Bubbles.

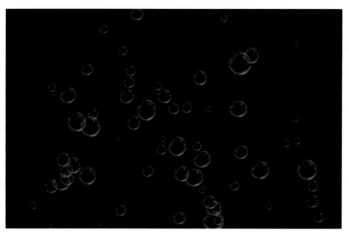

**2** By default, Foam emits bubbles from a point in the center of the layer. In the Producer area of the effect controls, increase the Producer X Size value to its maximum (0.45). This will make bubbles emit across the width of the entire layer. Adjust the Y value of the Producer Point value to put the emitting line of bubbles on the bottom of the comp (720 will work). Then, in the Physics area, increase the Initial Speed value to 2 so that these bubbles travel upwards like fizz.

**5** Import an image (I used bottle.jpg from Exercise Files>Media>Images) and bring it into this comp. Choose this new layer from Rendering>Environment Map in the Foam effect controls. Increase Reflection Strength to 1. You can now see your layer reflecting in the bubbles! You gotta admit, for bubbles, that's a pretty cool trick, and we've only scratched the surface of what Foam can do. By the way, I also switched back to the default bubbles for the above image because they have softer edges than most other bubble presets.

# Custom Particles

T HE TRUE POWER OF PARTICLES COMES FROM USING A CUSTOM OBJECT AS A PARTICLE. It's as simple as that.

If Foam can only emit bubbles, then we would rarely use it. But if we tell Foam to replace those bubbles with any object of our choosing, then it becomes infinitely more valuable. If we replace those bubbles with, for example, a graphic of a fighter plane, then Foam will shoot out loads of fighter planes, making an entire squadron!

In this easy example, we're going to take a simple graphic from Photoshop and prep it for use as a particle. Then we'll have Foam use that graphic instead of bubbles. And life will be complete.

**1** Open the Custom Particles.aep project and go to the Custom Particles START comp. It's pretty complex, so it might load a little slowly. We're going to take the music note graphic on the right, and change two properties to tell Foam to use those as particles instead of the bubbles.

**3** Select layer 10, the sixteenth notes layer, and precompose it by pressing ⌘ Shift C ctrl Shift C, and check Open New Composition. I've created a mask around the sixteenth notes for you already. Notice all the stuff on this layer (when the mask mode is set to None). Now press ⌘ K ctrl K to view the Composition Settings for this precomp. Change the dimensions to 428 x 484 and center the masked notes.

**2** Foam has been applied for you on layers 14-17. Choose one of those layers, and in the Foam effect, change Rendering>Bubble Texture to User Defined. Then, in the Bubble Texture Layer drop down right below that, choose the sixteenth notes layer (layer 10). The problem here is that Foam is seeing the entire layer, which is a black and white layer that consists of multiple shapes.

**4** Now that the notes are precomposed, the music notes and dark red tint (from the Tint effect) are "baked in", and can be seen by the Foam effect when used as a custom particle. Here, I've adjusted the Foam effect (as described in step 2) on layers 14-17 so that they emit music notes instead of bubbles. These music notes can now float around, pop, wobble, and do anything else bubbles do! Note that layers used as custom particles do not need to be visible.

**HOT TIP**

To keep things simple, we've used a still image here, but Foam is capable of using movies as particles! Think of the possibilities!

**SHORTCUTS**
MAC WIN BOTH

# Particles

# Simple Rain

**W**ANNA MAKE RAIN IN A HURRY? The CC Rain effect provides semi-believable rain in a split second. You apply it, and badda-bing – you're good to go.

And such is the case with many of the Cycore effects, as we'll see. They lack the professional flexibility of the After Effects particle effects (like Particle Playground and Foam), but they certainly win in the speed department. If you're not picky about quality, or if you're just doing a quick comp sample, the speed of the Cycore effects just can't be beat.

Later in this chapter, we'll use the Cycore effects to create snow. Then we'll look at how to create more complex weather systems using Foam.

**1** This is going to be challenging to see in screenshots, so I'm going to exaggerate my settings for the purpose of these screenshots. In the real world, we don't seem to need that much rain to tell our eyes that it's raining. Additionally, this rain looks a lot stronger when it animates, as opposed to just looking at a still frame. That being said, open the Rain.aep project, and go to the Rain START comp, where there's an uberstock video clip and a black solid layer waiting for you.

**3** First, let's handle the compositing issue. In the Timeline panel, change the blend mode of the solid layer to Lighten. This will remove the black of the solid layer, and show your rain on the subject below.

**2** Apply the CC Rain effect to the solid layer in this comp. It instantly applies fairly decent automatically-animating rain to this layer. We have two problems here though: this rain applies to this layer and doesn't allow for compositing through to the layer beneath, and this is made worse by the second problem, which is that this is very pixelated and blocky rain.

**HOT TIP**

CC Rain can also be used in conjunction with the equally easy to use CC Drizzle. CC Drizzle creates the look of rain hitting a wet surface. Just know that CC Drizzle works like many Cycore effects, in that it uses the color of the original layer. So if you use a black solid, you won't see anything.

**4** Now we need to soften this rain. Apply the Fast Blur effect and take the Blurriness value up to about 2 or 3. In a pinch, you could just apply the CC Rain effect to a layer that you wanted rain on, but then if you wanted to soften the rain, you'd be stuck because this Fast Blur would also blur the original layer. Note that in this screenshot, I have increased the Amount value in CC Rain so that you can see the rain more clearly. In the screenshot at the beginning of this cheat, I also applied the Color Balance effect to make the temperature of the piece a little cooler.

# Basic Snow

THANKFULLY, BASIC SNOW IS JUST AS EASY TO MAKE AS BASIC RAIN. Thanks again to another wonderfully easy Cycore effect, we can also instantly apply a single effect and have some decent looking snow (complete with automatic snowfall).

For my liking, the effect comes on a little strong at first. So we'll also look at how to temper the effect, and enhance it for a more realistic look.

Now, automatic effects like this are great in a pinch. But for a professional production, you'll want more control. So be sure and check out the benefits of creating snow from scratch in the next cheat.

**1** Open the Basic Snow START comp in the Basic Snow.aep project. It contains a photo I took of a snowy neighborhood. There's snow on the ground, but none in the air. This is a great reason to create digital snow.

**3** But again, as with CC Rain, it does not remove (or allow you to remove) the layer that the effect is applied to. So again, in the Timeline panel, change the blend mode of the black solid layer to Screen so we can remove the black and have the snow show through.

**2** Apply the CC Snow effect to the black solid layer on top of the neighborhood image. As with CC Rain, the results are pretty good right off the bat, and the particles also auto-animate.

**4** I see two problems with the default settings. First, it's not really deep enough from a 3D perspective. It looks like a shallow facade of snow. Secondly, the snow particles are much too large for my liking. To fix these problems, I reduced the Flake Size value to about 1.5, and added the Fast Blur effect with a low Blurriness value. Then I pressed ⌘ D ctrl D to duplicate this entire layer. Then I took the Flake Size in the CC Snow effect on the bottom layer even lower, to about 1. This creates another layer of depth. Perhaps it needs another one?

# Windblown Snow

T'S NOW TIME TO TAKE OUR SNOW MAKING CAPABILITIES UP A FEW NOTCHES. We're going to be creating our own custom snow, using Foam.

You might be asking why we would want to make snow, when we just made basic, quick, easy snow in the last cheat. The reason is because, frankly, that snow isn't good enough. We ought to expect more of our snow. Real snow is so light that even the slightest breeze moves it powerfully. If we were creating a cartoon – fine, use CC Snow. But for a realistic setting, we need to have two forces control our snow: one for telling it how to fall, and another force for acting on it while it falls. Foam gives us these capabilities, and once you see it animate, you won't be able to settle for anything less. Now, in these screenshots, you won't get the power of this, so you'll really have to trust me and try this out on your own.

**1** Open up the Windblown Snow START comp in the Windblown Snow.aep project. It again contains a background image and a black solid. Apply Foam to the black solid. Thankfully, it removes the content of the layer it was applied to so we don't have to worry about any additional compositing there.

**3** Increase the Producer>Producer X Size value to its maximum. Drag the Producer Point to the top of the screen so that our snow falls from the top down. Increase the Physics>Initial Speed value to about 2.5. The snow is now falling upwards, so we can't see it. Change the Initial Direction value to 180 degrees. Adjust the Bubbles>Size and Producer>Production Rate as desired. There's still a big problem here. Don't the particles look squashed to you?

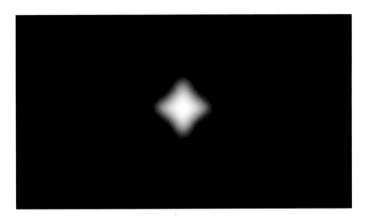

**2** This comp also contains a shape layer that will serve as the custom particle we'll be using. Because I've softened the particle with the Fast Blur effect, we'll need to precompose it. If you'd prefer, you could just use this layer and then apply Fast Blur to the completed snow. Select the shape layer and press ⌘ Shift C / ctrl Shift C to precompose it. Then in the Foam effect controls, change Rendering>Bubble Texture to User Defined, and then in the Bubble Texture drop down, choose the precomposed shape layer.

**4** The particles look squashed because Foam squishes the entire layer onto a square for each particle. Our layer was 1280 x 720, so it got squashed a lot on the X axis. Go back to the precomp layer and double click it to open it. Press ⌘ K / ctrl K to open the comp settings, and make the comp size even, like 500 x 500. Then to add wind, increase the Physics>Wind Speed value. Add the Fast Blur effect and duplicate the layer as desired. These settings are great for book screenshots, but they're overdone for professional snow. You should probably use much smaller snow than this (and perhaps a little more blur and a little less opacity as well).

**HOT TIP**

If you're having problems with the snowfall not being strong enough at the beginning of the layer, you can trim the layer and drag it in time to compensate. In other words, if you trim off the first few seconds while the snow is getting started and then drag the layer a few seconds earlier in time, no one will ever know! Also remember that because we applied Foam to a solid, we can extend the beginning of the ending of the layer in time as far as we want.

**SHORTCUTS**
MAC WIN BOTH

# Molten Gold

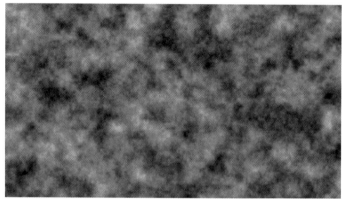

S O WE'RE NOW GOING TO VENTURE OFF INTO UNCONVENTIONAL TERRITORY. Sometimes it pays to just see what particle effects are out there and what they're capable of. I think I've used them all at one point or another.

In this cheat, we're going to take a look at the relatively obscure Cycore effect, Mr. Mercury. This effect is great at creating blobby liquids. I just used this effect in an iPhone game that I did some post production work on. Interestingly enough, I used it to create digital vomit. It's gross, but it had to be done. There really isn't a better and faster liquid simulator in After Effects, and it worked perfectly for the job.

I recently discovered how to make Mr. Mercury look metallic. It's super easy, and with a quick tweak, we can even play the role of alchemist as we turn a simple solid layer into gold.

**1** Start off in the Molten Gold START comp in the Molten Gold.aep project. Apply the Fractal Noise effect to the Deep Red Solid layer. Just leave the settings at their defaults. Then apply the Tint effect. In the Tint effect controls, click the color swatch for the Map White To and choose a golden color.

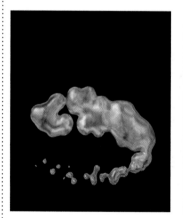

**3** Next, ⌥ *alt* click the stopwatch for the Producer property and link it to the Position property of the null object in this comp, which will take the path in a dollar sign shape. Reduce Velocity to 0 to have the particles stick to the shape a bit more.

**4** The gold is still melting too much. Take the Gravity value to 0 as well, and that should help things. You might also want to reduce the Radius X and Radius Y values to 0.5, and the Blob Death Size to 0.4.

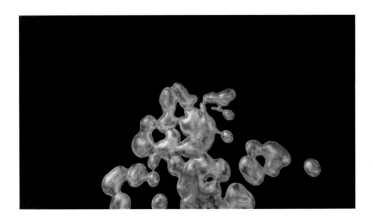

**2** Then apply the CC Mr. Mercury effect to this solid. Instantly, we have flowing molten gold. How about that!

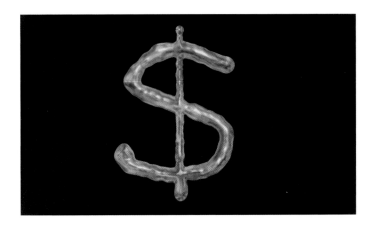

**5** Another cool attribute of this molten gold is that it is (somewhat) 3D. Although you'll need to fork out some extra cash to get the HD version of the Cycore effects to control the lighting here with an After Effects light, there is a pretty complex lighting system built into the effect. Compare this screenshot to step 4. You'll notice a change in the direction and angle of the lighting. That can help you add a 3D shimmer, and make this gold way more attractive.

**HOT TIP**

You may also want to try adding the Glow effect to the Mr. Mercury effect. The results of this can be seen in the intro screenshot of this cheat. It helps the gold to feel more hot and molten.

**SHORTCUTS**

MAC WIN BOTH

# Particles

# Light Ribbons

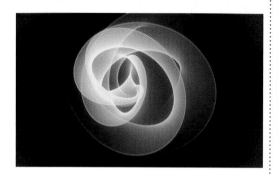

THIS THING RIGHT HERE IS WHY I LOVE AFTER EFFECTS SO MUCH. I'm sitting here right now in my office trying to get this book written to meet my publisher's deadlines, and I can't for the life of me stop playing with this exercise!

We're going to be looking at another old After Effects effect called Radio Waves that just really isn't appreciated enough. Interestingly enough, it was created by Brian Maffitt, my After Effects hero. Brian also created Shatter, Foam, and Colorama, among others. His creativity really shows in these effects that are still viable, and challenge us to find new and more creative uses for them.

Radio Waves generates concentric circles in its default state. It was designed to simulate the emitting of radio waves. But as we'll see, the capabilities of this effect go far beyond that. In this cheat, we'll look at an effect that is incredibly beautiful (especially when animated), but really hard to describe. So, I'm calling it light ribbons.

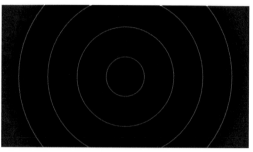

1 Open the Light Ribbons.aep project and go to the Light Ribbons START comp. For now, ignore the For Light Ribbons layer, and apply the Radio Waves effect to the layer called empty solid (which, true to its name, is just a simple black solid). The Radio Waves effect creates concentric circles emanating from the center of the comp. It also replaces the content of the layer, showing the background layer beneath it.

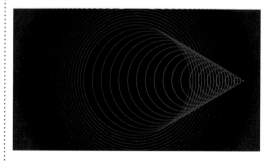

4 Concentric circles are all fine and good, but when you animate the Producer Point, it creates much more interesting animations. Here we see the Producer Point animated from the center to the right of the comp about 2 seconds later.

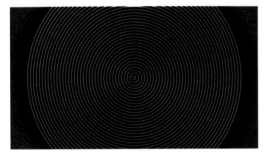

**2** For this cheat, the key property here is Frequency, which controls how often the radio waves are emitted. Increase the Frequency value to 10, and notice the difference.

**3** One of the features that I like about Radio Waves is that the particles fade out when they "die". To see this in action, decrease the Lifespan (sec) value to about 4.

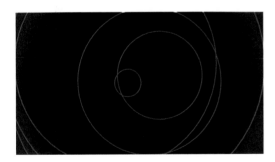

**5** So that about wraps up our Radio Waves primer. Now delete the empty solid layer, and turn on the visibility of the For Light Ribbons layer. This layer has Radio Waves applied for you, and I've applied a wiggle expression to the Producer Point value, so it jumps all over the place over time.

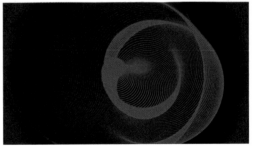

**6** It's not much to look at now, so increase the Frequency value to 50 (for now), and decrease the Lifespan (sec) value to 3.5 (for now). Now that's what I'm talkin' 'bout.

**HOT TIP**

The concentric circles of Radio Waves can also be used to create rain drizzle on a wet surface, or psychic brain waves emitting from someone with extreme mental powers. What else can you do with this effect?

continued...

# Light Ribbons (continued)

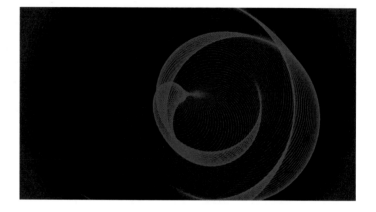

**7** The Stroke area in Radio Waves provides options relative to the opacity and appearance of each wave. Take the Profile to Bell to add some fall off to each ring. Then take the Start Width down to 2, so that the waves start a little thinner.

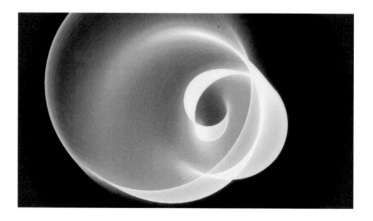

**9** Apply the Glow effect. Take the Glow Threshold to 70 and the Glow Radius to 40. Adjust all parameters to taste. And there you have it.

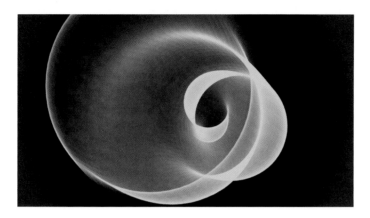

**8** OK, brace yourself. Increase the Frequency value to its maximum – 500. This will slow things down significantly, but the beauty is far worth it. Also, in the Stroke area, change color from blue to a pale gold. Take the Opacity value down to 0.3. I also took the Fade-in Time value up to 1.

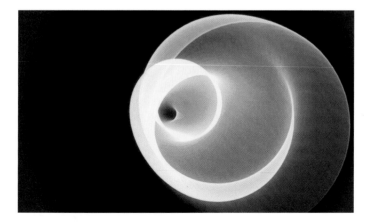

**10** As you move in time, you'll notice that the wiggling of the Producer Point will create these beautiful ribbons of movement that really need to be seen to be believed. Here's a few seconds later in the same comp. Note that if you're seeing undesirable lines in the shapes, these can usually be removed by playing around with settings. I also might go back and reduce the lifespan of these waves so that the outer edges are a little softer.

# Steam

SOMETIMES, WE MAKE "PARTICLES" WITHOUT PARTICLES. This is because sometimes it's preferable to fake the results of particles using another method. This might be for a variety of reasons – anything from the fact that faking it is sometimes easier or faster, to the fact that sometimes faking it actually looks better than using real particles.

In this cheat, we're going to create pretty realistic steam, like the type that comes off of a hot beverage in the winter time. But we're not going to use a particle generator to do it. But if we do it carefully (and we will), then we'll still have total control over this, including the ability to animate it in a very organic way.

Now, don't get me wrong. I'm a huge fan of particles. But slavish devotion to a particular way of doing things is never a good idea, and knowing multiple methods to achieve results always is. So here we go.

1 Open the Steam.aep project and go to the Steam START comp. Here you'll find a stock video clip courtesy of uberstock. In this clip, the cutest girl you've ever seen has some kind of hot beverage on an apparently cold day. The thing is, steam can be really hard to capture on video, and we're not getting too much here. I think we can add a lot to the vibe of the piece if we add some fake steam. Isn't she just adorable? Holy cow.

3 With the solid layer selected, select the Pen tool in the Tools area at the top of the interface, and click a rough mask around the area above the cup where the steam would be. Press the **F** key to reveal the Feather value for the mask, and increase that until the edges of the steam are soft enough for you.

**2** On the solid layer on top of this video, apply the Fractal Noise effect. In the Fractal Noise effect controls, reduce Brightness to –45, uncheck Uniform Scaling in the Transform area, take Scale Width to 20 and Scale Height to 700. Then, in the Timeline panel, change the blending mode of the layer to Screen. It's already looking a little steamy (you know what I mean).

**4** This steam really comes alive by applying the Turbulent Displace effect to this. In the Turbulent Displace effect controls, take the Size value down to 40. Also, take the Opacity of the layer down to about 70%. I also applied the Tint effect and changed the Map White To value to a pale yellow orange to composite a little better in this warm-toned scene.

**HOT TIP**

To bring this steam to life, animate the Y position of the Offset (Turbulence) property in the Turblulent Displace effect controls. Animate it from a high number to a lower number over time. This will automatically create rising steam that continues to warp. For added realism, you may also want to gradually animate the Evolution value of Fractal Noise over time.

**SHORTCUTS**
MAC | WIN | BOTH

# 3D Fireworks

N THIS CHEAT, WE'RE GOING TO LOOK AT CREATING A 3D PARTICLE SYSTEM. We've used CC Particle Systems II several times, but here we're going to be introduced to CC Particle World. It's basically a beefed up, 3D version of CC Particle Systems II, with many (most?) of the same controls.

We're going to be creating an extremely simple and rudimentary fireworks system. It's kind of crappy because CC Particle World (like CC Particle Systems II) allows you to emit simple lines. Those lines would be perfect for fireworks, but they don't give you any controls over the look of those lines (such as size or opacity falloff). I think the lines are meant to be kind of a working view so you can see the particles. But they create these fairly cool simple fireworks in a pinch. They are unique because they are also 3D.

So the purpose, then, of this cheat is twofold: to show you how to create quick fireworks, and also to show you native 3D particles in After Effects.

**1** Open the 3D Fireworks START comp in the 3D Fireworks.aep project. This comp contains some buildings and sky stuff that I made (it's all locked so don't worry about accidentally messing something up), and a black solid layer. Apply CC Particle World to the black solid called Fireworks.

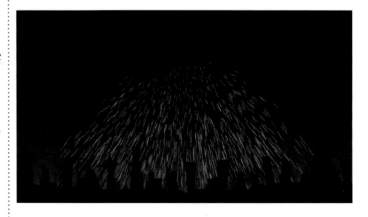

**3** While you can spend a while perfecting this result, the real trick in creating fireworks comes from animating the Birth Rate value. If you click the stopwatch for this property at any point (say, at 7 frames in), and then on the next frame change the value to 0, the particles will stop creating an apparent explosion. The animation is shown here at frame 12, and the particles are obviously dissipating.

**2** Assuming the effect is selected in the Effect Controls panel, you'll see the familiar default particles that we saw with CC Particle Systems II. But then you'll also see all these crazy widgets everywhere. These are to help with moving it in 3D, which we'll do in just a bit. Remember that the helpers disappear when the effect is no longer selected in the Effect Controls panel.

**4** But again, the magic here comes from the 3D-ness of these particles. While you can open the Producer controls to move this emitter in 3D space, you'll need to use the widget in the upper left hand corner in order to rotate it in 3D. Once rotated, you can create some interesting effect. Above we see the bottom side of the fireworks (at frame 12, as in the previous screenshot), as if we were standing under the fireworks as they went off. It kinda looks like fiery rain, or maybe like we're going through warp speed. This effect will allow you to create sparkles and smoke trails with the added benefit of being able to move them in 3D space!

**HOT TIP**

If all the 3D widgets are bugging you, just open the Grid and Guides area in the CC Particle World effect controls to control what helpers you're seeing.

# Psychic Waves

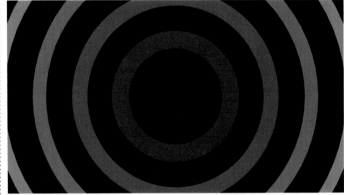

SOMETIMES, BORING PARTICLES CAN BE MADE AWESOME by other effects that we apply to them. Here, we're going to use a pretty basic and simple application of the Radio Waves effect as our foundation. Then, we'll use these waves as a map to displace the pixels on a video layer from uberstock.

I've actually seen this look (or something similar) on several movies and TV shows lately. It's often used when superheroes read someone else's mind, or think powerful, destructive thoughts. You could also use this effect to visually show the attractive woman from Chapter 4 sending out flirty vibes. Either that or she's having the mother of all headaches.

**1** Start out with a new comp and solid, 1280 x 720. Apply the Radio Waves effect to the solid. In the Stroke area of the Radio Waves effect controls, change the color to white. Then bump up the Start Width value to about 77, and change the Fade-in Time value to about 10. If you want, you can use the Psychic Waves.aep project as a reference.

**3** Import a video layer into this comp. You may need to go back to the precomposed waves to adjust the position of the producer. Apply the Displacement Map effect to the video layer. Take the values for Use For Horizontal Displacement and Use for Vertical Displacement to Luminance. Take Max Horizontal Displacement to about 75, and Max Vertical Displacement to about 45.

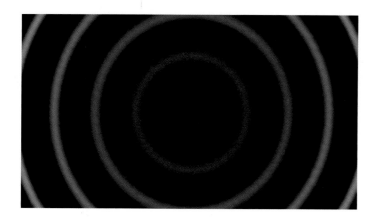

**2** In the Stroke area, it's important to change the Profile drop down to Sine. This will make the edges of the rings soft, so that it will create a better displacement map. Displacement maps really don't like hard edges. Then, select this layer and press ⌘ Shift C ctrl Shift C to precompose it. If we didn't do that, the displacement effect we're going to add wouldn't see the radio waves. Be sure to turn off the visibility of this precomposed layer.

**4** To make the effect more pronounced, turn on the visibility of the precomposed radio waves and take the Opacity of that layer down to 30%. Also, notice the tearing on the sides of the image. For a quick fix, go to the Displacement Map effect controls and check the Wrap Pixels Around option. It's hard to see the results as clearly in a still shot, but the displacement rings animate out with the radio waves, and I think it's a pretty cool effect.

**HOT TIP**

You could also use this same Radio Waves displacement map with FreeformAE. In that case, you'd be creating actual three dimensional ripples!

SHORTCUTS
MAC WIN BOTH

# Particles

# Particle Deflection

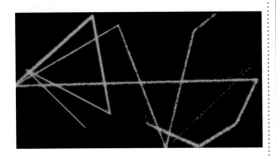

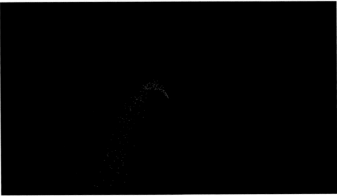

ONCE UPON A TIME, PARTICLE PLAYGROUND WAS THE KING OF THE PARTICLES. These days, most people find it far too confusing (unless you know the difference between Persistent and Ephemeral Property Mapping), not to mention slow to render, and just ignore it completely. Heck, it's still just an 8 bit effect. And these days, if you're a native effect and you're still only 8 bits, it basically means that Adobe hates you.

Now that's not to say that some 8 bit effects don't have their merit. Certainly, most old effects are still extremely useful, depending on the circumstances. Particle Playground is one of those.

In this cheat, we're going to learn some Particle Playground basics, and we'll also explore one of the features that Particle Playground does really well that most other particle systems in After Effects don't: the ability to bounce particles off of a "wall", using a simple mask. If these walls are used well, you can create some interesting effects from cool geometric patterns to a swirling tornado.

**1** I've created Particle Deflection.aep for you as a reference, but we're going to start from scratch. Create a new comp and solid, each at 1280 x 720. Apply Particle Playground to this solid. Holy parameters, Batman! That's a lot of properties! The way that Particle Playground works is that there are 4 different emitters to choose from (Cannon, Grid, Layer Exploder, and Particle Exploder), and Cannon is the only one on by default. Change Cannon>Direction to see these particles a little better. Its default settings create a fountain of tiny red squares.

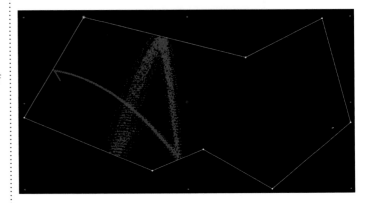

**3** From here, just play around with the settings. In the Cannon area, I changed the Particles Per Second to about 700, Direction Random Spread to 0, Velocity to 250, and Velocity Random Spread to 10. I also adjusted the Direction so that the particles point at the mask wall that we made. Hey look, isn't that the Star Trek logo?

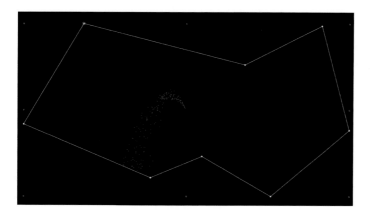

**2** And here is one of the (many) great limitations of Particle Playground. There are no settings to change the life of the particles, opacity over time, the shape of the particles, and so forth, without using another layer as a map, which brings it's own set of challenges. For this cheat, we're going to stick to the default particle shape. With this layer selected, press **G** to select the Pen tool. Then click around the layer to create a closed mask. Then, in the Particle Playground effect controls, choose the mask you just created from Wall>Boundary. Now the particles bounce off of the mask! Way sweet!

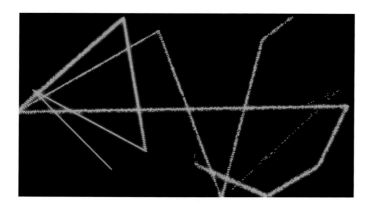

**4** For the final result, I also took the Gravity>Force value to 0. Note that the results will vary wildly as the position and angle (i.e. Direction) of the Cannon are changed. I also changed the Cannon>Color and added the Glow effect.

**HOT TIP**

Another cool feature of Particle Playground is that the Info panel will give you a readout of how many particles exist on the current frame. This is especially important if you're using the Grid emitter because the amount of particles on screen can get ridiculous pretty quickly.

**SHORTCUTS**
MAC WIN BOTH

# Star Field

**Y**OU NEVER KNOW WHEN YOU'LL NEED TO RECREATE OUTER SPACE. To that end, I wanted to provide a cheat here on creating your own custom star field.

This is extremely easy to do poorly, and just slightly more challenging to do well. You see, Cycore has a nice little effect called CC Star Burst that will do 99% of the work for us, creating a star field that automatically animates as if a camera was zooming through the galaxy.

The problem is that the default settings aren't all that great. So we'll fix those, and then we'll also look at a few other things you can do to play with the look of your star field.

**1** Create a new white solid and comp at 1280 x 720, and apply the CC Star Burst effect. It's VERY important that your solid is white! The CC Star Burst effect uses the color of the layer it's applied to when creating stars. If you had a black solid layer, you wouldn't see anything. Now, back to these stars – what's the deal? Oh my [way too big] stars. I'm not sure that there's a place in the entire universe where you could possibly be that close to so many stars at once.

**3** To make these stars stand out a little bit more, you can add several effects (such as Glow). I applied the 3rd party effect Trapcode Starglow here. That effect adds a little glow, but it also adds some nice little spikes of light, turning these into a little bit more of a star shape. It's subtle, but subtle often means better.

**2** In the Effect Controls panel, take Size down to 60, Grid spacing to 2, and Scatter to about 315. So now our stars look better, but if you press the spacebar, they still animate way too fast. Take Speed all the way down to 0.2. In many cases, even this is too fast.

**4** To make these stars look like they're going through warp speed, I applied the CC Radial Fast Blur effect, increasing the Amount to about 90. I also changed the Zoom drop down to Brightest to make the light streaks pop more. In this screenshot, you're seeing some cool purple and blue streaks, which were created from the Starglow effect. For compatibility reasons, I have not included the Starglow effect in the Star Field.aep project.

**HOT TIP**

If you take the Speed value down all the way to zero, the stars will be stationary. You can then increase their size back up a bit to create some very quick dust particles.

239

# Confetti

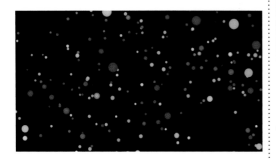

THIS IS GOING TO BE THE QUICKEST, EASIEST CHEAT in the entire book. We're making confetti. Ready? Here we go.

1 Make a comp and solid at 1280 x 720. Apply the Ramp effect.

3 Apply the CC Star Burst effect. BOOM. Confetti.

**2** Apply the Colorama effect.

**4** For better looking confetti, take Grid spacing to 15. Badda-bing. Done.

# Water Surface Disruption

W E'RE NOW GOING TO LOOK AT A COUPLE OF RARELY USED EFFECTS: CAUSTICS AND WAVE WORLD. These two effects aren't really particle effects, but if you're looking for a liquid surface, they may be your best bet. I have yet to see a particle system create the surface of water as quickly and as attractively has does the pairing of these two effects.

So, we're going to take this cheat and the next one looking at these interesting buddy effects. The Wave World effect is intended to create liquid-like displacement maps. And that's it. The purpose of the Caustics effect is to create a watery looking surface using displacement maps like the ones created by Wave World. It's a match made in heaven (if the mind of Brian Maffitt is heaven).

In this cheat, we'll create the illusion that we're disrupting the surface of water by dragging a finger on it. In the next cheat, we'll create flowing rivers of delicious milk chocolate using the same effects. Who doesn't love that?

**1** This cheat is pretty involved, so I've already animated the image of my hand moving around the comp for you in the Water Surface Disruption START comp in the Water Surface Disruption.aep project. Apply the Wave World (NOT the Wave Warp) effect to the waves displacement layer.

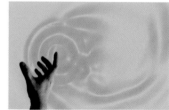

**4** Now the waves displace in the same place that my finger seems to touch. Take Simulation>Grid Resolution to 100. Select the my finger. tga layer and press ⌘ D ctrl D to duplicate it. Turn off the visibility of the original.

**5** Select the original hand and ⌘ ctrl click the waves displacement layer and press ⌘ Shift C ctrl Shift C to precompose these layers and call it waves DIS and turn off its visibility. Apply the Caustics effect to the water layer. Choose the waves DIS layer from the Water>Water Surface drop down.

 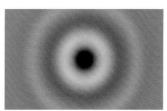

**2** The default view shows you a side view of the displacement map it's creating for you. The empty planes above and below the white wave area represent the highest (brightest) and lowest (darkest) points of the wave. Any part of the wave higher or lower will get clipped to white or black respectively.

**3** In the Wave World effect controls, change the View to Height Map. This is what your displacement map will actually look like. Waves emanate from the Producer 1 point, which is in the center by default. ⌥ alt click the stopwatch for the Producer 1>Position property, and drag the expression pickwhip to the Position property of the my hand.tga layer.

**6** Also in the Water area of the Caustics effect controls, increase Smoothing to about 13. I've also changed the water color to be a little more faded and slightly more green, and played with the lighting controls a little bit. Note that the Caustics effect will also allow you to use a composition light as the main Caustics light source if desired.

**HOT TIP**

In the last screenshot, you'll notice water bouncing off of the edges of the "pool". This effect is created by going to the Simulation> Reflect Edges drop down and choosing All (or whatever surfaces you'd like to have ripples reflect from).

SHORTCUTS
MAC WIN BOTH

243

# Flowing Chocolate

DELICIOUS, DELICIOUS CHOCOLATE. In this cheat, we're going to make flowing rivers of chocolate, and not only that, but we're going to create the (very believable) illusion that this chocolatey goodness is flowing over some text. It's a very realistic final result, and screenshots just don't do it justice. So I recommend that you open up this project and play the animation back to check it out.

For this, we're going to again be using the great partnership of Wave World and Caustics, although this cheat will be a bit more complicated. So, if you're looking for more information on these effects, check the previous cheat.

Also be aware that in order to have really clean final results like this, it will slow down your render time A LOT. If you have a weaker computer – that's fine. No one is judging you here. But you may not want to take the Grid Resolution up quite so high in the Wave World effect.

1 For this somewhat complex cheat, you'll want to open up the Flowing Chocolate.aep project. In the Flowing Chocolate START comp, you'll find this layer of text. It's turned off and should remain invisible. Apply the Wave World effect to the wave world layer, and change the View drop down in the Effect Controls panel to Height Map. Then in the Ground>Ground drop down, choose the chocolate outlines layer.

3 Select the wave world and chocolate outlines layers and press ⌘ Shift C / ctrl Shift C to precompose these layers so that Caustics can recognize them. Apply the Caustics effect to the caustics layer. In the Caustics effect controls, choose the precomposed waves from Water>Water Surface.

**2** Change the Y position of Producer 1 to 0, and Producer 1>Width to 0.4 so that this looks like a waterfall from the top of the screen. In the Ground area, change Steepness to 0.2 and Height to 0.42. Then, increase the Simulation>Grid Resolution value as much as your computer can take it. I used a value of 700, and you probably don't need more than that. Increasing this will slow down Caustics considerably, but the enhanced quality will be worth it. You can now see the grayscale waves dripping over the text in a very organic way. I love it.

**4** Change the Water>Surface Color to brown, and then increase Surface Opacity to its max value of 1. You may also want to increase the Smoothing value to about 9 so that you don't get those little tiny caustics lines. You can also go back inside the nested precomp to tweak Wave World if desired. The results will automatically show up in your chocolate. And again, the results really have to be previewed when animated to get the full effect. This trick can be used to create organic chocolate, paint, or any other thick flowing liquid.

**HOT TIP**

Try going back and opening up the nested composition with the blurred text in it, and removing the blur. Notice what effect that has on the final result.

SHORTCUTS

# Trapcode Form: 4D Fractal

TRAPCODE FORM IS AN EXTREMELY UNIQUE PARTICLE GENERATOR. In most particle systems, particles are emitted. In Form, those particles just are. There's no birth, no death. It's like a John Lennon song.

Form creates a grid of particles that is often displaced by a three dimensional fractal. This object is often called a 4D fractal because you can move it in all three dimensions, and then you also have the added dimension of time. It's a beautiful look that is quite easy to achieve, and it's getting quite popular.

This is tutorial will be a very basic introduction to Form, but the results will still be stunning. If you like this effect, you can buy it from Red Giant (redgiantsoftware.com). If you don't have it, you can go to the same website to download a free trial version (this goes for Particular in the next cheat as well).

**1** Make a new comp and solid at 1280 x 720 and apply the Form effect to the solid. By default, you can see the 3D grid Form creates for you. In the Base Form area in the Effect Controls panel, take Size X to 1100 and take Size Y to 600. That increases the size of the grid, but doesn't add any more particles. Increase the Particles in X and Particles in Y values to 400 each. In the Particle area, change the color from white to blue.

**3** To make this thing really pop, increase the Fractal Field>Affect Size value to 6. This makes it so that displaced particles actually change size based on the fractal map. It's those little wispy white highlights that really make me fall in love with these results. By the way, this is a result of having Particle>Transfer Mode set to the default value of Add.

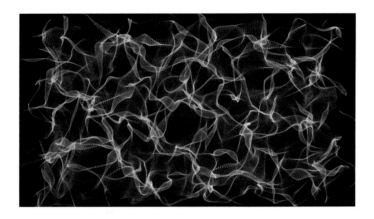

**2** In the Fractal Field area, increase Displace to 150. This uses a fractal noise pattern to displace particles in all three dimensions. This is already looking rather cool. Pretty easy, right?

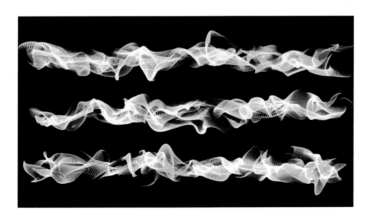

**4** Another one of the great things about this effect is that it is totally three dimensional. Here, I added a comp camera and rotated it so that I could see the bottom of these 3 fractal layers (I also increased Base Form>Size Z to spread them out a bit so you could see them more easily). As you can see, each is a separate, three dimensional fractal. You can add or subtract three dimensional iterations of these fractals by adjusting the Base Form>Particles in Z value.

**HOT TIP**

One of the best things about Form is that you can animate this fractal "passing through" your particles, without moving the particles! It's almost like a wave of displacement rippling through the scene. The effect is incredible, and it's really easy to do. Just animate the Flow X, Y, and/or Z values in the Fractal Field area of the effect.

# Particular: 3D Light Streaks

**W**ITHOUT A DOUBT, THE MOST POPULAR AND POWERFUL AFTER EFFECTS PARTICLE EFFECT IS PARTICULAR. Particular is also made by Trapcode (the same brain behind the Form effect that we looked at in the previous cheat).

Particular (version 2) is kind of like the particle system that everyone has always wanted. It can have After Effects lights shine on it, it's relatively easy to use, gives you control over every possible parameter you could ever want, and it also renders rather quickly for how great the results look.

Oh, and did I mention its particles are 3D? Yeah. So much so that they even show up in orthographic viewports! They respond to After Effects cameras, lights, and even depth of field! The more you use Particular, the more you will love it. I strongly urge you to at least download a free demo of it if you haven't played with it yet.

In this cheat, as with the previous cheat with Form, we're just going to scratch the surface as we introduce Particular. Also, as with Form, we're going to be making the quintessential particle creation – 3D light streaks, as initially made popular in an iPod commercial years ago.

**1** Open the Particular - 3D Light Streaks.aep project, and go to the 3D Light Streaks START comp. There is a light in this comp that I've already animated in 3D with the wiggle expression. Particular can use this as the emitter, which is really helpful. It's also important that the light layer is called Emitter. Apply Particular to the solid here. In the Emitter area in the effect controls, change Particles/sec to 2000, Emitter Type to Light(s), Velocity to 0, Velocity from Motion to 0, and Emitter Size for X, Y, and Z each to 0.

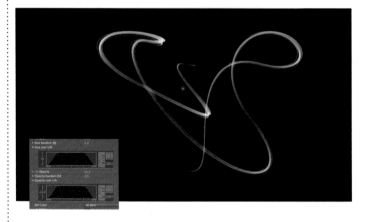

**3** Also in the Particle area, increase Life [sec] to about 6. Change Opacity to 35. Then open up the Size over Life and Opacity over Life to see this really cool graph that you'll see often in Form and Particular. You can manually click and drag a shape, or choose one from the presets on the right. I love that! I chose a hill-shaped preset for both.

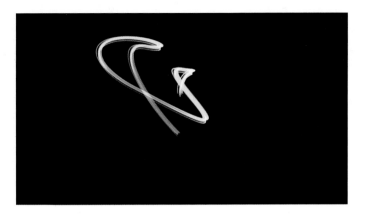

**2** In the Emitter area, take Position Subframe to 10x Linear. In the Particle area, change Particle Type to Streaklet, Size to 15, Transfer Mode to Add, and change the color to whatever you'd like. In the example at the beginning of the cheat, I used blue. Here I'm going to use the generic red/orange.

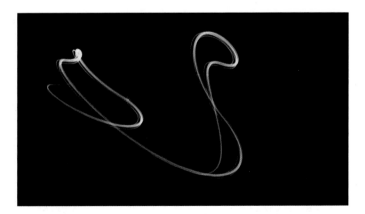

**4** Also remember that, like Form, this shape is completely 3D! Here is the exact same frame after rotating around the shape with an After Effects camera (no setup required for that, by the way). Particular is the new darling of the After Effects world and completely deserves its place as one of the most popular (if not THE most popular) After Effects plugins available.

**HOT TIP**

Both Form and Particular come with an impressive array of animation presets that are very well designed. You can use these as jumping off points in your projects, or to see what these effects are capable of. You could also use them as tutorials. After you apply them (discussed how in Chapter 10), you can then look at the settings in the Effect Controls panel that were used to create that effect.

# Particle Alternatives

THIS MIGHT BE SHOOTING MYSELF IN THE FOOT A LITTLE BIT. But I wanted to share with you an alternative to creating particles in After Effects, and that is to use live action video footage of particles, and then composite them into After Effects using blend modes.

The great downside of this of course, is that you completely lose control over the particles. Also, they are completely flat. and they will look like it. So if you're compositing in 3D, you're kind of stuck there. You also might have to spend some money getting footage of explosions and so forth, and the native effects in After Effects are free.

The great benefit to this of course, is that it typically looks much better. Creating a smoke trail is one thing, but creating an exploding building or a photorealistic flamethrower are entirely different challenges. Live action footage of almost any particle type is usually going to look much better than creating from scratch with a particle generator.

Another great benefit is that it's much, much faster. As much as I love Particular and could spend all day playing in it, that's just the problem: I can spend all day playing in it, trying to get the perfect settings. With stock particles footage, I find the clip I need and I'm done.

While there are many great resources all over the place for footage elements like this (from Digital Juice to Video Copilot), I've found a tremendous resource that I wanted to share with you. It's called Detonation Films (which you can find at detonationfilms.com). They have a huge assortment of clips, they look great, but the best part is how cheap it all is! I can't believe it. They even have a huge assortment of free effects clips! So, if you're thinking about trying out the live action particles thing, I recommend heading on down to their website and picking up a few of their many freebies. And even if you do want to fork out some cash for their other clips, you won't break the bank doing it. For example, I just saw a collection of HD (1080p) fire bursts on their site for $12. You can't beat that! I've personally used their stuff before in a variety of arenas, and I've found the quality to be just fantastic. Just so you know, Detonation Films is not paying me to say this. They don't even know that I'm mentioning them, actually. They're just good people with a great product, and an incredible price. And it's the combination of price and quality that makes it a good experiment to see if live action particles fit into your workflow.

You'll notice that I've used their clips a few times in the book already. I used a black mushroom cloud back in Chapter 4. And, after heavy color correction and stylizing, I've used one of their explosions in the Chad Show bumper piece we've seen throughout the book.

■ Good color makes all the difference in the world. We'll learn a massive amount of tricks to make your footage and graphics really pop and stand out from the rest.

# 9

# Color Correction

COLOR IS THE SECRET TO GREAT ART, motion or otherwise. Whether creating a movie or creating motion graphics, enhancing your art with color correction can make all the difference. If footage looks beautiful at first glance, it becomes instantly compelling.

In this chapter, we're going to have standard cheats, but I've arranged them in such a way that we'll also learn a great deal about the native color correction tools in After Effects and some color correction concepts and best practices along the way.

As with Chapter 8, we'll start with native effects, then adventure into 3rd party effects: Color Finesse (which is included for free with After Effects) and Magic Bullet Looks.

# Reading a Histogram

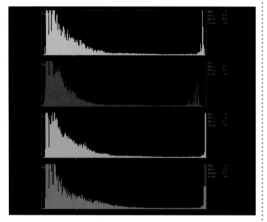

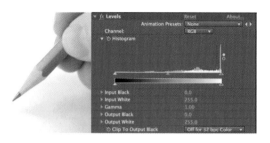

1 Open the Histograms.aep project and go to the 01 comp. Here you'll find a video clip from uberstock.com. It mostly shows a piece of paper. There are a lot of bright tones in this image, and not much in the way of shadows. But what about the pencil lead? Isn't that dark? The histogram will tell us! Apply the Levels effect. The histogram is a readout of the brightness in our image. The dark tones are represented on the left of the image; brights on the right. The higher the spike in the graph, the more of that particular value is in our image. In this histogram, we see huge spikes on the right (highlights), but really nothing in the shadow areas on the right. The shadows only seem dark compared to the rest of the image.

LEVELS IS PERHAPS THE SINGLE MOST FREQUENTLY USED COLOR CORRECTION tool out there. While it can correct colors as well, it is mainly used to correct luminance (i.e. brightness) issues.

The Levels effect is also unique in that it does something most effects don't. It gives you a readout showing you the various levels of brightness in your image. Also, as of After Effects CS5, it can now show you the various levels of colors in your image. It provides this information in the form of a histogram.

Histograms are extremely helpful, not just in After Effects, but you'll also find them in Photoshop, Color Finesse (shown above), video editing software, and still and video cameras. Knowing how to read them correctly can really help you understand what is actually happening in an image, as opposed to what it seems like is happening. Knowledge of histograms can also help prevent you from damaging an image. So this info will help us throughout this chapter.

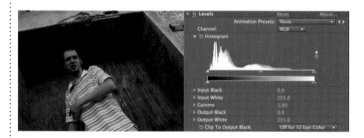

3 OK, let's put this to use a bit now. Move to the 03 comp where we have another Zen Chemists clip. Apply the Levels effect to this clip. Here we have a lot of shadows, and some decent midtones, but the image seems lackluster because there aren't any highlights. What we can do is drag the right most arrow (the one below the histogram, NOT the one below the gradient) to the left. This forces the tones that are the brightest in the image to go all the way to white. Make sure to stop dragging at the very first pixel in the histogram.

2 Let's move to the 02 comp. This clip is from a music video I directed by the
Seattle rap group Zen Chemists. Apply the Levels effect. If you never saw this
image, could you guess how the tones were distributed? There is tons of contrast
here – huge spikes on the left (shadows) and right (highlights) of the histogram,
but not much in the way of midtones. This histogram tells us that there might be
too much contrast in this image. While contrast is great, in most cases it's better
to have a better balance – at least some highlights, some shadows, and some
midtones.

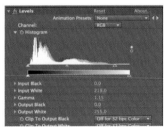

4 It's very important to look at the
histogram and NOT the image!
In this case, things might appear to
look OK, but I've actually dragged the
slider too far, beyond the blue and cyan
pixels in the histogram. This forced too
many pixels to white, and lost highlight
details, such as in the collar of his shirt.
That's not good.

5 This is what the histogram
probably should look like in this
case. Visually, the results are very
similar, but the highlights are not
blown out (i.e. all pushed to white). To
add additional brightness, I dragged
the midtones slider (in the middle) to
the left a bit. You can see how much
the histogram has helped us – to both
identify problems and to fix them
without creating more of them!

HOT TIP

The Levels effect
doesn't make
any adjustments
by default. So
you can feel
free to apply the
Levels effect at
any time to any
layer just to see
its histogram. I
often apply this
after applying
multiple
effects to make
sure that my
luminance
values are still
where they
should be.

# 9 Color Correction

# Cinematic Color: Warmth

**C**OLOR CORRECTING SHORT FILMS IS ONE OF MY FAVORITE THINGS TO DO. If used appropriately, color can be used to help shape the story the way a supporting character can. I'm well aware that there are many filmmakers that would disagree, saying that color correction gets in the way of the actual story. To me, the soundtrack helps tell the story, as does the wardrobe, and the props, and the location – why not color as well?

In the next few cheats, we're going to create different vibes with the same uberstock video clip. This clip intentionally has no inherent emotion to it – just a girl with a drink. Using color, we can help the audience begin to feel how the director of photography and screenwriter are already trying to get them to feel. As we'll see, color correction has a massive impact on the emotional response of an audience to a scene.

**1** So here's this clip from uberstock.com in its default state. Again, notice that there really isn't too much emotion here, meaning that this frame is not happy, sad, scary, etc. You'll find it in the Warmth FINAL comp in the Cinematic - Warmth. aep project. Apply the Color Balance effect to this clip, which is perhaps my favorite cinematic color adjustment tool.

**3** Color correction is a constant balancing act; a kind of push/pull motion, where you adjust one component (such as the shadows, or the contrast), and then that throws off another component (such as the highlights, or the saturation). So balance adding red, removing green (to add magenta), and removing blue. Above are the settings that I settled on.

2 The Color Balance effect allows us to play around with the balance of
different colors. The task at hand is to make this warmer, perhaps to create
sympathy for this character or to show how she is thought of fondly by someone
else. To create warmth, we add warm tones. But there's no yellow or orange here.
In this case, it pays to know a bit about color theory. Removing blue actually adds
yellow. Thus, adding red and removing blue will create an orange color.

4 There's definitely a much more welcoming feel with the color changes we've
added. I'm worried that this is feeling a little too strong to feel warm, though.
Let's lighten things up a little bit by applying the Levels effect, and then dragging
the slider in the middle of the histogram to the left. This image now tells a much
different story than the original image.

**HOT TIP**

Be careful as
you're going
back and forth
with your color
changes. If you
subtract too
much blue,
the image will
become too
yellow, which
makes the
image look
too vintage.
If you add too
much red, the
image will feel
too intense.
Again, like color
correction itself,
it's a balance.

# Cinematic Color: Horror

**1** So let's start in the Horror START comp in the Cinematic - Horror.aep project. This again uses the same clip from uberstock.com as seen in the previous and next cheats. Again, this is the default state, which is comparatively emotionless. We want to create the illusion at a single glance that either this woman means trouble, or that she's in grave danger. Perhaps she's drinking something sinister?

**N**OW WE'RE GOING TO TAKE A TRIP TO THE DARK SIDE. We're going to take the same clip from the previous cheat, and make it feel like it's something out of a horror movie. And all of this, just by changing the color a little bit.

It's often good to reflect on what colors mean to us. Why are red/orange/yellow associated with love? Why are cyan/green/blue associated with horror? This discussion is kind of getting away from the subject of an After Effects book, but it really pays to understand the psychological effects of color.

**3** Now, apply my beloved Color Balance effect. Here, we want to remove red – the color of warmth and safety. The opposite of red is cyan, which is basically green and blue, and we need a bunch of both of those colors. Above are the settings I used.

2 This image has way too much color in it to be scary. First step, apply the
Vibrance effect. Take the Saturation value down to –70. Ah, much better (and
by better, I mean worse – you know what I mean!).

4 I love the colors here, but it needs to be more intense from a luminance
perspective. So, check the Preserve Luminosity checkbox. I also applied
the Levels effect, and brightened the highlights and darkened the midtones.
Desaturated? Check. Greenish-blue tint? Check. Intense contrast? Check. Well,
folks, it looks like we've met the qualifications for a creepy movie color motif.

**HOT TIP**

With the Color
Balance effect,
it's generally
a good idea
to add more
color when
you want a
brighter image,
and subtract
colors when you
want a darker
final result.
The purpose of
the Preserve
Luminosity
checkbox is
to attempt to
compensate for
the gain/loss of
light from the
adjustments
of the Color
Balance
properties.

# Cinematic Color: Flashback

THE FLASHBACK IS THE BANE OF THE SCREENWRITER. Nevertheless, as After Effects professionals, we are often called upon to create the illusion of a flashback through color correction.

In our final cheat, we're going to go back in time. But this is only one way to create this effect. There really isn't a rule book on what it looks like when you go back in time. I don't think so, anyway. Some movies create the look of vintage film, with dust and scratches. Some flashbacks just desaturate the footage. In this cheat, we're going to give our flashback a dreamlike quality, and also an aged look. In my feeling, memories are kind of like that – exaggerated, dreamlike, and yet still old and faded a bit.

1 Open the Flashback START comp in the Cinematic - Flashback.aep project. This is the now-familiar uberstock video clip in its default state. Shown for comparison.

3 The next step is to add some yellow. We could use Color Balance, but a better way to do it in this case is to apply the Curves effect. In the Curves effect, change the channel drop down from RGB to Blue. Then drag the upper right point down to the first line, as shown above. This reduces the amount of blue light, adding yellow.

**2** Apply the Vibrance effect and reduce Saturation to –25. Then apply the Glow effect. In the Glow effect controls, take Glow Threshold to 25%, Glow Radius to 35, and Glow Intensity to 0.4. The Glow effect creates the diffuse glow that adds some dreamy softness to our image.

**4** The final step is kind of a naughty one. This is something you should normally never do. But we're going to degrade the quality of the image to create a more vintage look. In the Curves effect, change the channel back to RGB. Then drag the lower left point upwards a bit to taste. This lightens the shadows. Again, that's usually a very bad practice, because it washes out the image. But in this case, that's exactly what we want.

**HOT TIP**

It's a good idea when color correcting to always look out for flesh tones. It's a common amateur mistake to have blue or yellow flesh after color correcting. This is one of the reasons that I love Color Balance so much, as it lets you play with the colors a lot and still look believable. Our yellowing of the skin here is perhaps bordering on a bit too much.

# Day for Night

IGHT SHOOTS ARE EXPENSIVE. Because of that, they will often shoot footage in the day time that the script says should be at night. The director will then hunt down a color person and ask them to digitally make it look like it's nighttime. This type of shot is called a "day for night" shot.

That may seem very foreign to you if you've never heard of this idea, but day for night shots are used all the time in the broadcast world. So, I'm going to show you some ideas for both creating the effect, and what type of shot make it easier or harder to make this trick work and look good.

1 Open the Day for Night START comp in the Day for Night.aep project. This simple comp contains a video that I shot of some stuff in the light of day in Seattle.

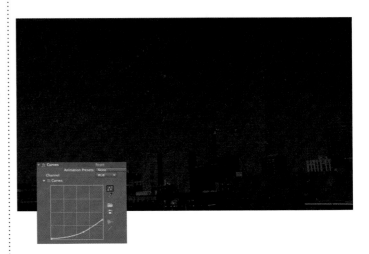

3 Now let's make it night. Apply the Curves effect. The upper right corner represents the highlights in the image. Dragging them downwards reduces the brightness of the brightest areas of the images, which is what happens at night. I then dragged the middle of the curve downwards (as shown above) to further reduce the brightness of the midtones.

**2** Other than in Las Vegas, nighttime is usually very desaturated. There's not that much light, and what little there is naturally is from the moon, and that's typically a very dim blue light. So apply the Vibrance effect and reduce the Saturation value to −85.

**4** Now we have to add a blue moon-ish tint. Apply the Color Balance effect. I took Shadow Blue Balance to 8, Midtone Blue Balance to 20, and Hilight Blue Balance to 15, and check Preserve Luminosity. Not bad.

**HOT TIP**

This shot works OK for day for night purposes. But be very careful. Intense sunlight can create shadows that make it impossible for a believable day for night shot. Even in our shot here, some of the windows have very bright highlights, which is a clue to our fakery. Additionally, notice the front of our buildings. They are bright on the front on completely black on the sides. The moon doesn't typically create such directional light, and when it does, it's never that powerful. Just something to watch out for.

# Reference Monitor

REFERENCE MONITORS ARE USED TO HELP YOU KEEP COLOR CORRECTIONS IN CHECK. After Effects does not offer a reference monitor, per se. Thankfully, however, there is a fairly easy way to set one up.

As we go forward in this chapter, you may want to use this technique to check your work. Color is a wacky thing. If you make subtle changes over time, you'd be surprised at what you'll let yourself get away with. But when you compare your work with the original, it's often surprising how drastic your changes have been.

1 Open the Reference Monitor.aep project, which contains an uberstock video clip. Setting up a reference monitor is kind of an interface trick. So just note that mine is currently just a standard layout.

3 This will create the Layer panel and Composition panel side-by-side. But the problem is that they're the exact same view, and effects applied to either layer will show up in both panels.

**2** Double click the layer in the Reference Monitor comp to open it up in the Layer panel. Click and drag on the grip marks (or the color swatch) to the left of the padlock next to the name of the Layer panel at the top of the interface. Dragging this panel over the Composition panel will show you several drop zones. Release your mouse as it highlights the one on the left side, as shown above.

**4** At the bottom of the Layer panel, uncheck the Render checkbox. Now, when you apply effects, you can see the original layer (in the Layer panel) side-by-side with the color adjusted version (in the Composition panel).

# Before and After

SIMILAR TO REFERENCE MONITORS, WE CAN ALSO QUICKLY VIEW BEFORE AND AFTER snapshots of our comps. After going through the last cheat, you may feel that changing your entire interface may be too much effort. Although this is not a constant view like the reference monitor, it is a very quick view of a previous state of your image. In addition, the reference monitor thing only allows you to see the original content of the layer. This trick allows you to see the before and after of anything you want. So you can see the before and after when adjusting parameters if you want to. Check the "hot tip" on the opposite page for information on how to save and preview up to 4 previous states of your work.

1 Open the Before After.aep project. This contains another uberstock video clip of someone who is apparently very excited about color correction.

3 Now, in the Tint controls, change the Map White To value to green.

2 Apply the Tint effect to this layer. Let's say we're not sure what color we want
to tint this – red or green. In the Tint effect controls, click the Map White To
color swatch and change it to red. Then, at the bottom of the Composition panel,
create a snapshot by clicking the camera icon. You'll hear a sweet little camera
noise indicating that it now remembers the current shot, as if it had taken a
photograph of it.

4 At the bottom of the Composition panel, click the Show Snapshot button
(to the right of the camera icon) and while you hold that button, it shows
you the picture it took when you clicked the camera icon back in step 2. This is a
great feature for quickly comparing the before and after state of anything in After
Effects, not just with effects (e.g. chroma key settings, lighting changes, design
and layout changes, etc.).

**HOT TIP**

You can actually
take up to
4 different
snapshots. The
Show Snapshot
button just
shows you the
last snapshot
that was
taken. To take
snapshots,
press Shift+F5,
Shift+F6,
Shift+F7, or
Shift+F8.
Press the
corresponding
F key to see
that snapshot.
For example,
after taking a
snapshot with
Shift+F7, press
F7 to view it.

# Colorizing

OLORIZING IS ONE OF THOSE THINGS that I find myself doing all the time. Whether it's recoloring a flat layer from Illustrator, or a pasted shape from Photoshop, or a black and white texture like fractal noise, or even a full color image, it seems like I'm always colorizing.

The "problem" is that there are so many tools to add color in After Effects that it can be confusing as to what does what. Most are really easy to use though. So, this cheat is going to be a little different. It's going to be six mini-cheats in one as we look very briefly at a host of ways to add and change color.

Note that for this power cheat, we'll be using the Colorizing.aep project. Each comp is numbered with its corresponding step number and effect name. For example, we'll be looking at the Leave Color effect in step 6, and the comp with those files is in the comp called 06 LEAVE COLOR. Also, in each comp, you'll find a visible layer called START (which is the layer for you to play with), and an invisible layer called FINAL so you can see the finished product for reference if you'd like to.

1 TINT. The easiest effect in the bunch is Tint. There are three controls – one for remapping black, one for remapping white, and one for blending the results into the original layer. In this case, we have a black shape on a black background. Apply Tint. Change the Map Black To color to blue. Done.

4 BLACK & WHITE. Before CS5, I used to use Hue/ Saturation to colorize a full color image with one color tint. CS5 provides a much better way with the Black and White effect. Apply Black & White to this image and check the Tint checkbox. The conversion is muddy. Take Reds to 110, Yellows to –100, Greens to 110, Cyans to –50, and Blues to –150. This makes the robots' headbands all bright (and the same color), and darkens the pirates a bit, and the waves a lot. The composition is much better now.

**2** TRITONE. For those times when you want a bit more control over colorizing (e.g. Shadows, Midtones, and Highlights, instead of just black and white like in the Tint effect), try the Tritone effect. Apply the Tritone effect to this grayscale fractal noise pattern. Change the Highlights color to RGB values of 250, 250, 150. Change Midtones to 200, 100, 0. Change Shadows to 75, 0, 0.

**3** COLOR BALANCE. By now, you know how much I love Color Balance. I use it whenever I can, even to colorize. It's useless for colorizing when colors are flat – in other words, just solid white or black. But when there are shades of gray (like in a fractal noise pattern), Color Balance can work its magic. Here, I subtracted red and added green and blue as we did earlier in this chapter.

**5** COLORAMA. The most powerful effect to colorize that I've ever seen is the Colorama effect. It's so powerful that people often avoid it. Its colorization features are so rich, that we can almost recolor this matte painting by Daniel Johnson. Change Output>Use Preset Palette to Fire, and change the Blend With Original value to 30%.

**6** LEAVE COLOR. Although technically not a colorizing effect (just the opposite actually), the Leave Color effect allows you to remove color from an image, except for one color. I'm including it here, because the final result creates the illusion that you've colorized a black and white image. We have this clip from uberstock (flip back a few pages if you want to see it in full color). Apply Leave Color. Change Amount to Decolor to 100%, Tolerance to 4.5%, and Edge Softness to 3.2%. Then use the Color To Leave eyedropper to click the red drink that she's drinking.

**HOT TIP**

In Chapter 10, we'll use the Colorama effect all over the place, and learn a little bit more about it there as well.

# Hue Shift

SOME COLORIZING JOBS CALL FOR A
DIFFERENT TOOL. In this case, the standard
tricks just won't work, so we're going to use
the good old faithful Hue/Saturation effect to
aid us here. I actually use Hue/Saturation far
more than the amount of cheats about it in this
chapter might suggest. It may not be the best
solution in every instance, but in my experience,
it's usually the fastest. We'll also look at
adjustment layers a bit in this cheat as well.

**1** Here are some Illustrator graphics that I assembled in After Effects. You can
find this in the Hue Shift.aep project. In the Hue Shift START comp, press
⌘ ⌥ Y ctrl alt Y to create a new adjustment layer. As in Photoshop,
adjustment layers affect all layers beneath them, and that's really the most
efficient way to colorize this entire composition. Apply all effects to this
adjustment layer.

**3** However, when I apply the Hue/Saturation effect and change the Master Hue
value to 135 degrees, only color tones shift.

2 Because there is only one color besides gray (including black and white), you might be tempted to use Tint and Tritone, but they don't work because they will shift some of the grays that we want left alone (notice the wings especially).

4 And not only did our adjustment layer help colorize this entire comp in one fell swoop, but we can also move it up and down in the layer stack to change which layers are affected by it. In the Timeline panel, drag this layer beneath the Rock logo precomp layer (layer 2) to have the Hue/Saturation color adjustment only affect the layers beneath the Rock logo precomp.

# Stylizing

CLOSELY RELATED TO COLORIZING IS THE PROCESS OF STYLIZING. Essentially, stylizing is when we change the look of footage so much that the look is no longer organic. We might create a painterly look on live action video, or we might posterize footage to make it look cartoony.

In this case, I wanted to have an explosion in the background, but I wanted it to feel very cartoony. A real explosion wouldn't match the feel of the piece, or the very limited color scheme I've created here. But how do you go about creating cartoony explosions?

I decided to take some sweet explosion video footage from Detonation Films and stylize that using a series of effects in After Effects. The result is kind of an interesting cocktail of color tweaks and stylizing adjustments.

1 In the Stylizing comp in the Stylizing.aep project, I've gone ahead locked all layers except for the Detonation Films explosion footage. I've also turned off the visibility of that crazy dude in the middle. This looks very organic, and it doesn't match the style or color of the piece at all.

3 I then applied the Cartoon effect to make it look even more stylized. Honestly, I'm not a big fan of this effect. It usually looks bad, and it takes forever to render. But it worked in this case, so I went with it. In the Cartoon effect controls, I took Fill>Shading Steps to 2, and Edge>Softness to 95.

2  The first step was to apply the Levels effect and enhance the contrast a lot
as described earlier in this chapter. I brightened the highlights a little, and
darkened the shadows a lot. It's already looking a lot more stylized.

4  At this point, I think I'm happy with the explosion. It definitely looks stylized
and fits in better with the rest of the project. Now, I want to just apply the
Tint effect, and change the Map White To value to be the same green as used in
the rest of the project. Yep. I like it.

HOT TIP

In the final
version of this
project, I also
applied the
Roughen Edges
effect to smooth
out and stylize
the edges of the
explosion.

273

# Faking Dimension

**1** So we have this really cool art by Dan Grady in the Faking Dimensions START comp in the project of the same name. I want to add some moon light on his head to give it some apparent roundness.

COLOR DOESN'T JUST MAKE STUFF LOOK PRETTY. In some cases, we can use color changes to simulate lighting, and thereby create the illusion of volume.

To accomplish this, we're going to use a layer style because it will give us a lot of flexibility. In After Effects CS3, Photoshop layer styles became native to After Effects. If you aren't familiar with those, I strongly recommend checking them out. I find those little guys extremely helpful quite often.

**3** Open the layer properties in the Timeline panel, and in the Layer Styles>Gradient Overlay>Blend Mode drop down, choose Screen. Now our white outline is back.

2 Select the robot captain head layer. Right click on it and choose Layer Styles>Gradient Overlay. This initially replaces the content of the layer with a gradient. Unfortunately, that also means the stroke around the edges of our object have been replaced as well.

4 Also in the Gradient Overlay settings, change the Angle to about 250 degrees, and adjust the Offset to put the gradient in the correct place. If desired, you can click the Edit Gradient text to open the Gradient Editor and make changes to the gradient. I made the white a little darker and more blue. You can also select the actual text that says Layer Styles in the Timeline panel and press ⌘ C ctrl C to copy this style, and then ⌘ V ctrl V to paste it onto other layers (as shown in the initial screenshot at the beginning of this cheat).

HOT TIP

I usually use the Ramp effect for this type of thing because there are fewer options and they're easier to get to. But in this case, we needed to use the layer style because the layer styles allow you to blend modes, which allowed our outlines to show through. The Ramp effect doesn't allow blend mode blending.

SHORTCUTS
MAC WIN BOTH

# Secondary Color Correction

PRIMARY COLOR CORRECTION IS WHAT WE'VE DONE SO FAR in this chapter. Primary color correction is when your adjustments change the entire image. It's usually a good idea to start out the color correction process with primary color correction.

But even after adjusting colors in the document, there are often places where certain colors are still not the way you'd like them to be. Secondary color correction is the process of tweaking certain colors without affecting the rest of them.

In this cheat, we'll do some light secondary color correction with my favorite quick and easy tool for the job – Hue/Saturation. In the next cheat, we'll continue on as we discuss spot color correction.

1 We're going to be using this cute clip of my kids from the short film *The Young are the Restless.* You'll find this in the Secondary CC START comp in the project of the same name.

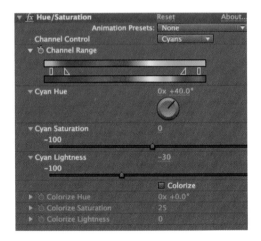

3 It looks much better after the primary color correction, but I don't like the way the colors in their outfits work in the scene. The cyan sleeves on my daughter are distracting. Apply the Hue/Saturation effect, which is pretty good for secondary color correction. Change the Channel Control drop down to Cyans to work on only those color tones. Above are the settings I used.

2 First, I'm going to do some primary color correction. It's important to do that first because sometimes color problems can be exaggerated or diminished by doing the main (primary) color correction. Here, I added Levels and Color Balance and adjusted them as we've done earlier in this chapter.

4 Now her sleeves look much better! And this doesn't need to be keyframed – every frame with those same color tones will be adjusted in the same way automatically. If there are some areas of the sleeves that aren't changing, you can change the Channel Control drop down to Greens, and make changes there.

**HOT TIP**

You can get even more control over the color ranges selected by Hue/ Saturation by adjusting the sliders in the Channel Range graph.

# Spot Color Correction

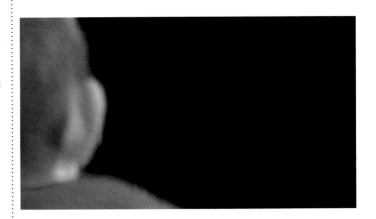

1 Open the Spot CC START in the Spot CC.aep project to begin where we left off in the last cheat. Because of the limitations of CMYK ink, you're not getting the full effect here, but the boy on the left is far too bright. I used a very shallow depth of field for this shot, and both the boy and the background are out of focus, while the girl (who is the subject) is in sharp focus. But the boy is so bright still that it's distracting. Using Roto Brush, we'll isolate and adjust just the boy.

**S**POT COLOR CORRECTION ISOLATES CERTAIN AREAS, even as secondary color correction is used to isolate certain colors.

We're going to continue where we left off in the last cheat with the clip from *The Young are the Restless*. Here, we're going to use the new Roto Brush tool to isolate a character, and then perform some spot color correction.

3 When you switch back to the Composition panel, you'll see only the boy. Now we can spot color correct. Darken and desaturate this layer (with Levels, Vibrance, etc.) as you see fit. Then press ⌘ D ctrl D to duplicate this layer.

2 Double click this layer to open it in the Layer panel. As described in Chapter 4, select the Roto Brush tool and select only the boy. Remember that you can draw while holding ⌥ alt if you want to subtract from the selection (as shown above). In the Roto Brush effect controls, take the Feather value up to 100%.

4 Put the top copy into the Multiply blend mode and reduce its Opacity value to 50%. On the bottom copy, delete the Roto Brush effect and the other effects you added in step 3. And that's it! Because Roto Brush will automatically trace content from frame to frame, we don't need to worry about doing anything else for this scene. Before CS5, I would usually do something like this with a mask, but then you would have to animated it to follow the subject. Roto Brush makes this process much easier.

**HOT TIP**

Once you're happy with your Roto Brush settings, make sure to click the Freeze button (in the Layer panel) to cache your Roto Brush settings and save them with the project. Not only that, but it will also make rendering the matte go much faster from frame to frame.

SHORTCUTS
MAC WIN BOTH

# Color Finesse Basics

**1** We'll be working in the Color Finesse.aep project with one of my favorite uberstock.com video clips.

**C**OLOR FINESSE IS ONE OF THE MANY 3RD PARTY EFFECTS THAT SHIP FOR FREE with After Effects. Although I really love After Effects' native color correction tools (and use them more often, honestly), Color Finesse is truly a professional powerhouse of color correction features.

In Color Finesse, you'll find all kinds of graphs to display information about the current image, as well as a host of color correction tools. Many of the color correction effects we've used in this chapter so far can be found in Color Finesse.

Know that Color Finesse does come with After Effects CS5, but unfortunately, it is a separate download and installation, and it even has its own serial number. It's very common for After Effects users to miss this one altogether for that reason.

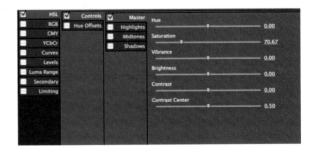

**3** In the default state, all effects are turned off and there is no change. Change the Saturation value to 70. As soon as you make the change the property is activated, as it were. As we look left, we can see that this is part of the bigger Master property, which is under the HSL>Controls category. Note that we have all of these parameters for highlights, midtones, and shadows as well.

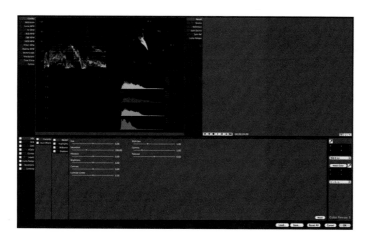

**2** Apply the Color Finesse effect to this layer (it's actually called SA Color Finesse 3). Then, in the Effect Controls panel, click the Full Interface button to launch the main Color Finesse window. Wow look at all that stuff! On the left, we see a bunch of monitors, including a waveform monitor, vectorscope, and a histogram per channel, as well as one for the composite. On the right side of the interface, we see our footage. Note that we're not seeing it above because the screen capture software I'm using won't capture it. But it's there. The bottom of the interface has all of our effects.

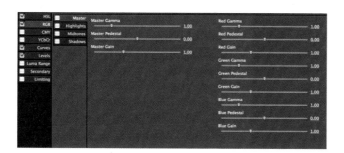

**4** Click on the RGB tab on the far left to get access to controls similar to Color Balance, only much more detailed and powerful. As checked above, there are also adjustable levels, and a much more powerful curves system. And this only skims the surface of the possibilities with Color Finesse. We'll explore a few extra features in the following cheats.

**HOT TIP**

As mentioned earlier in this chapter, color correction is a constant push/ pull as you go back and forth when you make changes. As you change luminance, saturation and color balance will often need to be fixed afterwards. Color Finesse gives you (in most cases) the most powerful tools for the job all in one place.

# Color Finesse "Looks"

E VEN IF YOU DON'T USE COLOR FINESSE, YOU CAN STILL EASILY TAKE ADVANTAGE OF it's incredible selection of preset "looks". As we'll talk about later in this chapter, one of the most popular 3rd party effects for After Effects is Magic Bullet looks. One of the reasons that it is so popular is that it has so many impressive looks that you can apply with the click of a button. Many of those "looks" as they are called resemble film stock quite a bit.

The great secret is that Color Finesse has a massive library of looks that are just as easy to apply! Many of these attempt to recreate the look of particular film stocks as well. Even if you don't ever want to master Color Finesse, you can still easily take advantage of these presets.

What we're going to do here is take just one video clip, and apply a bunch of different looks and see what we can come up with. Think of this cheat like a Color Finesse presets sampler.

1 We're going to use the Color Finesse Looks.aep project for this cheat. This is another clip of one of my kids from the short *The Young are the Restless*. This is the original untouched color from the camera.

2 Apply Color Finesse and click the Full Interface button. On the left side of the interface (where all the charts and monitors are) choose Gallery. You will see two folders. Open the one that says Settings Presets (System). You will see a lot of folders that contain different preset looks. Open a folder and double click a look to apply it. Note that each time you apply a look, it completely replaces whatever was there before.

6 Filters>Tobacco 2 Tiffen.

7 Filters>Tropical Blue1 Tiffen.

**3** Open 35mm Filmstocks>Eastman Kodak and double click Eastman 5231 Plus-X B&W to apply it.

**4** Now try 35mm Filmstocks>Fuji Films>Fuji 8563 Eterna 250D.

**5** This is Filters>Coral 4 Tiffen.

**8** Gels>Rosco Cinegel>Rosco Cinegel_3304_Tough Plusgreen Windowgreen.

**9** Misc>Faded Color Neg 1.

**10** Processing>Bleach Bypass.

**HOT TIP**

If you're really into emulating film, you may want to try to check out the Add Grain effect, which allows you to add film grain that matches specific film stocks. Some of the film stocks you can match the grain of with Add Grain, are some of the same film presets in Color Finesse!

# Using Color Lookup Tables

S O WHAT HAPPENS WHEN YOU WANT TO REUSE A COLOR ADJUSTMENT? Or say you wanted to use a color correction look that someone created in a different application? What do you do then?

Well, the industry decided a while back that this could be a problem. So they created a type of file called a Color Look Up Table (LUT). These files are cross platform and, because they are an industry standard, can be used by many applications. And as of After Effects CS5, you can add After Effects to the list of applications that can take advantage of this technology.

In this cheat, we're going to both create a color LUT and apply one. It's surprisingly easy to do.

1 We're going to start with the Make Color LUT comp in the Color LUTs.aep project. This is a video clip courtesy of uberstock.com.

3 Now move on over to the Apply Color LUT comp. Apply the new Apply Color LUT effect to this footage. As soon as you apply it, a browser will pop up. The only thing you can do with this effect is to use a color LUT with it. So navigate to the color LUT you made in step 2 and click OK.

2 Apply the Color Finesse effect and click Full Interface. Make some drastic changes. Feel free to use one of the presets that we looked at in the last cheat. I desaturated this a lot, and removed some red, and then faded the image a bit. When you're done, in the Color Finesse interface, choose File>Export>Settings to Autodesk 3D LUT>Smoke, and save your color LUT file.

4 Instantly, the color is changed with the exact same settings you created in step 2. Using Color Finesse, you can create color LUTs for most popular programs out there. Using the new Apply Color LUT effect, you can now apply them from outside applications as well. But these color LUT files are not only good for sharing, they're great for creating a library of your own custom looks.

# Improving 3D Renders

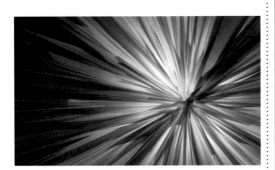

I REALIZE THAT THE AUDIENCE FOR THIS CHEAT MAY NOT BE THAT LARGE. But it's just astonishing how much more beautiful you can make 3D renders using color correction tools in After Effects.

For me, I'm honestly not that good at 3D apps, but I can make stuff that looks halfway decent thanks to After Effects. So, it's almost like After Effects makes me a better 3D artist. Hopefully someone out there will benefit from this tiny 2 page tidbit.

1 We're going to be using the 3D Renders START comp in the Improving 3D Renders.aep project. This contains a 3D project that I created in Cinema 4D. It's really not much to look at, but it's the best I could do.

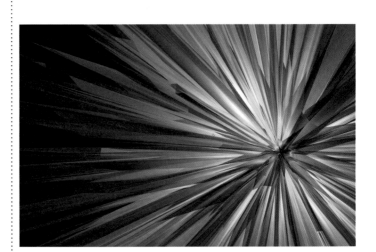

3 Next, let's improve the colors a little bit. Apply the Color Balance effect. Increase blues and greens and decrease reds as desired. OK, now I'm starting to have a little hope in this 3D image.

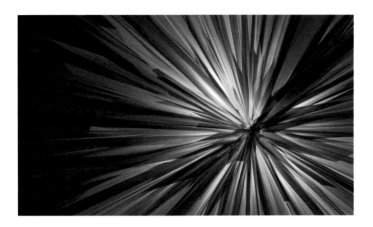

2 Let's first apply the Levels effect and punch the highlights and adjust the midtones as discussed in the beginning of this chapter. It doesn't look quite so bad after that.

4 For the final step, let's make this really pop by applying the Glow effect. In the Glow effect controls, take Glow Threshold to 35%, Glow Radius to 50, and Glow Intensity to 0.2. Wow. I have to admit, I love it. These amazing color correction tools here in After Effects really breathed a whole new life into this 3D render.

# Checking Dark Areas

I REALLY LOVE INTENSE CONTRAST. But the challenging side of that is that often, shadow areas look black on my monitor, and then when I see my final product in some other arena, I can see problems in the darkness that I missed when I was working on my computer.

After Effects actually has a very quick fix to this problem. It will allow you to temporarily adjust the exposure using a little obscure button in the interface. That little button doesn't actually change anything in your document, so there's no way to accidentally render your comp with it on. It's really a great feature that doesn't get a lot of attention.

**1** In the Checking Dark Areas.aep project, you'll find this clip from the short film *I Hate Basketball* by Jef Faulkner. I was visual effects supervisor on this film, which features a gang of possessed basketballs as its antagonist. In this shot, several crew members are throwing out the army of basketballs. I was charged with removing the crew, but I can't see them.

**3** With the exposure raised, I can now see all the background activity that I need to remove. But I certainly wouldn't want to inadvertently render this looking like that.

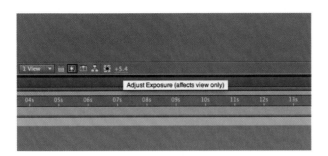

**2** At the bottom of the Composition panel, you'll find the Adjust Exposure value. It's the numbers on the right end of the buttons at the bottom of the Composition panel. Increase this value to temporarily raise the exposure of this view. I took it to a very high value of 5.4. Also note that when you've adjusted this property, the button immediately to its left glows letting you know that you've tweaked this option. Reset the exposure by clicking that button.

**4** Thankfully, it's impossible to render with this adjustment turned on. It's a preview feature only, so you don't have to worry about turning it off. I love that. Note that you can also use this feature to find the darkest pixels in the image. Turn it up full blast, and whatever pixels don't get turned white are the darkest pixels in that frame. I find this feature very helpful.

# Magic Bullet Looks

**M**AGIC BULLET LOOKS IS, ALONG WITH TRAPCODE PARTICULAR, THE MOST POPULAR AFTER EFFECTS PLUGIN on the market today. And there's good reason for that. It's a great color correction tool, but it's even more than that. It is laid out in a very intelligent and useful way. If you want to build your look using various customizable components, you can do that. Or if you prefer, you can instantly click to choose from a massive library of well designed and extremely diverse looks.

Similar to what we did a few cheats back with Color Finesse's "looks", we're going to just go through a sampler of what Magic Bullet Looks has to offer.

Remember that this is a 3rd party plugin that does not come with After Effects CS5. If you don't own this plugin, you can download a free trial of it from www.redgiantsoftware.com.

1 In the Magic Bullet Looks.aep file, you'll find the uberstock clip that we'll be using as we take our tour through Magic Bullet Looks.

4 Here I chose Basic>Basic Warm.

**2** Apply the Looks effect (in the Magic Bullet category of effects). In the Effect Controls panel, click the Edit button to open the full Magic Bullet Looks interface. If you hover your cursor over the right side, you can see the tools. Here you can drag individual components (such as Saturation, Exposure, Vignette, or tons of others) on to your footage in the center of the interface.

**3** On the left side of the interface, you'll find the looks. These are tons of presets that you can instantly apply to your footage. I find that these are a little heavy handed and need to be toned down a bit to use professionally, but they'll make the changes extra easy to see in the screenshots.

**5**  Popular Film>Blockbuster.

**6** Music Videos>Berlin.

# Shooting Filmlike Video

ALMOST EVERYONE THAT SHOOTS VIDEO WANTS IT TO LOOK LIKE FILM. And hey, I'm totally in that boat myself. Film just looks better than video. But many people really aren't aware of what it means to shoot video like film. Oftentimes, people will just add tons of contrast and call it filmlike. While most major motion pictures do have more than their fair share of contrast, that's not what makes it inherently filmlike. Following just a few tips can really help you shoot video that will not only look more professional and filmlike, but it will also help you achieve better results in your post production color correction.

The first thing that you should do is to make sure that you are shooting at 24 frames per second, and that those frames are progressive (i.e. not interlaced). Our eyes are quick to detect the difference in 24 and 30 frames per second. Although 30 frames per second looks cleaner (especially when animating), there's just something very filmic about 24p. And perhaps it's my ignorance, but I find that it's kinda challenging taking regular 29.97 frames per second video and converting it to 24p and making it look good.

Perhaps the most striking way that video is different from film is in its limited dynamic range. Point a film camera at a bright sunset, and you'll get beautiful footage. Point a video camera at a bright sunset, and you'll either get blown out highlights or very, very dark footage. Video just can't capture dark darks and light lights at the same time. So, in order to make your footage look more like film, make sure that your exposure is low enough so that your highlights are not all blown out. Also, once highlights are blown out, there's no way to recover them in post. Once that detail is lost, it's lost. Most of the footage that I shoot is a little too underexposed because I'm just so paranoid that I'm going to blow out the highlights.

Now, you have to be very careful that you don't follow my bad example an underexpose too much. The reason is that video gets really grainy when it is underexposed. Although in theory we can lighten dark footage, sometimes underexposed footage is just too dark to work with because the noise can make it unusable. In my opinion, when shooting filmlike video, I think it's best to slightly underexpose the footage. It's much easier to brighten dark footage than darken light footage, but again, you don't want to underexpose too much.

While we're talking about my opinion, allow me to share another one with you. Now if you're working with a talented director of photography, they may not go along with this one, but I like to also shoot flat. This means that I shoot very low contrast, with as little processing as possible. If the camera allows me to adjust things like saturation and sharpness, I usually turn that stuff down or even all the way off. My footage isn't much to look at on its own (and this is why directors of photography don't like to shoot this way, because it doesn't let them show off their skills!). But the reason I do this is so that I have the most control in post production.

When I first bought my Canon 7D camera, everyone raved about how great the footage is right out of the box. But I hated it! It looked great, but it already had tons of contrast. But what happens if I want less contrast? Or what happens if I want to remove the sharpening? If I shoot it flat, then I have much more control over the final product. In some cases, such as when I made the short film *The Young are the Restless*, I knew I wouldn't have time to color correct in post, so I tried making the footage look more rich on its own. But most of the time, I try to record footage that is as bland as possible.

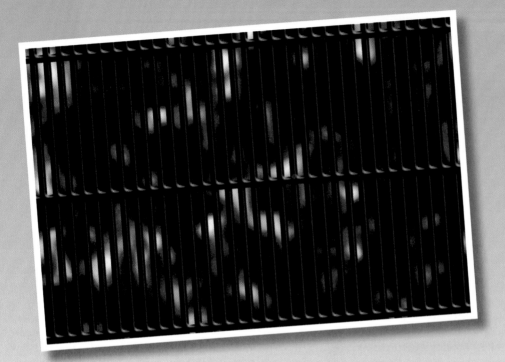

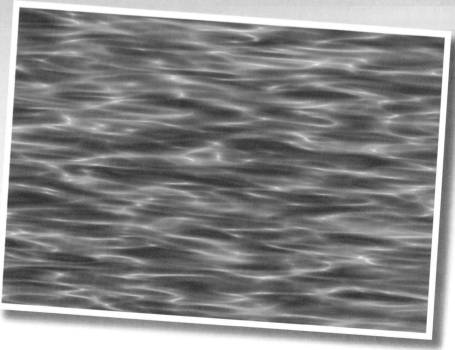

■ In this chapter we're going to look at several After Effects tools for creating textures from scratch. We'll make fire (including hot coals and a grill), water, TV noise, curtains, and much more – all from scratch.

After Effects

# 10

# Backgrounds and Textures

CREATING ANIMATED BACKGROUNDS is perhaps one of the things I find myself doing very frequently, and most After Effects users would probably agree. Whether putting something behind a client logo, compositing something on a background element, or creating an interesting track matte, knowing how to create animated textures from scratch is a necessary weapon in the arsenal of the cheating After Effects user.

In this chapter, we'll not only look at how to create a variety of textures from scratch with fun recipes, but I'll show you a few ways to come up with your own textures. Then we'll look at how to use After Effects features to quickly create an entire library of your own custom textures.

# Fire Texture

THIS TRICK IS AN OLDIE BUT A GOODIE. It also helps demonstrate the versatility of the Fractal Noise effect. It's important to remember that as cool as this fire is, it is limited to remain forever as a background. Fractal Noise is an impressive pattern generator, but don't make the mistake of thinking it can act as a particle system.

Although Fractal Noise probably won't single-handedly create the class of explosion that Tom Cruise might walk away from in slow motion, it can be very useful in adding texture to components of that explosion. Later in this chapter, we'll use this same fire as the basis for other cheats.

**1** Create a new comp. Let's just go with the standard NTSC DV preset for right now. Create a new solid by pressing ⌘Y/ctrl Y and make sure the dimensions of the solid match the dimensions of the comp. The color of the solid will be completely replaced by the Fractal Noise effect, so it is irrelevant. Apply the Fractal Noise effect (NOT the Fractal effect) to the solid. Poor Fractal Noise ain't much to look at with its default settings.

**3** Maybe it's just me, but this gray stuff is getting tough to look at. And even if you're not visually bored yet, it's really hard to look at this and envision what our fire will look like. Now we have color, but it looks like a TV weather pattern. So let's apply the Colorama effect to this. In the Colorama effect properties in the Effect Controls panel, open up the Output Cycle area and from the Use Preset Palette drop down, choose Fire. OK. Now we're talking.

2 Change the Fractal Type (the drop down at the top of the Fractal Noise
effect in the Effect Controls panel) to Dynamic Twist. This basically adds a
twist to the noise pattern being generated, and this extra twist is going to make
our noise look more fiery in a moment.

4 This texture is already pretty fiery as is. And fire comes in a wide variety
of fiery flavors – camp, bon, candle, explosion, flamethrower, etc. Each
has their own distinct shape, texture, and movement. So the fire we're creating
in this cheat maybe just a jumping off point for your own custom fire. But for
our purposes here, there's just too much fire, and it's just not as intense as I'd
like it to be. You can address both of those concerns by increasing the Contrast
parameter. I'm going to use a value of 300, but you can use whatever you'd like.

continued...

**HOT TIP**

Our fire is
already looking
more believable.
However, in my
own opinion,
it seems like
the majority of
that realism is
coming from the
color scheme
and not from
the fire itself.
So be careful
that you don't
use Colorama's
wicked cool
colorization as a
crutch, and just
settle for any
old texture.

SHORTCUTS

# Fire Texture (continued)

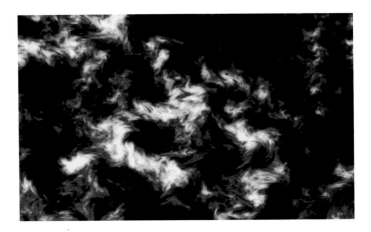

**5** At this point, I'm liking the contrast, but I still think there's too much fire. Whenever you want to get rid of some of the noise in Fractal Noise, try taking down the Brightness parameter. It works in kind of an interesting way. It doesn't darken every pixel. It allows white to stay white. Often, this has the effect of thinning out the noise. A value of around −40 works for me.

**7** OK. We got some fire going on here, but it still is too "noisy" for what I'm looking for; too much texture. I'm kinda going for a look as though the camera is shooting something on the other side of the fire and the depth of field is creating blurry fire. The Complexity property controls how many virtual layers of noise are being generated, and in this case, we've got too many. With this property, a little adjustment can make a fairly big difference, so be careful. I'm going to take Complexity to 3.6.

**6** I want this to look like campfire-style fire. Fire in a campfire has a definite direction. So open up the Transform area in the Fractal Noise effect, uncheck Uniform Scaling, and increase the Scale Height property a lot. No, seriously. A LOT. I'm going to try a value of 1000. Note that you can only go to 600 with this property if you use the slider.

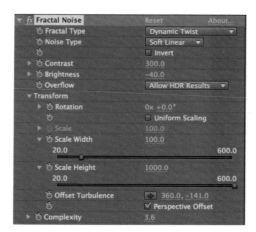

**8** Alright! This fire looks pretty awesome! But what about animating it? Typically, we bring to life the patterns created by Fractal Noise by animating the Evolution property. But here, Evolution doesn't work, because it will make the flames go both up and down simultaneously. That's not what flames do! In this case, we only want the flames to travel upwards. To do that, animate the Y axis of the Offset Turbulence parameter in the Transform area of the Fractal Noise controls from a larger value to a smaller one. Unfortunately, this property moves all of the virtual layers of noise in one solid unit. For added realism, enable the Perspective Offset parameter, which will move the noise layers as if they were staggered in 3D.

# Candle Flame

THIS IS GOING TO BE A QUICK CHEAT, but quite fun nonetheless. We're going to start where we left off in the last cheat (where we learned how to make a fire texture with the Fractal Noise effect). So, if you just jumped here, back up a few pages and do that tutorial first. With a very quick adjustment, we can turn that wall of fire into a very realistic candle flame.

Technically, this doesn't really count as a background or a texture, I realize. But the real point of this chapter is to expand on what you can do with textures you create in After Effects. And this is a great eye opener as to what Fractal Noise is capable of.

**1** Because Fractal Noise generates random patterns, this will take an artistic eye on your part. Fiddle with properties (such as Evolution, Offset Turbulence, Scale Width or Scale Height) until you see a candle flame shape at the bottom of the comp. In this image, there's a flame on the right side that I'm liking.

**4** Select your layer and press the **F** key on your keyboard. This will show the Mask Feather property. Increase this property just a little to soften the edges of the mask we just created. I went with a value of 15, but I'm wondering if even that isn't too much feathering here.

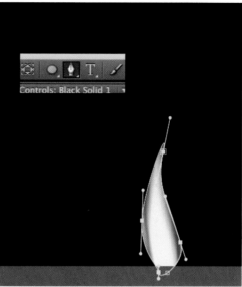

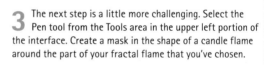

**HOT TIP**

Wondering why we precomposed this layer? If we didn't precompose before feathering the mask, the Colorama effect would have made all of our semi-transparent feathered edges completely opaque. And that would have looked terrible.

**2** Precompose this layer by selecting it in the Timeline panel and choosing Pre-compose from the Layer menu at the top of the interface. You can also use the keyboard shortcut ⌘ Shift C ctrl Shift C. Choose the option Move all attributes into the new composition. I'll explain why precomposing this layer is important in the tip on the side.

**3** The next step is a little more challenging. Select the Pen tool from the Tools area in the upper left portion of the interface. Create a mask in the shape of a candle flame around the part of your fractal flame that you've chosen.

**5** In the previous figure, you may have noticed that my flame isn't perfect. With this flame, the hotspot should be in the center of the candle where it is burning brightest and the colors SHOULD get darker as they go away from the center. But on the left side of my flame, they get brighter alongside the edge. So double click the precomp to go back to Fractal Noise and reduce the Brightness value. I'm also going to adjust my mask. And while I'm at it, I think I'll just take that Mask Feather down to a more realistic value of 8. Ahhh.... now that's a more believable candle flame!

# Creative Playing

I'VE DECIDED THAT I WANT TO TAKE A LITTLE BREAK from the whole "cheat" thing. What I want to do here is to just play around. Sometimes as After Effects users, we lose sight of the big picture – that After Effects is just the most fun application on the planet, and it's a beautiful thing to just create and explore. Creative playing is also just a great way to become more familiar with the application and problem solving in it. However, it can be a little intimidating to just venture off the beaten path and just play around in After Effects, especially if you're new to the program.

So I wanted to just start from scratch and experiment with you watching. I have no idea where we'll end up, but I'm just going to play around the way I do when I'm goofing off when no one is looking and I don't have any hardcore deadlines. I'm hoping that you'll benefit from the process, and even more, I'm really hoping that what we make here isn't total crap because that would be embarrassing. But oh well. There is joy in the journey, right?

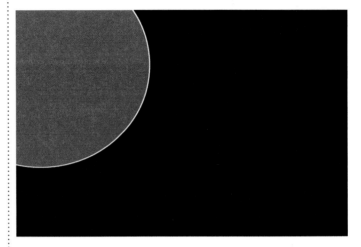

**1** Well, first things first. We have to start with a new comp. Let's just start with a standard NTSC DV preset comp. And I think instead of starting with a solid, I'm going to start with one of my favorite AE features: a shape layer. So, I'm going to select the Ellipse tool in the Tools panel, and I'm going to just click and drag to create a circle in the Composition panel. I'm going to hold **Shift** while I'm creating it to make it a perfect circle. I'm not really feeling it in the center though. I think I'll put it in the upper left corner, which you can do by just clicking and dragging once the shape has been created.

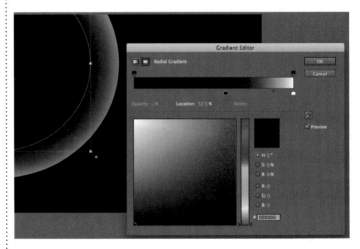

**3** I'm going to increase the stroke thickness by clicking on the number to the right of the word "Stroke" at the top of the interface. I think I want a thick stroke, so I'm going to try a value of 130. Similar to what we did with the fill, click on the word stroke in the Tools area, but this time change the stroke to a radial gradient (the option on the far right). I think I want the gradient stroke to be black on the inside, and then gradually fade to white on the outer edge. Here are the settings for the gradient that I went with and the result. As you can see, I made the left side black and the right side white, and then scooted the black swatch to the right so that the black center would be larger. Cool.

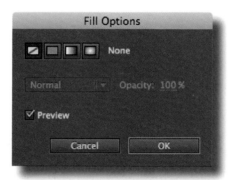

2 The first adjustment I want to make to this is to adjust the default red fill and white stroke. They're not working for me. I actually don't think I want a fill here. So, I'm going to click the word "Fill" in the Tools area at the top of the interface with the shape layer selected, and then click the None button on the left.

4 Now let's add a gradient background. Press ⌘ Y ctrl Y to create a new solid of any color. Drag it below the shape layer in the layer stack in the Timeline panel. Right click on the new background solid and choose Layer Styles>Gradient Overlay. I'm really thinking that I want a warm color scheme. So, I'm going to open up the layer properties for this solid layer, and then Layer Styles>Gradient Overlay. For the Colors property, click on Edit Gradient. Click on the first gradient color stop and select an orange color, and change the gradient stop on the right to a deep red.

continued...

**HOT TIP**

OK, this looks terrible so far. This sounds more like advice in a self-help book than a software book, but you've got to have enough faith in yourself to allow yourself to play around! Many extremely talented artists are working the night shift at the local fast food restaurant because they are paralyzed by a fear of failure. Instead of getting discouraged about how bad something looks, ask yourself what could be done to improve it, even just a little. You'll be amazed at how asking such questions will often yield powerful answers and solutions, whereas self-doubt rarely does.

SHORTCUTS
MAC WIN BOTH

303

# Creative Playing (continued)

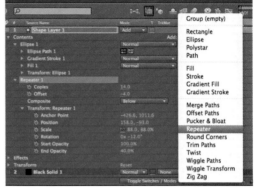

**5** Dang it all to heck! I did that backwards – I wanted orange on top and red on bottom. Stupid confusing layer styles gradient editor! Oh well. Just find the Reverse option in the Gradient Overlay area and click Off to change it to On. Now, we need to blend the shape layer into this background better. I'll use a blend mode for that. In the blend mode drop down for the shape layer, change the blend mode from Normal to... um... let's try Add.

**6** Next, let's add more shapes. The most powerful way to do that is by adding a Repeater operation to the existing shape layer. Open the shape layer's properties in the Timeline panel and on the right you'll see a tiny circle with an arrow in it that will allow you to add all kinds of adjustments to your shape layer. Go ahead and choose Repeater. This will add a whole new area (Transform:Repeater 1) and will allow you to make and transform multiple copies of your object.

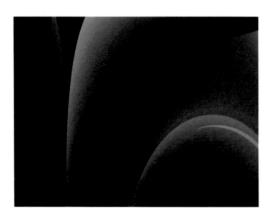

**9** Now I think I might try to see what this shape would look like if I changed the blend mode from Add to Soft Light. Pretty sweet. But it's a little dark. What if we now duplicated the layer? After putting this layer into the Soft Light blend mode, duplicate the layer by pressing ⌘ D ctrl D.

**10** I like this, but it's a little too dark still. I think I'm going to create a new adjustment layer by pressing ⌘ ⌥ Y ctrl alt Y. Make sure that this adjustment layer is the topmost layer in the layer stack in the Timeline panel. I think I'm going to brighten this with two of my "go-to" brighteners – the Levels effect and the Glow effect. Here are the settings I used.

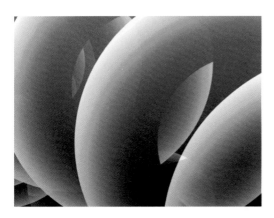

**7** In the Repeater 1 area, I increased the Copies value to 14, then just started playing around until I found a design that I liked. As the author of this book, I would love to say that I knew ahead of time exactly what settings to use, but in reality, I just kept goofing around until it looked cool. I adjusted Anchor Point, Position, Scale, and Rotation in the Transform:Repeater 1 area, which allowed me to control the look and behavior of the repeated copies.

**8** I like the way this looks. But I want to try something else. There's just so much there to play with. So, I'm going to try a distort effect to kind of change the proverbial scenery. Let's apply the Polar Coordinates effect. In the Effect Controls panel, I'm going to adjust the Interpolation value to about 36% or so. You may want to use a very different value or just skip this step altogether. But I actually like the shape I'm getting now.

**HOT TIP**

If you'd like to see my projects from this section, I've created a folder of the steps here called Creative Playing in Chapter 10 of the Exercise Files.

**11** So here's the final result. I kinda like it! Pretty impressive, coming from a single, unattractive circle!

**12** You might be wondering now, well how exactly does this thing animate? You could try several things. Try doing a slow animation of the Interpolation property of the Polar Coordinates effect on the duplicate of the shape layer. You'll also get really cool results by playing with the Offset property in the Repeater 1 area of the main shape layer. The possibilities are endless. Just keep playing!

**SHORTCUTS**

# 10

# Hot Grill

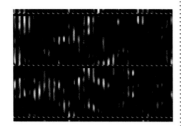

L AST IN OUR SERIES of fire-like backgrounds, we're going to look at how to create a hot grill. What is this hot grill cooking? You decide what goes on it! Possibly some text? Perhaps it's cooking up your logo? This trick is even cooler when brought to life with the Evolution parameter. Because hot coals are not directional like the campfire-style fire we created previously, the oscillation created by Evolution creates a very organic hot coal animation.

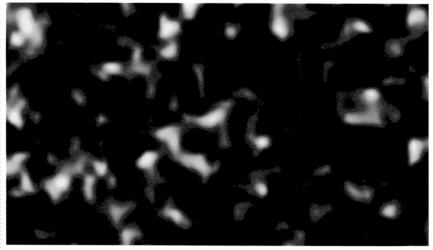

1 Create a new comp using the HDV/HDTV 720 29.97 preset. Then create a new solid of the same size and, using the Fractal Noise and Colorama effects, create some fire as we did at the beginning of this chapter. Except this time, don't mess with the scaling, and take complexity down to 2. That will give us a nice blurry look to the coals. I'm going to name this layer Fire.

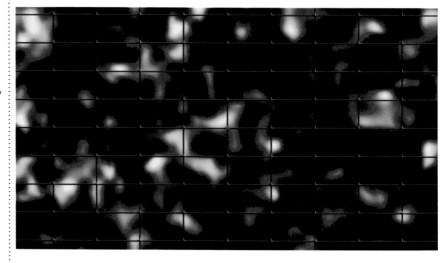

3 Apply the frequently-ignored Grid effect to the Grill layer. Our first order of business is to hop on over to the Effect Controls panel and change the Color value in the Grid effect from white to black.

2 Create another new solid, but this time change the size. Leave the Width value at 1280, but increase the Height value to 800 pixels. I'll explain why a little later on. I'm going to name this layer Grill.

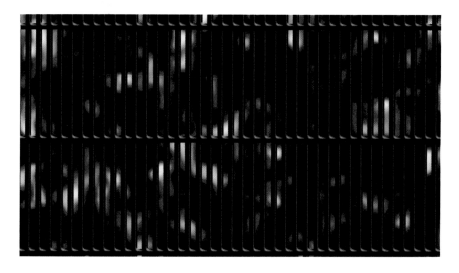

4 This "grid" looks less like a grill and more like a tennis net. Next time we have a doubles match with our BBQ, we'll be sure and remember these settings. For now, we want a grill! So, in the Grid effect, increase the Border value to about 20, increase the Y value of the Corner value to about 700 or so, and increase the X value of the Anchor property somewhere between 700 and 740. And we're done! I really like the lowered Complexity value on the fractal fire because it gives the illusion of blur created by a shallow depth of field, which adds more believability. To bring this to life in a very realistic way, just animate the Evolution property in the Fractal Noise effect on the Fire layer.

# It's Curtains For You!

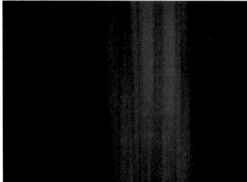

C REATING A PROMO FOR AN INDEPENDENT FILM or play? Want to create a video to reveal a new product line? Aspiring to reach the top of the cutthroat drapery industry? Then you may one day want to create curtains from scratch in After Effects!

1 Create a new comp. Use the HDV/HDTV 720 29.97 preset. Create a new solid with matching size. Apply the Fractal Noise effect to this solid. When creating curtains, there are a variety of ways to achieve the effect. The way I use is just one of the many ways, so feel free to improvise and use your own settings. I'm going to use Dynamic for the Fractal Type. Open up the Transform area, uncheck Uniform Scaling and increase the Scale Height value a bunch, to about 3000.

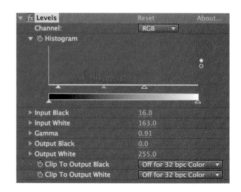

4 This next step is optional, but I'm going to apply the Levels effect to give these curtains more punch. By dragging the right slider to the left, the highlights are brightened. By dragging the left slider to the right, the shadows are darkened. For more info on color correction, check out Chapter 9. If you feel like following along, here are my Levels settings.

**2** The previous figure is looking very curtain-ish. But there is too much texture. Take the Complexity value down to 5.5. There's still too much going on here texture-wise, but if I lower the Complexity value any more, the curtains will appear blurry. The solution? Change the Noise Type at the top from Soft Linear to Spline. This is a more advanced calculation of the noise used to create this fractal noise. It takes a little longer to process, but in this case it makes our curtains look much more realistic.

**3** I think that's all that we need to do with the Fractal Noise effect here. I think they need more contrast, but I'm going to add that with the Levels effect. First, let's add some color by applying the Tint effect to our curtains. In the Tint effect controls, click the Map White To color swatch and change the white color to a deep red.

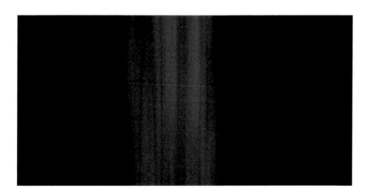

**5** The final touch here is to add an After Effects light. First, make the layer with the curtains a 3D layer by clicking the box in the 3D Layer column in the Switches area of the Timeline. Then create a new light by going to the Layer menu at the top of the interface and choosing New>Light. From the Light Type drop down in the Light Settings dialog box, choose Spot. All other properties can stay at their defaults. The spot light not only adds more focus and interest, but the falloff of the light on the sides of the image really heightens the realism.

**HOT TIP**

If you wanted to animate the curtains opening, you could create two smaller comps, each with their own fractal curtains. Then combine them in a larger comp and have them opening using Position. For added realism, use an effect from the Distort category of effects or the Puppet tool to bend the curtains in realistic and organic ways.

# Background Bars

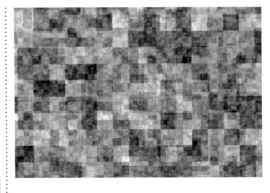

1 Create a new comp using the HDV/HDTV 720 29.97 preset. Create a new solid with matching settings. Apply the Fractal Noise effect. The key to achieving this effect is to change the Noise Type from Soft Linear to Block.

FREQUENTLY IN THE WORLD OF BROADCAST, we see this background of animated fractal bars. For example, this type of background was seen in the intro to *The Bernie Mac Show* on Fox.

This trick appears really complicated, as if someone has animated a series of bars by hand. In reality, this is an extremely simple and quick trick, made so by the ever powerful Fractal Noise effect.

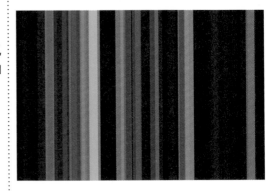

4 The final step is to colorize these bars. For that, we're going to apply the Tritone effect. That effect allows us to recolor our layer using three colors: one for highlights, midtones, and shadows. I'm going to use a light blue for the highlights, a slightly dark red for the midtones, and a very dark blue for the shadows. Then all you need to bring this to life is to animate the Evolution property and those bars will shuffle around horizontally in a very organic way.

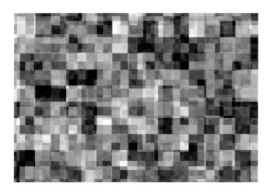

**2** There's too much going on here. Lower the Complexity value to 2.5.

**3** Can you guess how we make these squares into bars? That's right! We open up the Transform area, uncheck Uniform Scaling, and increase the Scale Height value all the way up to about 9000. If you see wacky horizontal lines, you may need to adjust the Y axis of the Offset Turbulence property. A value of −640 worked for me. And there's our bars!

**5** If you wanted to get creative, you could also use these bars as textures in other instances. Here, we see the fractal bars as the background texture and as the texture using the text as an alpha matte. This example is kinda lame, honestly, but you can see that with a little more effort it could yield a pretty cute result.

# Basic Water

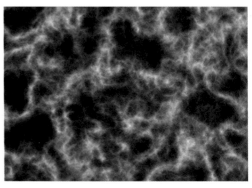

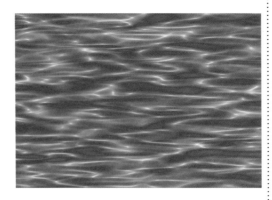

**SUPPOSE IT WOULDN'T BE FAIR TO THE ELEMENTALS** if we were to cover the making of fire and skip over water. So here it is. As before, we'll be using the versatile Fractal Noise effect to make our water.

Be forewarned that making water is a little more challenging. If you ever watch large amounts of water, like in a pool, you'll notice little "whips" of light. These are called caustics. Thankfully, Fractal Noise has an option called Wrap Back which makes it much easier to create these caustics. We'll also delve a little deeper into the powerful colorization tools in Colorama. In the next cheat, we'll keep the party going by making this water look even more realistic.

**1** Create a new comp using the HDV/HDTV 720 29.97 preset. Create a new solid layer of the same size and apply the Fractal Noise effect to it. Change the Fractal Type to Smeary, the Noise Type to Spline, and check the Invert checkbox (right below Noise Type). It's not much to look at yet, although this texture could be used as the basis of an electric texture.

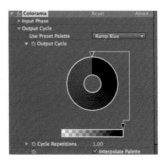

**4** Apply the Colorama effect, which essentially converts all colors in an image to shades of gray and then allows you to recolor it using a gradient. Yes, it's complex. But it gives you more power to recolor a layer than anything else, even in Photoshop! Open the Output Cycle area in the Colorama effect controls. That color wheel indicates the colors that will be used to remap the colors in your artwork. As a jumping off point, change the Use Preset Palette value right above the color wheel to Ramp Blue. This wheel contains two triangles, one blue, one black. The highlights are mapped to blue (at the top), then the values at the bottom of the circle are mapped to gray, and the black color stop (also at the top) is mapped to black.

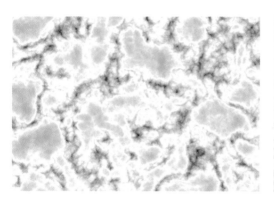

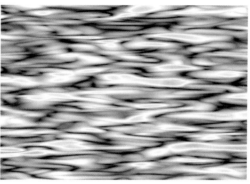

**2** In other cheats, we've played around with Contrast and Brightness. They behave as expected. But we're going to turn that world upside down. In the Overflow drop down, change the setting from Allow HDR Results to Wrap Back. This will make it so that when we brighten white areas or darken white areas, they begin to "wrap back" in the other direction. This creates really psychedelic effects, but it can also be used to create caustics when making water. With Wrap Back selected for the Overflow property, change the Contrast value to 137, and the Brightness value to 62, and prepare to have your mind blown.

**3** To make this come a little closer to the appearance of water (and to help this render faster), take the Complexity value down to 1.9. Then open the Transform area in the Fractal Noise effect controls. Uncheck Uniform Scaling, and take Scale Width to 170 and Scale Height to 25.

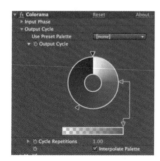

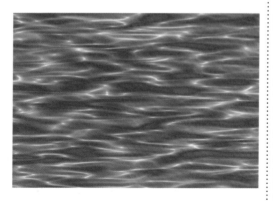

**5** Double click on the blue color stop at the top of the color wheel and your system's color picker will pop up (Mac or Windows). The color pickers on both systems feel kind of archaic, but they both do the job. For this color stop, use the RGB values of 0, 50, 100, respectively. Then click right outside the wheel at about the 7 o'clock position to create a new color stop, and use the RGB values 25, 70, and 150. Click at about the 3 o'clock position and create a color stop with the values 25, 100, 200. Finally, click the black color stop that is hiding behind the first blue stop, and change that stop's value to pure white (0, 0, 0).

**6** If desired, apply the Hue/Saturation effect and tweak the Master Hue value a little bit to add more of a green tint. Here I used a value of –20. Nice water!

**HOT TIP**

If, while fiddling around with the color stops on the Output Cycle color wheel in the Colorama effect controls, your top most colors get moved a little bit, hold down the *Shift* key while moving them back into position. That will force them to snap back to the position that they should be in.

**SHORTCUTS**
MAC WIN BOTH

# Better Water

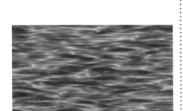

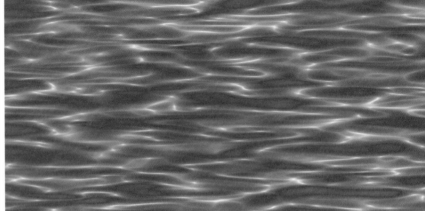

WE'RE GOING TO BE CONTINUING HERE WHERE WE LEFT OFF in the last cheat, where we learned how to make basic water.

In real life, water is just a complex thing. Aside from the caustics discussed in the last cheat, there are multiple colors and reflections that add complexity to its appearance. To create more beauty in our water, we're going to duplicate the layer we've made and make a few more adjustments.

1 You may either continue where we left off in the last cheat, or you can open the Advanced Water. aep project from the Chapter 10 folder in the Exercise Files folder, and start with the Advanced Water START comp.

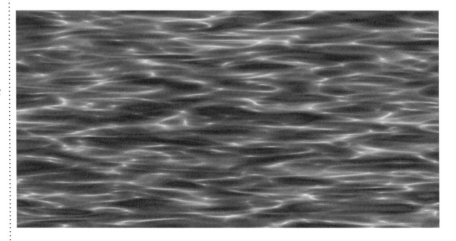

3 In the Fractal Noise effect on the duplicated (top) layer, open up the Evolution Options area and adjust the Random Seed value until you're happy with the results. Essentially, the Random Seed value takes all of your settings and gives you a random version of them. This makes it so that our duplicates are not exactly the same, which adds a lot of complexity to our water.

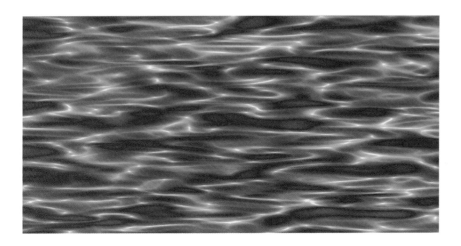

2 First, just duplicate the Basic Water layer by selecting it and pressing ⌘ D ctrl D. Then put the duplicated layer (the one on top) in the Soft Light blend mode. This adds more contrast, but not much else. We'll fix that in the next step.

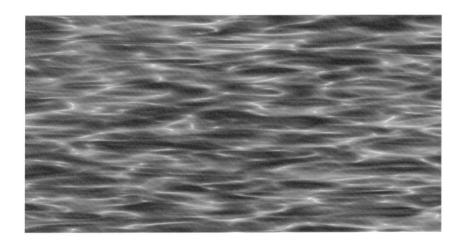

4 This last step is an optional one. I like the way it looks when the colors of the original and the copy are slightly different. So, I'm going to go to the Hue/Saturation effect controls on the duplicate layer and further reduce the Master Hue value to add more green. A value of about −40 looks good on my screen, but you can use whatever looks best for you.

SHORTCUTS
MAC WIN BOTH

# TV Noise

O NE OF THE THINGS THAT YOU MAY BE CALLED UPON TO DO on occasion is to create TV noise – the static that is on a TV set when it can't find the channel. Although this phenomenon isn't really all that common anymore with the phasing out of rabbit ear antennas and analog TV signals, it is one of those cultural things that still has significant value. Like 8 bit video games, LP records, and old black and white movies, analog TV static has retro appeal. It also has symbolic significance and is used to suggest a communication disconnect. This effect is also often used in connection with horror movies to add grungy texture to broadcast messages.

1 Open the TV Noise.aep project from the Chapter 10 folder of the exercise files, and go to the TV Noise START composition.

3 Now, if the previous step got your noise the way you like it, feel free to skip this step. But I think that this noise needs a little bit of random color. To get that random noise, I'm going to apply (what else?) the Noise effect. After Effects has 6 effects with the word "noise" in it, so make sure that you apply the one that is simply called Noise. Leaving the other settings the same, take the Amount of Noise value in the Noise effect controls to about 80% or so. The difference is subtle, but I like it much better than having just plain black and white noise.

**2** Apply the Fractal Noise effect to the Noise layer. In the Fractal Noise effect controls, take the Complexity down to 3.0. In the Transform area of the Fractal Noise effect controls, take the Scale value down to 3.0 as well.

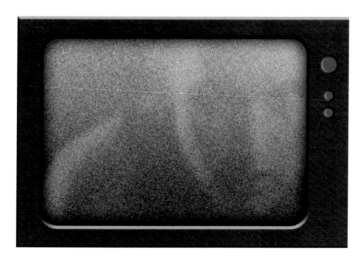

**4** At this point, you could also add a video layer. I've brought in a clip from uberstock.com into the TV Noise DONE comp. I'm going to put the video clip directly on top of the Noise layer in the layer stack in the Timeline panel. I'm going to put the video in the Soft Light blend mode, and reduce its Opacity value to about 50%. It still looks a little too clean and crisp to me. I'm not buying that this is a noisy image. So I'm going to apply the Fast Blur effect, and take its Blurriness value to about 40.

**HOT TIP**

This noise looks OK, but what about animating it? Typically, we bring Fractal Noise to life with the Evolution parameter, but that creates smooth animation over time. Instead, open up the Evolution Options area in the Fractal Noise effect controls, and animate the Random Seed value. Every time the Random Seed value changes, it gives you a completely different image, which creates more believable noise. To animate the Noise effect, simply animate the Amount of Noise value over time (e.g. from 80% to 90%). Like Random Seed, any adjustment in this property will create an entirely new noise pattern.

# Ornate Vintage Patterns

**1** Open the Ornate Vintage.aep project from the Chapter 10 folder of the exercise files. In this project, open the Ornate Vintage START composition. I've already created a blank background for you. This layer is just a simple solid with a radial Gradient Overlay layer style applied to it.

O NE DAY, WHILE PREPARING SOME VIDEO TRAINING TUTORIALS, I just happened to play around with some of the Cycore effects that ship with After Effects (the Cycore effects are the ones with the "CC" prefix). One of the Cycore effects that I played with was CC Kaleida, which can be used to instantly create extremely rich and ornate patterns. What's even better is that with a slight tweaking of a single parameter, that ornate pattern can look completely different. When you're looking for a great Victorian or steampunk texture, or even if you're just looking for a little more complexity in a background, this is a great effect to be aware of.

**4** Before we go any further, let's make this look a lot better by changing the blend mode of the new solid layer we've created from Normal to Overlay. This will remove the gray base and create transparency there so that the green gradient shows through underneath.

**2** Create a new solid layer the same size as the comp and make sure it is on top of the Background layer in the layer stack in the Timeline panel. To this solid layer, apply Fractal Noise. The reason why we're doing this before applying the CC Kaleida effect is because CC Kaleida needs something to turn into a pattern. And certainly, there is not a better pattern generator than Fractal Noise. After applying Fractal Noise to this new solid layer, then apply the CC Kaleida effect.

**3** Right away, we have a beautiful texture, but we can make this better. In the CC Kaleida effect controls, reduce the Size value to about 7, or whatever looks good to you.

**5** If the texture is too intense for you at this point, you can reduce the contrast in the Fractal Noise controls. Remember that the pattern that we're seeing here is being generated by Fractal Noise and distorted by CC Kaleida. So any changes you make to the Fractal Noise effect will noticeably affect the appearance of the final image. Here, I left the CC Kaleida settings exactly the same, and just increased the Fractal Noise Contrast value to 200 and changed the Fractal Type to Threads. And look at how different the pattern became! This effect really is infinite in its possibilities!

# Cells Through a Microscope

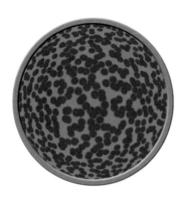

**B**EING ABLE TO CREATE CELLS in a petri dish, or as if looking through a microscope, or as a solid background is one of those things that you may not use all the time, but it does come up on occasion. After Effects has a built in effect called Cell Pattern that does the bulk of the work for you.

Not only does this effect look pretty good in these screen shots, but it animates in an extremely organic way. Further, if you're familiar with Fractal Noise, Cell Pattern will be a piece of cake. One of the most powerful features of Fractal Noise is that it allows you to play with multiple layers of noise. Cell Pattern has only one, so it's much easier to master.

**1** Open the Cells.aep project in the Chapter 10 folder of the Exercise Files folder, and go to the Cells START comp. I've set this up a little bit for you here. I've created a gray ring indicating the microscope, and I've also created an adjustment layer with the bulge effect applied so that the center of what we're seeing in the "microscope" looks distorted as when you look through a cheap microscope with lens distortion.

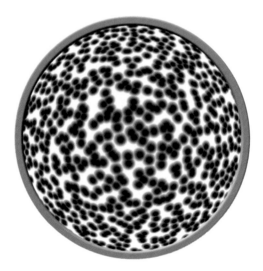

**3** In the Cell Pattern effect controls, increase Contrast to about 300, increase Disperse to its maximum value (1.50), and take Size to about 20 or so.

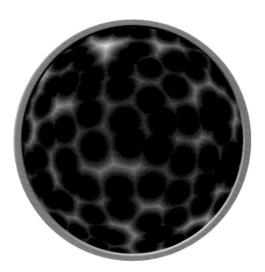

2 Select the Cells layer and apply the Cell Pattern effect. Like Fractal Noise, Cell Pattern is a grayscale pattern generator. As you can see the default settings of Cell Pattern already look fairly cell-like. For the first adjustment, simply click the Invert checkbox to invert this pattern. It creates a really cool X-ray type of look.

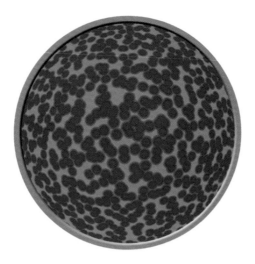

4 Now we need to colorize this. Apply the Colorama effect. In the Colorama effect controls, open up the Output Cycle area. In the Use Preset Palette drop down, choose the Moldy preset, which seems quite appropriate.

# Retro Video Game Maze

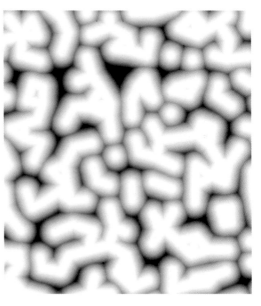

**1** For this cheat, we're going to just start from scratch. Create a new composition that is 800 x 800. Create a new solid to match that size, and apply the Cell Pattern effect to it. Change the Cell Pattern value in the Effect Controls panel from Bubbles to Tubular.

**W**ITH A SMALL AMOUNT OF FIDDLING, you can take the cells of the Cell Pattern effect and turn them into all kinds of things that make great backgrounds. In this cheat, we're going to turn the Cell Pattern cells into the walls of a maze, like the kind you might find in an 8 bit video game with a certain yellow chomper and some ghosts.

**4** Finally, we need to colorize this. Apply the Tritone effect. For the Highlights color value, I used a light blue color. For the Midtones value, I used a medium blue, and I left the Shadows black.

**2** This looks too blobby. Increase the Contrast value to about 1000.

**3** Make these tubes more orderly by reducing the Disperse value. This is a tough one. I used a value of 0.08, but there's wiggle room here depending on what you want. If you take the value lower, you'll start getting less "walls" and more dots. If you take the value higher, you're going to start to notice warping as the tubes begin to disperse.

**5** If you wanted to give it more of a video game look, you could apply the Glow effect. Here, I used a Glow Threshold of 60%, a Glow Radius of 25, and a Glow Intensity of 1.5.

**HOT TIP**

Although I didn't mess with the Size property, feel free to explore the difference that this parameter makes to your maze. Essentially, it is like a zoom control in this instance.

# Quick Variations

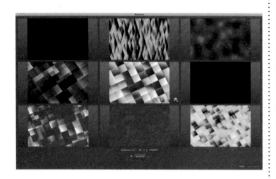

M ANY TIMES, WHEN I'M CREATING BACKGROUNDS for something, I'm not exactly sure what I'm looking for. I'm just kind of experimenting until I find something that I like. But there are so many options! Going back and forth between different choices in texture and color takes so long, and it also really interrupts the creative process.

To remedy this, the After Effects developers came up with something that I think is incredibly brilliant and useful to all users of the program. It is called Brainstorm. It allows you to select a single property, or multiple properties, or an entire effect, or even multiple effects, and just randomize the values to show you a multitude of different options at a glance. This works with shape layers, effects, animation, and all over After Effects in places where it's easy to get stuck because of all the options available to you. Later in this chapter, I'll show you how to use Brainstorm in conjunction with Animation Presets to quickly create an entire library of your own custom backgrounds.

1 Open the Brainstorm.aep project from the Chapter 10 folder of the exercise files. Open Comp 1. In this comp, I've created a solid layer and I've applied Turbulent Noise (which is almost identical to Fractal Noise) and the Tritone effect at their default settings.

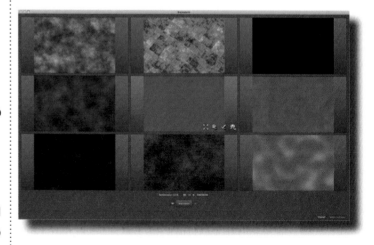

3 Initially, Brainstorm usually isn't all that impressive. That's because the default value for the Randomness parameter in Brainstorm is a very conservative 25%. This means that Brainstorm can only have about 25% wiggle room. Let's go crazy. Give her all she's got, captain. Take Randomness all the way up to 100%. Then press the big button that says Brainstorm on it to get 9 more variations of these two effects.

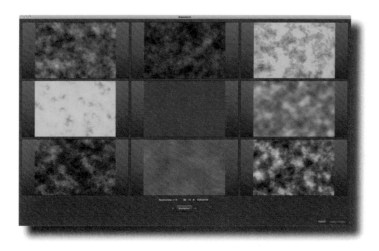

**2** In the Effect Controls panel, click on the Turbulent Noise effect and, while holding the **Shift** key, click on the Tritone effect. This selects both effects, and allows Brainstorm to randomize all properties of both. Making sure both effects are selected, press the Brainstorm button in the Timeline panel (the button looks like a little light bulb in a thought bubble).

**4** Each time you press the Brainstorm button, After Effects will give you 9 more variations. It also saves each variation temporarily. Like a web browser, you can press the left facing arrow on the left side of the Brainstorm button to go back to previous brainstorms, or the right arrow to go to the next ones you've made. Keep clicking the Brainstorm button until you find a pattern you like. I kinda like the rusty red texture at the top. I'm going to hover my mouse over that square. Four buttons will appear. The leftmost button shows a dot with four arrows pointing away from its center. Click this to maximize the tile that you like.

continued...

SHORTCUTS
MAC WIN BOTH

# Quick Variations (continued)

**5** Like the person across the crowded room at the party, on closer inspection this tile isn't as attractive as I thought it was. But I'm getting closer. I'm going to put my cursor over the tile to get the four Brainstorm buttons again. Now the leftmost button will restore the tile size. Now what I'm going to do is put my cursor over that same tile again, but this time, I'm going to choose the rightmost option, which looks like the Brainstorm icon. Click that button to tell After Effects that it's on the right track. This tile will be included in the next brainstorm, and After Effects will also try to make the other tiles match this one more closely. So, before hitting the Brainstorm button again, take down the Randomness value to about 50%.

**7** If you create animation with the objects that you're mixing up in Brainstorm (say, in this situation, with the Evolution property) before entering Brainstorm, you can preview your existing animation with the brainstormed tiles by pressing the play icon in Brainstorm! They thought of everything!

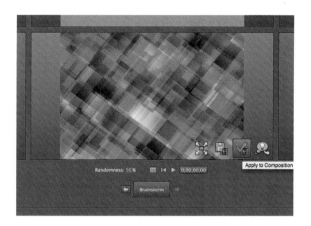

6   Now that After Effects is in the ballpark, it didn't take many more Brainstorms before I found the
    pattern that I liked. So I'm going to use the bottom center image from the previous figure. Hovering
my cursor over this tile, I'm going to choose the checkmark with the composition icon on it. This will
apply these settings to the effects in my project. It's just that easy!

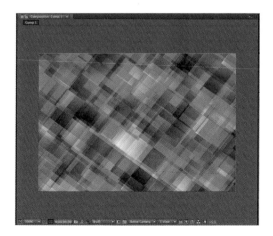

8   Now I'm back in my comp, and I can see the pattern Brainstorm helped me to create. Never
    before has there been a way in After Effects to preview so many options so quickly and with such
little effort. This is just an ingenious feature. I should also point out that it's a great way to learn the
application as well. As Brainstorm creates textures, you can apply them, and then look at the settings to
see how you can create a similar effect on your own.

# Animation Presets

THIS CHEAT IS GOING TO BE MORE LIKE VEGETABLES for many of you. But just like many veggies, if you try it, you'll like it, and they're good for you! Most After Effects users want to just get in the program and go fast. We don't want to worry about things like making complex expressions, naming layers, or using animation presets. But all of these things are used by the pros because they save time in the long run.

Animation presets allow you to save the settings of an effect, or even multiple effects, and this includes not only keyframes, but expressions as well! Imagine if you had a massive library of backgrounds and animations that you had created, that you could apply at the touch of a button. Imagine how you could charge clients a fortune for a tiny amount of work because of the library of presets you've created. It's all possible with animation presets. In this cheat we will apply one and create one. Later in this chapter, I'll show you how to use Brainstorm to create an arsenal of preset backgrounds that you can use whenever you want.

I've also included a folder of animation presets in the Exercise Files folder for you to play around with. Though you may not redistribute or sell them, feel free to use them in your projects however you'd like.

1 First, let's apply an existing animation preset. Make a new comp using the NTSC DV preset, and make a solid of the same size. MAKE SURE that your current time indicator is at the beginning of your timeline. This is very important. The animation stored in animation presets will be applied wherever the current time indicator is. If your current time is 5 seconds when you apply the animation preset, then there won't be animation for the first 5 seconds. With the solid layer selected in the Timeline panel, go to the Animation menu at the top of the interface. Choose Animation>Apply Animation Preset. Navigate to Exercise Files>Media>Animation Presets. Choose the EXPLOSION OF FURY!.ffx preset.

3 Now let's create an animation preset from scratch. Choose File>Open and navigate to the Maze.aep project in the Chapter 10 folder that we created earlier in this chapter. In the Maze DONE comp, select the Black Solid 1 layer, and notice the effects we've applied to this: Cell Pattern, Tritone, and Glow. With the Effect Controls panel selected (you can tell if it's selected if it has an orange highlight around it), press ⌘ A ctrl A to select all of the effects.

**2** With that last step, you've instantly created a churning aerial explosion, created by Fractal Noise and Colorama. It also uses expressions. You've created it instantly without any effort. Here are the parameters changed from their default values. It would take a while to input all of this information, even if you knew exactly what you were doing, even longer if you were just fiddling around. Think of all the time saved by animation presets!

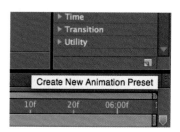

**4** With all of these effects selected, create a new animation preset by clicking the Create New Animation Preset button at the bottom of the Effects and Presets panel (not the Effect Controls panel). Alternatively, you could also choose Save Animation Preset from the Animation menu at the top of the interface. Navigate to a place on your hard drive to save the new FFX file, and you've created an animation preset that you can use again in an instant! I recommend giving it a distinct name so you can find it easily later on.

**HOT TIP**

After Effects might warn you about this, but if you save your animation preset in the Presets folder inside of the After Effects application folder, then your preset will show up in the Effects and Presets panel when doing searches. If you save your preset outside of this folder, you'll have to navigate to it manually when you want to use it.

**SHORTCUTS**
MAC WIN BOTH

# Presets and Adobe Bridge

L IKE ANIMATION PRESETS, THE USE OF ADOBE BRIDGE is one of those things that many people avoid, but can really come in handy. Adobe Bridge is a file browsing application that comes with After Effects for free. It really is a tremendous file browser, allowing you to preview most movie and audio files, and file types that you typically can't browse in large batches including Photoshop (PSD) and Illustrator (AI) files. For After Effects users (especially motion graphics designers), that feature alone is worth using Bridge.

However, it gets even better than that. You can also import files into After Effects straight from Adobe Bridge. This applies to animation presets as well. Presets that ship with After Effects (including the very valuable text presets) have a visual representation, but all presets can be applied from Bridge.

**1** We're going to launch Bridge from After Effects, so please close it if you've launched it from another application. Bridge intelligently remembers which application it was launched from. If you double click an image in Bridge, it will open in Photoshop if you opened Bridge from Photoshop, but will import into After Effects if you launched Bridge from After Effects. You can launch Bridge from After Effects by going to File>Browse in Bridge. But there's a better way. In the flyout menu of the Effects and Presets panel, choose Browse Presets.

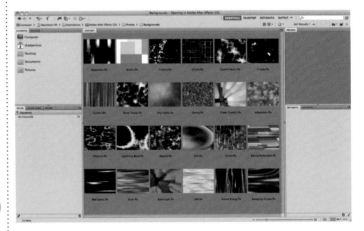

**3** Double click the Backgrounds folder to open it and browse all of the cool background presets that After Effects ships with.

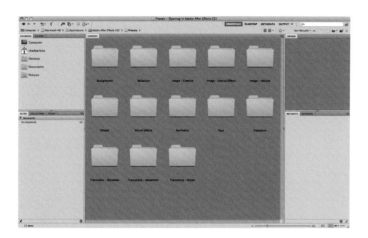

2 Opening Bridge by using this command will take you straight to the Presets
folder in the After Effects application folder.

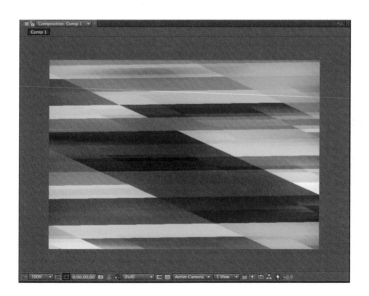

4 Go back to After Effects and create a new comp using the NTSC DV preset
and a new solid of the same size. Make sure that the layer (not the comp)
is selected in the Timeline panel. Then go back to Bridge, and double click the
Racing Rectangles.ffx preset. It will instantly apply the animation preset to your
solid in After Effects! Bridge is a very efficient way to browse large amounts of
assets and presets, and bring them into your projects as well.

# Library of Custom Textures

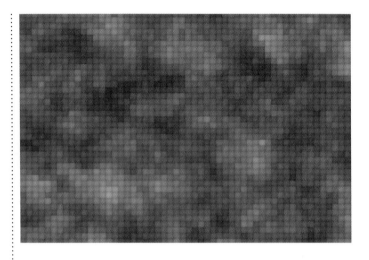

E ARLIER IN THIS CHAPTER, we learned how to use Brainstorm and create animation presets. In this quick cheat, we're going to look at another feature of Brainstorm that you can use to create your own library of custom background textures. This trick will also work for creating animation presets of any type.

1 Open the Custom Library.aep project from the Chapter 10 folder of the exercise files. Comp 1 contains a simple solid with the Turbulent Noise, Tritone, and CC Ball Action effects applied to it. As we'll soon see, the CC Ball Action effect is capable of yielding some really cool results.

3 This is a tremendously easy way to create an entire repository of cool effects. After you've closed Brainstorm, you can go back to your Project panel, and open up your new collection of comps. Open them up and save those new creations as your own animation presets.

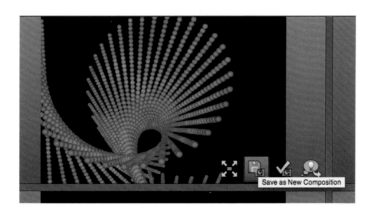

**2** Select the Effect Controls panel and press ⌘ A / ctrl A to select all of the effects applied to this layer. Then press the Brainstorm button in the Timeline panel to open up Brainstorm. Increase the Randomness value to taste and click the Brainstorm button until you find a variation that you like. Hover your cursor over the desired tile to see the pop up of the four buttons we saw earlier in this chapter. The checkmark button that we used previously applies the current brainstorm to your currently selected layer. But if you select the Save as Composition button, After Effects will perform the extremely kind gesture of creating a new composition for you in your Project panel with a new solid with the same settings and effects as your current setup.

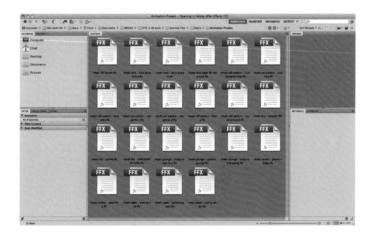

**4** In just a few minutes, you'll have a huge library of your own that you can draw from in a future pinch.

# Generic Background Texture Recipe: Generate, Distort, Stylize

AS A FINAL TIP IN THIS CHAPTER, I WANTED TO SHARE WITH YOU A RECIPE that has gotten me out of a few creative jams. The formula is to take any of the effects in the Generate category (which typically make stuff from scratch), tweak it with one of the effects in the Distort category, and then polish it up with one of the effects in the Stylize category. It sounds crazy, but it really works.

To demonstrate this, I'm going to pick a random effect from each category and hope for the best. From the Generate category, I picked 4-Color Gradient, which basically makes a gradient with four colors. So, I'm not off to the best start. I'm going to leave the settings at their defaults and then apply a Distort effect. Wave Warp was the effect selected from this category. I decided to adjust this one a bit. I'm going to take the Wave Type to Square and reduce the Wave Height value to about –190. Then, I'll apply the Stylize effect – Motion Tile. After reducing the Tile Height value to about 25, this is what I came up with. While it isn't the greatest texture I've ever seen, it's not too shabby considering it was totally random. I can even imagine using this background in a retro motion graphics piece.

While it might not work in every instance, I recommend giving this recipe a shot if you're ever in a creative pinch for a texture.

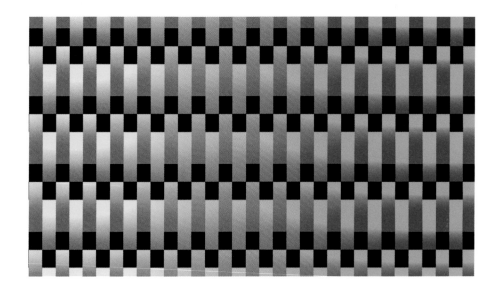

# Index

3D:
  applications, 58, 80-1, 110
  cameras, 42-3, 81
  CC (Cycore) effect, 72
  distortion, 68
  Environment application, 81
  fireworks, 232-3
  light, 46
  light streaks, 248-9
  motion blur, 110
  nested compositions, 78-9
  The Parallax effect, 50-1
  Photoshop, 55, 56-7, 76-7
  planetscape, 73-5
  postcards, 64-5
  renders, 286-7
  Repoussé feature, 52-5
  shadows, 126-7
  shatter scenes, 58-61, 61
  space, 71, 79, 127
  text, 8, 62-3
  Trapcode Stroke, 204-5
3D objects:
  applications, 80-1
  distortion, 68-71
  echospace, 76-7
  introduction, 49
  nested compositions, 78-9
  The Parallax effect, 50-1
  Photoshop, 56-7
  planetscape, 72-5
  postcards, 64-5
  Repoussé feature, 52-5
  shatter scenes, 58-61
  solids, 66-7
  text, 62-3
3DS Max application, 58, 80
4-Color Gradient effect, 170-1,
  334-5

## A

Active Camera view, 108
Add Grain effect, 283
Adobe Bridge, 330-1
After Effects projects (.aep):
  3D
    Camera Path, 42-3
    Distortion, 68-71
    Fireworks, 232-3
    Light Streaks, 248-9
    Planet, 72-5

Renders, 286-7
Text, 62-3
Animating
  the Blob, 146-7
  Masks, 200-1
Basic Shadows, 24
Basic Snow, 220-1
Before After, 266-7
Blending Away
  Dark, 96-7
  Light, 98-9
Blooming Flower, 10-11
Bouncing Ball, 140-1
Brainstorm, 324-5
Cells, 320-1
Chad Show Bumper Final, 78
Checking Dark Areas, 288-9
Cinematic
  - Flashback, 260-1
  - Horror, 258-9
  - Warmth, 256-7
Color Finesse, 280-1
  Looks, 282-3
Color LUTs, 280-1
Colorizing, 268-9
Compositing
  Animation, 106-7
  Color, 104-5
  Textures, 100-1
Compression of videos, 131
Controlling Shadows, 28-9
Custom Library, 332-3
Custom Particles, 216-17
Damaged Film, 16-17
Day for Night, 262-3
Depth of Field, 35
Distortion, 68-71
film Noir Lighting, 32-3
Fireball, 4-5
Flowing Chocolate, 244-5
Focus, 108-9
Growing Vines, 6-7
HDR, 162-3
Histograms, 254-5
Hue Shift, 270-1
Intro to Compositing, 94-5
Keying, 86-7
Laser Beams, 180-1
Lens Distortion, 39
Light
  Ribbons, 226-7, 228-9
  Whips, 168

Luma Key, 88-9
Luma Matte, 196-7
Magic Bullet Looks, 290-1
Mask Options, 188-9
Master Solid, 18-19
Matching Color, 112-13
Molten Gold, 1, 224-5
Motion Paths, 202-3
Multi Camera Render, 40-1
Multiple Mattes, 92-3
Negative Light, 30-1
Orient to Camera, 44-5
Ornate Vintage, 318-19
The Parallax Effect, 50
Parenting, 142-3, 147
Particle Deflection, 232-3
Puppet
  Overlap, 136-7
  Tool, 134-5
Rack Focus, 36-7
Reference Monitor, 264-5
Refine Matte, 90-1
Resizing Animation, 154-5
Restoring Opacity, 124-5
Searchlights, 174-5
Shatter Scenes, 58-61
Sheen, 176-7
Silhouettes, 166
Smoke Trail, 212-13
Spot CC, 278-9
Stained Glass, 27
Star Field, 239
Steam, 230-1
Stylizing, 272
Text Messaged Animation, 156-7
Tilt Shift, 12-13
Trapcode
  3D Stroke, 204-5
  Shine, 182-3
TV Noise, 316-17
Vegas, 194-5
Vignette, 190-1
Water Surface Disruption, 242-3
Waving Sail, 144-5
Windblown Snow, 222-3
Alpha channels:
  CG subway, 95
  failure, 125
  Glow effect, 179
  glow light effect, 178-9
  mask options, 188
  opacity, 124-5

premultiplied, 114-15
Track Matte, 199
video to shape layer, 193
Amazon (company), 156
Animation:
blob, 146-7
bouncing ball, 140-1
compositing, 106-7
displacement mapping, 152-3
introduction, 131
masks, 200-1
parenting, 142-3
photos, 148-9, 150-1
Photoshop, 148
puppets
duck, 138-9
overlap, 136-7
pin tool, 134-5
resizing, 154-5
text messaged, 156-7
Walt Disney, 158-9
waving sail, 144-5
Aperture adjustment, 35
Applications (3D):
3DS Max, 58, 80
Cinema 4D, 58, 80-1, 110, 176
Environment, 81
Maya, 58, 80-1
objects, 80-1

## B

Backgrounds and textures:
animation presets, 328-9
bars, 310-11
basic water, 312-13
better water, 314-15
candle flame, 300-1
cells through a microscope, 320-1
creative playing, 302-5
curtains, 308-9
fire, 296-9
generic recipe, 334-5
hot grill, 306-7
introduction, 294-5
library of textures, 332-3
ornate vintage patterns, 318-19
Presets and Adobe Bridge, 330-1
quick variations, 324-5
retro video game maze, 322-3
TV noise, 316-17
Bars, 310-11

Basic snow effect, 220-1
Basic water, 312-13
Bernie Mac Show, 310
Better water, 314-15
Bit depth, 184
Bit Point Float Color, 162
Black and White effect, 268
Blend modes:
align layers, 102-3
multiple, 105
Blob animation, 146-7
Blooming flower, 10-11
Blur:
compositing, 110
depth of field, 108
motion, 110-11
Bouncing ball animation, 140-1
Brainstorm effect:
description, 324-7
library of custom textures, 332-3
Brush Time properties, 7
Bubbles:
foam, 214-15, 216
windblown snow, 222
Bugs Bunny cartoon, 158
Burn Film effect, 17
Bywater, Kymnbel, 95

## C

Cameras:
3D, 42-3, 81
Canon 7D, 293
DV, 131
Focus Distance, 109
hand held, 107
HD, 131
multiple angles, 40-1
orient to, 44-5
Candle flame, 300-1
Canon 7D camera, 293
Captain Morgan, 182
Card Wipe effect, 64-5
Cartoon effect, 272
Cast Shadows feature, 24-5
Caustics effect, 242-3
CC (Cycore) effects:
3D, 72
bubbles, 215
Burn Film, 17
Cylinder, 69
Kaleida, 318-19

Light Rays, 183
Light Sweep, 177
Lights option, 29
Mr Mercury, 224-5
Particle Systems II
3D Fireworks, 232-3
Ink spatter, 14-15
Particles, 208-9
Smoke Trail, 212-13
Sparkles, 210-11
Particle World, 232-3
Radial Fast Blur, 239
rain, 218-19, 220
snow, 221, 222
Sphere, 72-3
Spotlight, 33
Star Burst, 73, 238-41
Cell Pattern effect:
animation presets, 328
cells through a microscope, 320-1, 322
stage lights, 170-1
Cells through a microscope, 320-1
Chocolate (flowing), 244-5
Christiansen, Mark, 112
Cinema 4D application, 58, 80-1, 110, 176
Cinematic color:
flashback, 260-1
horror, 258-9
warmth, 256-7
Citizen Kane film, 34
Clone Stamp tool, 149
CMYK ink system, 278
Color:
channels, 113
compositing, 104-5
HDR, 184-5
introduction, 252-3
matching, 112-13
"superwhite", 185
Color Balance effect:
3D renders, 286
cinematic color
horror, 258
warmth, 256-7
color composition, 105
colorizing, 269
day for night, 263
secondary color correction, 277
Color correction:
3D renders, 286-7

before and after, 266-7
cinematic color
  flashback, 260-1
  horror, 258-9
  warmth, 256-7
Color Finesse, 253, 280-1
Color Lookup Tables, 284-5
colorizing, 268-9
dark areas, 288-9
day for night, 262-3
faking dimension, 274-5
histograms, 254-5
hue shift, 270-1
introduction, 253
Magic Bullet Looks, 253, 290-1
primary, 276
reference monitor, 264-5
secondary, 276-7
spot, 278-9
stylizing, 272-3
Color Finesse:
  basics, 280-1
  effect, 285
  histograms, 254
  introduction, 253
  "Looks", 282-3, 290
Color Lookup Tables (LUT), 284-5
Colorama effect:
  Animation presets, 329
  basic water, 312-13
  Brian Maffitt, 4
  candle flame, 300-1
  cells through a microscope, 321
  colorizing, 269
  fire texture, 296
  fireball, 4
  hot grill, 306
  Star Burst, 241
Colorizing and color correction, 268-9, 270
Compositing:
  animation, 106-7
  blending away
    dark, 96-7
    light, 98-9
  color, 104-5
    matching, 112-13
  dark blending away, 96-7
  focus, 108-9
  garbage matte, 84-5
  green screen removal, 86-7, 94,

130-1
  guide layers, 128-9
  introduction, 83, 94-5
  light blending away, 98-9
  luma key, 88-9, 90
  manual shadow, 126-7
  mattes
    multiple, 92-3
    refinement, 90-1
  Mocha shapes, 120-1
  motion blur, 110-11
  opacity restoration, 124-5
  premultiplied alpha channels, 114-15
  restoring opacity, 124-5
  Roto Brush, 122-3
  textures, 100-1
  tracking with Mocha, 116-19
Compositions (3D nested), 78-9
Compression of videos, 131
Confetti effect, 240-1
Controlling shadows, 28-9
Creative playing, 302-5
Cruise, Tom, 296
Curtains, 308-9
Curves effect:
  cinematic color, flashback, 260-1
  damaged film, 17
  day for night, 262
Custom particles, 215-16
Cylinder effect, 69

**D**

da Vinci, Leonardo, 159
Daffy Duck cartoon, 158
Damaged film, 16-17
Dark areas, 288-9
Dark blending away, 96-7
Day for night effect, 262-3
Deflection of particles, 236-7
Depth of field:
  blur, 108
  creation, 34-5
  focus, 109
  "long" lens, 37
  miniatures, 13
Detonation Films:
  Library, 98
  particle alternatives, 250-1
  stylizing, 272

Difference blend mode, 102-3
Digital Juice, 250
Disney, Walt, 158-9
Displacement mapping, 152-3
Distortion (3D), 68-71

**E**

Edge Detection 17, 200
Easing in after effects, 159
Echospace (3D), 76-7
Ellipse tool, 191, 302
Energon cubes, 172
Energy cube, 172-3
Evolution parameter, 306-7, 317

**F**

Faking dimension, 274-5
Fast Blur effect:
  3D planetscape, 75
  basic snow, 221
  blending away light, 99
  CC (Cycore) Radial, 239
  HDR, 163
  rain, 219
  searchlights, 174
  star field, 239
  TV noise, 317
  windblown snow, 223
Faulkner, Jef, 84, 288
Fill effect, 167
Film noir lighting, 32-3, 66
Filmlike videos, 292-3
Fire breathing dragon, 2, 4-5
Fire texture, 296-9
Flowing chocolates, 244-5
Foam effect:
  bubbles, 214-15
  custom particles, 216-17
  windblown snow, 223
Focus, 108-9
Focus Distance (cameras), 109
Fractal Noise effect:
  3D planetscape, 72, 74
  animation presets, 329
  bars, 310
  basic water, 312-13
  better water, 314
  cells through a microscope, 320
  curtains, 309

damaged film, 16
fire, 296-9, 300
fireball, 5
hot grill, 306-7
light whips, 168-9
Luma Matte, 197
ornate vintage patterns, 319
searchlights, 175
steam, 231
TV noise, 317
volumetric light, 165
FreeformAE effect, 70-1, 72, 75

## G

Garbage matte, 84-5
Glow effect:
   3D renders, 287
   Animation presets, 328
   cinematic color - flashback, 261
   creative playing, 304
   energy cube, 173
   light, 178-9
   light ribbons, 228
   Retro Video Game Maze, 322
   star field, 238
Gradient overlay, 303-4
Grady, Dan:
   depth of field, 34
   faking dimension, 274-5
   multiple camera angles, 40
   The Parallax effect, 50
   parenting animation, 142
   puppet overlap, 136
Graph Editor:
   bouncing ball, 140-1
   easing, 159
   resizing animation, 154-5
Green screen:
   removal, 86-7, 94
   shooting, 130-1
Grid effect, 306-7
Growing vines, 6-7
Guide layers, 128-9

## H

Hand held cameras, 107
HDR (High Dynamic Range):
   color, 161, 184-5
   light effect, 162-3

Help feature, 20-1
*Heroes* (TV show), 8
High Dynamic Range see HDR
Histograms, 254-5
Hot grill effect, 306-7
*How to Cheat in Photoshop*, 148
Hue/Saturation effect:
   basic water, 313
   better water, 315
   hue shift, 270-1
   secondary color correction, 276-7

## I

*I Hate Basketball* (IHB), 84-5, 288
Illustrator, AI files, 330
   motion paths, 202-3
Ink spatter, 14-15
INSPIRE text, 168-9
Instant vignettes, 190-1

## J

Johnson, Daniel:
   motion blur, 110
   negative light, 30-1
   volumetric light, 164
Johnston, Ollie, 158
Jones, Chuck, 158

## K

Kaleida effect, 318-19
"Key" light, 46
Keying project, 86
Keylight effect:
   compression, 131
   green screen removal, 87
   luma key, 88-9
   multiple mattes, 92-3
   shadows, 46

## L

Laser beams, 180-1
Leave Color effect, 269
Lens Blur effect, 12
Lens distortion, 38-9
Lens Flare effect, 97, 181
Levels effect:
   3D renders, 287

cinematic color - warmth, 257
creative playing, 304
curtains, 309
histograms, 254-5
secondary color correction, 277
stylizing, 273
Library of custom textures, 332-3
Light effects:
   blending away, 98-9
   energy cube, 172-3
   glow, 178-9
   high dynamic rays, 162-3
   introduction, 160-1
   laser beams, 180-1
   Rays, 183
   Ribbons, 226-7, 228-9
   sabers, 180-1
   searchlights, 174-5
   sheen, 176-7
   silhouettes, 166-7
   Soft, 101, 304, 315
   stage, 170-1
   Sweep, 177
   Trapcode Shine, 182-3
   volumetric light, 164-5
   whips, 168-9
Lighting:
   film noir, 32-3, 66
   green screen, 130
   introduction, 22-3
   negative, 30-1
   secrets, 46-7
Looks effect, 291
Luma Key effect, 88-9, 90, 167
Luma Matte, 196-7, 198
LUT see Color Lookup Tables
Lux plugin (Trapcode), 165

## M

Mac computer, 1
McDonalds, 182
Maffitt, Brian:
   radio waves, 226
   shatter effect, 58
   water surface disruption, 242
Magic Bullet Looks:
   color correction, 290-1
   Color Finesse "Looks", 282
   introduction, 253
Manual shadow, 126-7

Mask Feather option, 191, 300
Masks:
  animation, 200-1
  instant vignettes, 190-1
  introduction, 186-7
  Luma Matte, 196-7
  opacity, 188
  options, 188-9, 191
  Track Matte, 198-9
  The Vegas effect, 193-4
  video to shape layer, 192-3
Master solid, 18-19
Matte:
  Choker effect, 130
  Luma effect, 196-7
  multiple, 92-3
  refining, 90-1
  Track, 198-9
Maya application, 58, 80-1
Mocha:
  shapes, 120-1
  tracking, 83, 116-19
Molten gold effect, 224-5
Motion Blur:
  compositing, 110-11
  hand held cameras, 107
  refining a matte, 90
  Roto Brush, 122
Motion paths and Illustrator, 202-3
Motion Tile effect, 334-5
Mount Doom, *Lord of the Rings*, 86
Mr Mercury effect, 224-5
Multiple camera angles, 40-1
Multiple mattes, 92-3
Multiply blend mode, 105

**N**

Negative light, 30-1
Nested compositions (3D), 78-9
Noise effect, 98, 316

**O**

O'Brien, Conan, 86
Opacity:
  3D Light Streaks, 248
  color compositing, 104
  light ribbons, 229
  masks, 188
  psychic waves effect, 235
  restoring, 124-5

Spot color correction, 279
  steam effect, 231
Orient to camera option, 44-5
Ornate vintage patterns, 318-19

**P**

Pan Behind tool, 175
The Parallax effect (3D), 50-1
Parenting animation, 142-3, 147
Particle Playground effect, 230-1
Particle Systems II effect:
  3D fireworks, 232-3
  particles, 208-9
  smoke trail, 212-13
  sparkles, 210-11
Particle World effect, 232-3
Particles:
  3D
    fireworks, 232-3
    light streaks, 248-9
  alternatives, 250-1
  confetti, 240-1
  custom, 215-16
  deflection, 236-7
  flowing chocolate, 244-5
  foam effect, 214-15
  introduction, 207, 208-9
  light ribbons, 226-7
  molten gold, 224-5
  psychic waves, 234-5
  rain (simple), 218-19
  smoke trail, 212-13
  snow
    basic, 220-1
    windblown, 222-3
  sparkles, 210-11
  star field, 238-9
  steam, 230-1
  Trapcode Form: 4D fractal, 246-7,
    248-9
  water surface disruption, 242-3
Particular effect, 248-9
Pen tool:
  candle flame, 300
  searchlights, 175
  steam, 230
Photo animation, 148-9, 150-1
Photoshop:
  3D, 56-7
  After Effects, 148
  animation, 148

animation and After Effects, 150
  bird shape, 201
  energy cube, 172
  histograms, 254
  PSD Files, 330
  Puppet Warp feature, 134
Planetscape (3D), 72-5
Polar Coordinates effect, 30
Postcards (3D), 64-5
Premultiplied alpha channels, 114-15
Presets and Adobe Bridge, 330-1
Previews in After Effects, 115
Primary color correction, 276-7
Primatte Keyer Pro software, 87
Psychedelic effects, 102
Psychic waves effect, 234-5
Puppet:
  animation, 138-9
  overlap, 136-7
  Overlap tool, 136-7
  Pin tool, 134-7, 139
  Starch tool, 137
  tool, 138-9, 150

**Q**

Quick variations, 324-7

**R**

Rabinowitz, Aharon, 79
Rack focus effect, 23, 36-7
Radial Blur effect, 179
Radial Wipe effect, 10-11
Radio Waves effect, 226-9, 235
Rain effect (simple), 218-19, 220
Ramp effect, 275
Red Giant software:
  Echospace, 76
  Primatte Keyer Pro, 87
  Trapcode Form: 4D Fractal, 246
Redgiantsoftware.com, 246
Reference monitors, 264-5
Refine Matte effect, 90-1, 130, 166
Repoussé feature (3D), 52-5
Resizing animation, 154-5
Retro Video Game Maze, 322-3
Roto Brush tool:
  compositing, 83, 122-3
  Refine Matte effect, 90
  Spot color correction, 278-9
  video compression, 131

Roughen Edges settings, 5

# S

Science Fiction Museum, Seattle, 46
Searchlights, 174-5
Secondary color correction, 276-7
Shadows:
   3D, 126-7
   casting, 24-5
   controlling, 28-9
   "key light", 47
   keylight, 46
   manual, 126-7
   stained glass, 26-7
Shapes:
   creative playing, 304
   introduction, 187
   layers, 192-3
Shatter scenes (3D), 58-61
Sheen light effect, 176-7
Shine Effect, 182-3
Silhouettes, 166-7
Smoke trail effect, 212-13
Smudge tool, 172
Snow effect:
   basic, 220-1
   windblown, 222-3
Soft Light:
   compositing textures, 101
   creative playing, 204
   TV noise, 317
   water, 315
Solids:
   3D, 66-7
   master, 18-19
Sparkles effect, 210-11
Sphere effect, 72-3
Spilled Ink Animation, 95
Spot color correction, 278-9
Spotlight effect:
   curtains, 309
   film noir lighting, 33
Stage lights effect, 170-1
Stained glass shadows, 26-7
Star Burst effect, 73, 238-41
Star field effect, 238-9
Starglow effect (Trapcode), 238
Steam effect, 230-1
Stylizing, 272-3
Sunsets, 120-1
Superman (character), 86

"Superwhite" color, 185

# T

Talking bird, 2, 8-9
Temporal alignment, 102-3
Text:
   3D, 8-9, 62-3
   INSPIRE, 168-9
   messaged animation, 156-7
   satirical, 167
   tracked, 8-9
Textures, compositing 100-1
   see also backgrounds and textures
The Young are the Restless, 46, 276,
   278, 293
Thomas, Frank, 158
Tilt shift, 12-13
Tint effect:
   before and after, 266-7
   colorizing, 268
   curtains, 309
   hue shift, 271
   stylizing, 273
   volumetric light, 165
Track Matte, 198-9
Tracked text, 8-9
Tracking with Mocha, 83, 116-19
Transform Data option, 119
Trapcode:
   3D Stroke plugin, 195, 204-5
   Echospace plugin, 76
   Form: 4D fractal effect, 246-7,
   248-9
   Lux plugin, 165
   Shine light effect, 182-3
   Starglow effect, 238
Tritone effect:
   animation presets, 328
   bars, 310
   colorizing, 269
   hue shift, 271
   Retro Video Game Maze, 322
Turbulent Displace effect:
   blob animation, 146
   steam, 231
   waving sail, 144-5
Turbulent Noise effect, 325
TV noise, 316-17

# U

uberstock.com videos:
   compression, 131
   histograms, 254-5
   kid dancing, 192-3
   matte refining, 90
   steam, 230-1
   stock, 1
   Temporal Alignment, 102
   Track Matte, 199
   TV noise, 317
   woman flirting at bar, 117
UFOs (unidentified flying objects):
   Mocha shapes, 120-1
   motion blur, 110
   premultiplied Alpha Channels, 114
   smoke trail, 212-13

# V

The Vegas effect, 169, 194-5
Venetian Blinds effect, 71
Vibrance effect:
   cinematic color - flashback, 261
   cinematic color - horror, 259
   day for night, 263
Video Copilot, 250
Video to shape layer, 192-3
Videos:
   compression, 131
   filmlike, 292-3
   Zen Chemists, 190-1, 254-5
   see also uberstock.com videos
Vignettes (instant), 190-1
Vitruvian Man (da Vinci), 159
Volumetric light, 164-5

# W

Warner Brothers:
   cartoons, 158
   museum, 46
Warp effect, 165, 169
Water:
   basic, 312-13
   better, 314-15
Water Surface Disruption effect,
   242-3
Wave Warp effect, 146-7, 334-5
Wave World, 242-3

Waving sail animation, 144-5
Whips (light effect), 168-9
Wide angle lens, 39
Wikipedia.org, 159
Windblown snow effect, 222-3
Wrap Pixels Around option, 235
Write-on-effect, 7

# Y

You Yell You Kick (YYYK) image, 148-53

# Z

Z space, 39, 76, 79, 107, 143
Zen Chemists, 190-1, 254-5
Zombie Crush photography, 12, 148